Soviet Intervention
in Czechoslovakia,
1968

Soviet Intervention in Czechoslovakia, 1968 *Anatomy of a Decision*

Jiri Valenta

The Johns Hopkins University Press
Baltimore and London

This book has been brought to publication with the generous assistance of the Andrew W. Mellon Foundation.

The Johns Hopkins University Press, Baltimore, Maryland 21218
The Johns Hopkins Press Ltd., London
Originally published, 1979
Johns Hopkins paperback edition, 1981

Library of Congress Cataloging in Publication Data

Valenta, Jiri.
  Soviet intervention in Czechoslovakia, 1968.
  Bibliography: pp. 190–94
  Includes index.
  1. Russia—Foreign relations—Czechoslovakia. 2. Czechoslovakia—Foreign relations—Russia. 3. Czechoslovakia—History—Russian intervention, 1968– 4. Russia—Foreign relations administration. 1. Title.

DK67.5.C9V34   327.47'0437   78–20522
ISBN 0–8018–2168–1 (hardcover)
ISBN 0–8018–2540 (paperback)

Errata

In all references to "Bilak," an accent was omitted. *For* Bilak *read* Bilàk.

On pp. 78, 121, 151, and 185, an accent was omitted in "Ceausescu." *For* Ceausescu *read* Ceausçescu.

ריררד

To my wife, Ginny

Bureaucracy considers itself the ultimate purpose of the state. . . . The aims of the state are transformed into the aims of the bureaucracies and the aims of the bureaucracies into the aims of the state. Bureaucracy is a circle from which no one can escape. Its hierarchy is a hierarchy of knowledge. The higher circles rely on the lower in everything involving a knowledge of the particular while the lower circles trust the upper in everything involving an understanding of the universal, and thus each deceives the other.—Karl Marx

Contents

Preface

The Soviet military intervention in Czechoslovakia in August 1968 came as a surprise to most students and observers of Soviet politics. It was Alexander Dubček's ninth month of tenure. Only seventeen days had passed since the seemingly successful negotiations with the Czechoslovak leadership at Čierna nad Tisou and Bratislava, and the situation in Czechoslovakia seemed to be stable. The decision of the Soviet leadership to use military force at this time, without the prompting of some dramatic change in Czechoslovakia, has led many observers to doubt seriously the predictability of Soviet behavior in the management of future crises. The repercussions of the intervention for the Soviet posture in world politics have been striking, and in many quarters, particularly in Western Europe and in China, the invasion is vividly remembered a decade later.

When I visited the USSR in May and June 1968, I could not foresee that in a few short months the Prague Spring experiment would be abruptly terminated by Soviet military intrusion. I was, however, able to discern a deep interest and curiosity regarding the Prague phenomenon on the part of Soviet students and intellectuals. Indications of the overflow of Czechoslovak reformism on the intellectual communities of Leningrad and Moscow were unmistakable. Also unmistakable were the very real apprehension and hostility of Soviet officials with whom I came into contact. Still, I did not anticipate such a drastic action on the part of the Soviets, and I was as surprised by it as was the general public in both the East and the West. Later, when I began serious research on the crisis, I discovered that Soviet will and timing in the use of military force had been miscalculated not only by Dubček and his reformist supporters but also by many policymakers and analysts of Soviet politics in the West. Students of the behavior of other nations, including that of the United States, have likewise met failure at times in predicting conduct; thus students of Soviet behavior should be spared undue criticism for their miscalculation. In the future search for rational responses to Soviet foreign policy actions, it is essential to examine factors that shape decisions such as the one to invade Czechoslovakia in 1968. It is this premise which has guided the writing of the present study.

My original purpose was to explain the sudden turnabout in Soviet decisionmaking after Čierna and Bratislava. Were the negotiations there a smoke screen for military intervention, or did the Soviet Politburo simply change its mind on the Czechoslovak issue after these meetings, and if so, why? Later, faced with the intricacies of Soviet decisionmaking, my intention altered to one of elaborating a theoretical paradigm and developing a case study of Soviet management of the crisis. The goal of the book is therefore limited and specific. I have not written a history of the death of Prague reformism, since more qualified students are attending to this issue, but rather an analytic and interpretative essay focusing on the Soviet decisionmaking process.

Chapter 1 examines the problems underlying a conceptualization of Soviet foreign policy decisionmaking, with particular attention given to the role of bureaucratic politics in the Czechoslovak crisis. Chapter 2 analyzes Soviet decisionmaking in July 1968, at the peak of the crisis, including a number of ramifications: pressures on Czechoslovakia from the Warsaw Pact countries, signs of internal debate in the Soviet Politburo, and foreign policy linkages. Chapter 3 treats bilateral negotiations between the Soviet and Czechoslovak leaderships at Čierna nad Tisou and the multilateral conference of five Warsaw Pact countries at Bratislava prior to the intervention. Chapter 4 discusses the reactions of several bureaucratic elites and other groups in the Soviet Union and Eastern Europe to the outcome of the negotiations, and attempts to explain how organizational, domestic, and personal interests affected the preinvasion debate and the resolution of the crisis. Chapter 5 attempts to explain how and why the Soviet decision to intervene was finally reached and examines the timing of the decision. Here also the role of information is examined, together with the importance of the Soviet perception of U.S. response and the neglected issue of the implementation of the decision to intervene. Chapter 6 states my conclusions and reassesses the costs of the invasion as seen after a decade.

The study employs, then, a bureaucratic-politics paradigm as a methodological tool in explaining Soviet management of the Czechoslovak crisis. Richard Neustadt's thesis of "pulling and hauling" in government, elaborated in studies of U.S. foreign policy decisionmaking by Graham Allison, Morton Halperin, and others, is not a new one to students of Soviet politics. Indeed, the "conflict school," which deals with factional struggle and internal politics as they affect Soviet foreign policymaking, may be regarded as an intellectual forerunner of the "bureaucratic-politics school."[1]

My conceptualization of Soviet foreign policy decisionmaking is far from definitive. Attempts at conceptualizing Soviet decisionmaking are still in their infancy, and the task is not an easy one. Analysts are hampered by a

ack of reliable data, owing to the secretive nature of Soviet decisionmak-
ng. Unlike students of politics in Western societies, the student of Soviet
politics has neither historically valid documents nor access to primary ma-
erials. There are no Daniel Ellsbergs or Jack Andersons in the Soviet
Union. Instead, the analyst must track the infrequent and often puzzling
bits of evidence in the Soviet press and in the testimonies of witnesses. This
study was developed in a similar way, starting with a systematic examination of all available sources. I am fully aware that the study, written without
access to confidential Soviet documents, cannot be definitive. I venture that
it has benefited, however, from my being able to follow events closely in
both Czechoslovakia and the Soviet Union, and from my sense of the
moods in both countries. Interviews after the invasion with many former
Czechoslovak politicians and advisers to the Dubček regime and with
Czechoslovak intellectuals and newspapermen provided much valuable information. I wish to express appreciation particularly to Zdeněk Mlynář,
Ota Šik, Jiří Pelikán, Eugen Loebl, Karel Jezdinský, Josef Hodic, Přemysl
Janýr, Radoslav Selucký, Dušan Havlíček, Antonín Šnejdárek, Larisa Silnický, František Silnický, and Karel Král. Unfortunately, many other
Czechoslovak officials and Soviet citizens with whom I had informal discus-
sions in Czechoslovakia throughout 1968 or during my visit to the Soviet
Union in May and June 1968, as well as Soviet and East European immi-
grants whom I interviewed in the United States, Western Europe, and
Israel, wish to remain anonymous. They also deserve my thanks. I am indebted as well to several high officials of the Johnson administration—
Dean Rusk, Walt Rostow, Henry Owen, and Morton Halperin—for sharing
their knowledge with me. A similar debt is owed to the national security adviser to President Jimmy Carter, Zbigniew Brzezinski.

During my research, several persons were of great help in answering questions and sharing special knowledge. In Vienna, Austria, a former high official of the Austrian Communist Party and editor of *Tagebuch,* Franz
Marek, and the head of the Jewish Documentary Center, Simon Wiesenthal, were kind enough to answer my queries. In Paris, I owe special thanks
to the editor of *Svědectví,* Pavel Tigrid, and to Michel Tatu of *Le Monde;* in
Bern, Switzerland, to the staff of *Ostinstitut,* particularly Laszlo Revesz;
and in Washington, D.C., to Victor Zorza of the *Washington Post,* who
kindly allowed me the use of his private files at his home in England. I am
equally indebted to Professor William Griffith for allowing me access to his
useful collection of documents at the Center for International Studies at the
Massachusetts Institute of Technology.

Appreciation must also be expressed to others who made valuable comments on drafts of the study. Foremost is my adviser and teacher at the
School of Advanced International Studies of The Johns Hopkins University, Herbert Dinerstein, for his encouragement and support from the

beginning and for his assistance in writing this manuscript. Others who made valuable comments on the book as a whole were George Liska, Jerome Gilison, Bruce Parrot, Bennett Ramberg, and Allan Foley of Johns Hopkins; the late Josef Korbel of the University of Denver; Morris Rothenberg of the University of Miami; and Malcolm Palmatier of The Rand Corporation.

I have benefited from valuable comments by and discussions with my former colleagues at the Brookings Institution, especially I. M. Destler, now at the Carnegie Foundation. I owe thanks for many useful comments to scholars at other institutions: David Burke of the Naval Postgraduate School, Monterey; Melvin Croan of the University of Wisconsin; Galia Golan and Ted Friedgut of the Hebrew University of Jerusalem; A. Ross Johnson of The Rand Corporation; and Andrew Gyorgy of the Sino-Soviet Institute of George Washington University. For their valuable criticism I would also like to thank many of my students in the program of Soviet and East European studies of the Department of National Security Affairs, the Naval Postgraduate School, Monterey, California.

I would like especially to thank my dear wife, Virginia Lyda, to whom the book is lovingly dedicated, for putting up with me and the Soviet invasion during preparation of the manuscript, for her constant help and encouragement, and for her many valuable insights.

Finally, I wish to record my gratitude to several institutions for their varying degrees of support and encouragement: The Johns Hopkins University, the Brookings Institution, and the Naval Postgraduate School. Particular thanks are due David Schrady, William Tolles, and Patrick Parker of NPS for their encouragement in the final preparation of the book.

The failures and shortcomings of the book are my own.

Soviet Intervention in Czechoslovakia, 1968

I *It is a little simpleminded to talk of "the Russians," because we are sure there are important contradictions, and even struggles, within the Soviet Party itself.*—Lucio Lombardo Radice, leading theoretician of the Italian Communist Party

Soviet Foreign Policy Decisionmaking and the Czechoslovak Crisis: Conceptualization

At the very peak of the Czechoslovak crisis on August 3, 1968, Secretary General Leonid Brezhnev and other members of the Soviet delegation to the Bratislava Conference, together with the leaders of several East European countries—East Germany, Poland, Hungary, and Bulgaria—appeared to reach a *modus vivendi* with Alexander Dubček's leadership. At the same time, Warsaw Pact forces were withdrawn from maneuvers on Czechoslovak territory. Many observers of Soviet politics interpreted these events as a victory for the Czechoslovak reformers. But only seventeen days later, on August 20, the mood was broken by the sudden military invasion of Czechoslovakia by its partners in the Bratislava agreement. Some skeptics among observers of Soviet politics had doubted that the rapprochement would endure. Very few had expected a Soviet military move so soon. Many political observers saw the Bratislava agreement as a sign that the Soviets had decided to compromise by adjusting to the new situation. U.S. government officials and officials of other North Atlantic Treaty Organization (NATO) countries had also considered intervention to be very unlikely, as had the Czechoslovak leadership and Dubček himself. True, President Lyndon Johnson and other high administration officials had been told by some of Johnson's advisers that an attack *could* (not

1

would) take place at any time with virtually no warning; but as former commander-in-chief of the U.S. Army in Europe General James H. Polk acknowledged, they "didn't think it would happen."[1] Even one of the most pessimistic members of the Johnson administration, former U.S. ambassador to the USSR Charles E. Bohlen, underestimated (as he frankly admitted) the Soviet timing on the use of military force. In a memorandum of August 13 to Secretary of State Dean Rusk, Bohlen described the Czechoslovak situation as "inherently serious," though he doubted that "any spectacular development" would arise during the rest of the month.[2]

Overall, the U.S. intelligence community failed to provide warning that the Soviet leadership had "decided to intervene with force." Although intelligence sources concluded that "the Soviets were capable of launching an invasion at any time," a review of U.S. intelligence performance by the Pike Committee indicates that the agencies "were not up to the difficult task of divining Soviet intentions."[3] After the Čierna-Bratislava negotiations, which ended on August 3, and until the invasion on August 20—i.e., during a period of roughly two weeks—U.S. intelligence "lost" track of the Soviet combat troops that were conducting maneuvers around the Czechoslovak borders, primarily in northern Poland. U.S. intelligence again "found" the Soviet troops when their tanks rolled through the streets of Prague, but only by way of Czech Radio news broadcasts! President Johnson learned about the invasion when Soviet Ambassador A. Dobrynin visited the White House and told him of it. NATO officials were also surprised by the intensity and timing of the invasion, learning about it only from an Associated Press dispatch. Why did most Czechoslovak and Western officials and analysts fail to predict the sudden Soviet intervention?

Rational Policy Paradigm

Recent American foreign policy literature has suggested that such failures often arise from a tendency to treat the state as a unitary actor, rather than looking within to analyze bureaucratic conflict and consensus-building. Many *ex post facto* explanations of the Soviet intervention in Czechoslovakia thus fit what Graham Allison has christened the "rational policy paradigm."[4] According to Hans Morgenthau, the Warsaw Pact invasion was aimed at preventing Czechoslovakia from shifting its orbit closer to that of West Germany: "It is an existential fact which has determined the fate of the nations of Eastern Europe for centuries that none of them can stand on their own feet but must lean on one or the other of its powerful neighbors to the East and to the West. . . . In the measure that Czechoslovakia moved away from Russia, it was bound to move closer to Germany. It was against this threat that the Soviet Union reacted, and may well have over-reacted, in 1968."[5] Similarly, Herman Kahn argues that the main concern of the Soviet Politburo about Czechoslovakia became the fear of a "German threat." As Kahn puts it, "The threat was that these events [in Czechoslovakia] might leave the Soviet Union militarily exposed; that the weakening of the Warsaw Pact, combined with the strengthening of West Germany (because of Czech recognition and trade), might one day culminate in a U.S.-backed West German attack on the USSR."[6] Another interpretation emphasizes the importance of ideological doctrine in Soviet decisionmaking: an example is the so-called Brezhnev doctrine of "limited sovereignty" of socialist states, which was actually the Soviet *ex post facto* justification of the isolated Czechoslovak incident.[7] In short, most published studies of the Czechoslovak crisis, whether critical of or sympathetic to the Prague Spring, depend in some degree upon a rational policy paradigm.[8] Consequently, most analysts appear to believe that the Soviet willingness to negotiate at Čierna and Bratislava and the early "soft" Soviet policy toward the Dubček regime were part of a ruse calculated to lull that regime, and the world, into a false sense of security while plans for intervention were being perfected.

Can explanations of Soviet foreign policy decisionmaking be improved by applying an additional explanatory model, a bureaucratic paradigm, to Soviet behavior? Does such an approach offer hope for more accurate predictions of Soviet behavior? This study seeks to test the approach by applying it to Soviet management of the Czechoslovak crisis in 1968. The key issue that this study addresses is why the Soviets invaded Czechoslovakia under such peculiar circumstances, i.e., only seventeen days after seemingly successful negotiations at Čierna and Bratislava had apparently resolved the issue. Several questions underlie the puzzle. Who were the central figures in this Soviet decision? How and in what degree did the perception of national security interests, accepted by the Soviet ruling elite, condition Soviet behavior during the crisis? What were the interests of Soviet policymakers, and how did these interests affect their stand on the Czechoslovak issue? Did the bureaucratic division of labor within the Politburo lead to development of a particular form of coalition politics? On what sources of information did the Soviet decisionmakers rely, and were these sources manipulated by some players during the crisis? If so, in what manners? Did external pressures have a significant effect on the Soviet decisionmaking process? What other factors shaped the decision? How and when was the Soviet decision to intervene in Czechoslovakia reached? How was it implemented?

Bureaucratic-Politics Paradigm

The bureaucratic-politics approach as applied here does not suggest that purely abstract institutional and organizational interests motivate Soviet foreign policy actions. It does not assume that the USSR is subject to the same pluralistic forces and bureaucratic behavior as the advanced industrialized societies of the West, or that the Western model of bureaucratic politics as developed by Allison and Halperin can readily be applied to Soviet decisionmaking.[9] The bureaucratic-politics paradigm as developed and tested here takes into consideration the distinctive features of Soviet politics, primarily the unique role of the Soviet Politburo, which minimizes organizational conflict, and the rules of the game circumscribed by Soviet political culture.

The general argument of the bureaucratic-politics paradigm can be summarized as follows: Soviet foreign policy actions, like those of other states, do not result from a single actor (the government) rationally maximizing national security or any other value. Instead, these actions result from a process of political interaction ("pulling and hauling") among *several actors*— in this case, the senior decisionmakers and the heads of several bureaucratic organizations, the members of the Politburo, and the bureaucratic elites at the Central Committee level. Bureaucratic politics is seen as based upon and reflecting the division of labor and responsibility for various areas of policy among the Politburo members. This division arises from two historical conditions characteristic of the post-Stalin era: (1) a highly developed bureaucratic political system and (2) a collective leadership within which no single leader possesses sufficient power or wisdom to decide (or willingness to accept responsibility for) all important policy issues.

The Soviet Politburo must constantly respond to a multitude of pressures. This study hypothesizes that Soviet foreign policy decisionmaking is affected by a number of constraints, among them shared images of national security, organizational interests, domestic interests, various personal interests and idiosyncrasies, the rules of the game and the sets of participants, and internal bargaining and maneuvering.

Obviously, Soviet national security interests include elements widely accepted by the ruling elite. Within their various career patterns, participants in Soviet decisionmaking share important broad characteristics, among them a Machiavellian drive for and appreciation of power. Soviet decisionmakers can be at once tough and flexible, and they share a similar Marxist-Leninist *Weltanschauung*. All are patriots believing in the might of their country, and certainly none wants the Soviet Union to be attacked by a hostile power. It appears reasonable to assume that, like their American counterparts, Soviet leaders share a certain *set of images of national security*.[10] This set of images conditions the basic answers to questions asked by the Soviet ruling oligarchy and key bureaucracies: Who are our friends, who our enemies? With whom shall we ally, with whom do we struggle? All Soviet decisionmakers might not agree that all accepted images accurately reflect the dynamics of world politics at all times. Yet in leadership debates they appear to argue within the boundaries set by images prevailing within the ruling elite.

The following are some of the images of national security shared by Soviet leaders: (1) The Soviet Union must try to avoid nuclear confrontation with the United States. (2) It is desirable to weaken the U.S. commitment to its NATO allies and to Japan. Contradictions among the Western countries should be exploited by the Soviet Union. (3) The Soviet Union must prevent the rise of an equal or superior power in Europe, such as a united Germany. (4) The Soviet Union should prevent the spread of anti-communism in the socialist commonwealth. The East European states are vital to the security of the Soviet Union, which should maintain maximum influence there. Thus, (a) the withdrawal of an East European country from the Warsaw Pact is not permissible; (b) the restoration of a multiparty system within any of the Warsaw Pact countries would jeopardize the responsibility and control of the Communist Party and must not be allowed; and (c) when faced with such a development in Eastern Europe as that described under (a) or (b), the Soviet Union should intervene to protect its interests. (5) China presents a challenge to the Soviet Union as a military power and as a participant in the international communist movement. (6) The Third World presents opportunities to the Soviet Union. These shared images of national security interests undoubtedly affect the attitudes of Soviet decisionmakers, who, in the internal debate, base their arguments upon them.

Despite the shared images of national security, senior Soviet decisionmakers differ on how various issues should be approached and resolved. As in Western societies, the Soviet decisionmaking process is political, not scientific. The decisionmakers are not necessarily cast in the same mold. Often their backgrounds and areas of bureaucratic experience contrast sharply, and often they assume different administrative duties and bureaucratic responsibilities and have different domestic and personal interests.

Organizational Actors

Foreign policy formulation among Soviet leaders proceeds within the context of organizations controlled and coordinated by the Politburo. The Politburo stands at the center of the decisionmaking process, where it makes the final decision on any critical foreign policy and national security issue.[11] Thus, it was the Politburo that made the crucial decision to intervene in Czechoslovakia. Besides the Politburo, the main organizational participants in the foreign policy decisionmaking process are the various departments of the Central Committee (CC) of the Communist Party of the Soviet Union (CPSU) and national security ministerial bureaucracies: the Ministry of Foreign Affairs, the Committee for State Security (KGB), and the Ministry of Defense and its various branches.

The pursuit of separate bureaucratic responsibilities, including responsiveness to constituencies, leads at times to various organizational conflicts such as disagreements over budgetary allocations, organizational values, scope of authority, organizational sense of mission, and self-image. The privacy surrounding decisionmaking and the controlled flow of information within a political system characterized by a centralized, competitive, bureaucratic environment tend to influence bureaucratic politics, and thus the final outcome of the decisionmaking process.[12]

Organizations less concerned about the budgetary implications of their missions, such as the bureaucracies of the Central Committee (the International Department, the Department of Liaison with Communist and Workers Parties [DLCWP]) and the Ministry of Foreign Affairs, are interested mainly in their influence on and self-image in the Soviet decision-making process. For example, the International Department tends to assess foreign policy decisions on the basis of their effect on its mission abroad, particularly in maintaining ties with its constituencies abroad, such as the Communist parties and the pro-Communist trade unions in the West and the "progressive forces" in the Third World.

Organizational differences may arise on various issues even among elements of the Soviet foreign policy establishment which share certain interests, as between the bureaucrats in the International Department, who supervise relations with nonruling Communist parties, and those of the Department of Liaison with Communist and Workers Parties, whose main concern is relations with ruling Communist parties and ultimately with preserving the *status quo* in Eastern Europe. The latter, rather more than the former, tend to focus on particular implications of foreign policy issues, such as their effect upon Eastern Europe.

The subdivisions of the Soviet military establishment, themselves organizations with expensive proclivities, are greatly concerned with the budgetary implications of policy decisions. As Roman Kolkowicz suggests, the Soviet military employ various means of influencing the policies of the Politburo.[13] Furthermore, Soviet force posture and strategic decisions may be affected, among other things, by intra-institutional conflicts of interest: organizational concerns and rivalries among subdivisions of the military establishment—the Ground Forces, the Strategic Rocket Forces, the Air Defense Forces, the Naval Forces, the Air Forces, and the Rear Services.[14]

As concerns another national security agency, the KGB, there is scattered evidence that some of its departments are unenthusiastic about détente, particularly as manifested in increased cultural exchanges between the USSR and Western countries. On the other hand, although détente may complicate the mission of the KGB departments responsible for domestic affairs, it may actually facilitate the mission of those departments responsible for collecting intelligence abroad. Moreover, the KGB had apparently tried in the past to influence important Soviet decisions with its own "maneuvers for influence." A well-known case is the attack with nitrogen mustard gas on a

West German technician in September 1964, an act apparently aimed at blocking Khrushchev's effort to visit West Germany later that year.[15]

Some Soviet bureaucracies are charged with missions that can be accomplished mainly at home. Examples of such bureaucracies are the Central Committee's Department for Propaganda, the Department for Science and Education, the Party Control Committee, and Party bureaucracies in Soviet non-Russian republics charged mainly with ideological supervision, indoctrination, and "Party discipline." Since the responsibilities of these departments are almost entirely internal, international developments and Soviet foreign policy actions are generally viewed for their effect on stated missions. As one source has observed, segments of the foreign policy establishment such as the International Department and the divisions of the Ministry of Foreign Affairs responsible for relations with Western countries are more likely to be interested in good relations with the Western countries than are the bureaucracies charged with ideological supervision and those responsible for political stability in various non-Russian national republics such as the Ukraine and the Baltic republics. The latter departments tend to view détente suspiciously, since it obviously makes their organizational mission of ideological supervision and indoctrination much more difficult.[16]

Needless to say, organizational concerns weigh more heavily in the interests of some Soviet decisionmakers than in those of others. Some members of the Politburo, themselves heads or overseers of Central Committee departments, depend for their power on the solidarity and performance of their respective bureaucracies, which may harbor differing interpretations of national security interests. Consequently, they may be more sensitive to their bureaucracy's orientation and tend to perceive issues through an organizational prism. In the Soviet Politburo and the Central Committee, a rough scale of organizational parochialism seems to exist, ranging from the Ministry of Defense and the KGB as the most parochial, to the International Department, the Ministry of Foreign Affairs, and the Presidium of the Supreme Soviet of the USSR as the least parochial.

Uncommitted Thinking; Personal and Domestic Interests

Soviet decisionmakers do not head organizations with homogeneous constituencies. Some run organizations without clearly defined missions and with rather informal organizational goals. Many have broad responsibilities involving general concepts and sometimes overlapping foreign and domestic interests. Although there are Soviet bureaucrats who seek the enhancement of their organizational independence, the pattern of overlapping in many instances probably does limit the validity of Allison's notion "Where you stand depends on where you sit."

Several senior decisionmaking "generalists" within the Politburo have especially diversified responsibilities and enjoy power and position that do not depend on the interests of bureaucratic organizations. Because they are relatively little influenced by organizational parochialism, their decisions are characterized by *uncommitted thinking*. Thus, during deliberations they take into account, in addition to personal interests, the many diverse factors of Soviet domestic and foreign policy. Moreover, some decisionmakers' constituencies may not be unified in their policy interests. It is conceivable that, as defined by the division of labor, a senior decisionmaker's bureaucratic responsibilities may put him (or her) at odds with a "natural" political constituency. Thus, some policy conflicts reflect basic bureaucratic differences, while others are essentially idiosyncratic.

Personal interests, varying backgrounds, previous political experience, and, as Robert Jervis has suggested, the intellectual formation, values, biases, and idiosyncrasies of the individual—in addition to organizational role—provide important clues to a given leader's position on a given political issue.[17] For example, in the Soviet environment, those decisionmakers who, as leaders of Party bureaucracies in various non-Russian republics, had to deal with the volatile "nationalism" issue share a background experience that can affect their stand on a variety of issues. Finally, each participant's position on an important issue is undoubtedly influenced to some extent by other personal factors—prestige within the Politburo, and the apparently unresolved question of succession.

The domestic interests of Soviet leaders likewise affect their stands on issues. In Soviet decisionmaking, the challenges of internal politics are much more real and forceful than the alleged threats of "U.S. imperialism," "German revanchism," "Czechoslovak revisionism," or "Chinese adventurism." As an example, in the early 1960s the main objective for Khrushchev and other supporters of arms control negotiations with the United States was to overcome the stiff opposition of certain segments of the Soviet armed forces. Khrushchev's management of the Berlin crisis in 1961 and his later policy aimed at rapprochement with West Germany were also affected by internal opposition, including that from the KGB.

The signals of other nations are often used in Soviet politics to advance domestic interests. In his domestic policy of reducing the military budget, Khrushchev needed to give proof to the representatives of the military-industrial establishments—"the metal-eaters," as he called them—that the United States was not so dangerous as they maintained and that the Soviet Union would still be well protected by its reduced forces. Domestic political constraints in Soviet foreign policymaking have become even more important in the past decade. Particularly under the more stable leadership of Brezhnev, Soviet decisionmakers are less immune than ever to domestic constraints and pressures.[18]

It is reasonable to assume that bureaucrats of the foreign policy establishment (the International Department and the Ministry of Foreign Affairs) are more concerned about the foreign affairs aspects of Soviet actions than bureaucrats whose primary responsibilities lie with domestic politics. Yet, since the domestic orientation usually prevails among the Soviet decision-making elite, it is reasonable to conclude that most leaders, when faced with a foreign policy issue, consider both its possible international consequences and also, perhaps even more importantly, its impact on domestic politics.

Rules of the Game

Who plays and calls the shots in the game of Soviet decisionmaking in foreign policy? Unfortunately, little is known of that particular game for which the rules and procedures are extremely well guarded. In discussing this subject, we must therefore limit ourselves to general observations. The actors in Soviet decisionmaking are influenced by the peculiarities of Soviet politics, the style of leadership, and the nature of the issue; they work in an exclusive, asymmetric bureaucratic environment. That internal conflict and bargaining in the Soviet Union are somewhat circumscribed can be explained in part by the Russian "political heritage" of insecurity, mistrust, and siege mentality and by Soviet political culture, especially the Leninist tenets of democratic centralism and Party discipline. Contrary to the political bargaining in the United States, where participants frequently look outside the system for support, participants in the more controlled Soviet environment seek support mainly *inside* the Central Committee bureaucracies. This is one of the principal differences between the Soviet and American political cultures and, ultimately, their decisionmaking processes. It is seen particularly in debates on important foreign policy issues. While interest groups and lobbies may become allies of senior decisionmakers in debates on various domestic issues such as education reform, economic reform, and agriculture,[19] the support of these groups is seldom invoked in foreign policy debates.[20]

Perhaps the most visible set of rules in foreign policy decisionmaking pertains to the Politburo. As stated, no single leader in the Soviet Union possesses enough power to decide alone the most important foreign policy decisions. Decisions are made more or less by the collective leadership, i.e., the members of the Politburo. The style of the collective leadership is symbolized by the Russian term *kollektivnost* (collectivity), which is considered "the highest principle of party leadership."[21]

With the restoration of collective leadership, and collectivity as the ruling principle of Soviet decisionmaking, in the post-Stalin era, the leadership became more stable and harmonious, developing a degree of cohesion. To prevent erosion of the authority of the collective leadership following Khrushchev's forced resignation, the functions of the Politburo were for

malized and institutionalized into a system providing for redistribution of
power, mutual control, and maintenance of countervailing power among
senior decisionmakers (mainly by separating the posts of First Secretary
[now Secretary General] of the Central Committee and Chairman of the
Council of Ministers).[22] That is, decisions are now made by the oligarchy of
the Soviet Politburo.

Mohamed Heikal, adviser to Egyptian Presidents Gamel Nasser and An-
war Sadat and former editor of *Al-Ahram,* pictured an incident of
consensus-oriented bureaucratic decisionmaking which occurred during the
Soviet-Egyptian negotiations in Moscow in 1970:

There was one rather odd incident during this meeting in the Kremlin. At one point
the door opened and a senior official from the Ministry of Foreign Affairs came into
the room and gave a piece of paper to Vladimir Vinogradov, Deputy Minister of
Foreign Affairs. Vinogradov gave the paper to Gromyko, the Minister of Foreign
Affairs, who read it, got up, and took it to Kosygin. Kosygin read it, and gave it to
Brezhnev. Brezhnev read it and gave it back to Kosygin. Kosygin then gave it to
Podgorny. Podgorny read it, and gave it back to Kosygin, who gave it back to
Brezhnev. Then Brezhnev signed it, and gave it to Kosygin, who signed it too. Then
Podgorny signed. Then Podgorny gave it to Gromyko, who gave it to Vinogradov,
who gave it back to the Foreign Office official. . . . The whole transaction took, I
suppose, about five minutes. It had begun while Nasser was speaking, but when he
noticed that everyone was taken up with something else he stopped. When it was all
over Brezhnev saw that the whole Egyptian delegation was staring at him, and
presumably felt that he ought to give some sort of explanation. "This is something
that concerns you too," he said. "We have received information that there will be an
attempt at a coup d'état against General Siad in Somalia tonight. We have accordingly decided to send him a telegram of warning. Now we have seen this telegram and
approved it." Later, as we were going out of the meeting, Nasser said to me: "Did
you see what happened?" "Over that bit of paper, you mean?" I asked. "Yes," said
Nasser. "It is too bureaucratic. If a telegram to General Siad in Somalia needs the
signature of all those three then we are in trouble."[23]

Although the collective leadership decides the most important issues,
such as sending troops or military advisers into a foreign country (troops,
Hungary 1956, Czechoslovakia 1968, Afghanistan 1980; military advisers,
Egypt 1970, Angola 1975, Ethiopia 1978), it does not require that all top
leaders participate on a day-to-day basis, deliberating all issues. Who - plays -
when depends partly on the subject. Players prominent in foreign affairs
appear to be heavily represented in deciding issues where national security
interests are at stake. For example, during the Cuban missile crisis of 1962,
the response to Kennedy's blockade was decided by a kind of Soviet "national security council," which resembled in some respects Kennedy's inner
circle.[24] The restriction of the Soviet decisionmakers' circle reflected not
only Khrushchev's leadership style in the last years of his tenure, but also,
and perhaps more importantly, the nature of the crisis, the managing of
which seemed to require smaller numbers than might have been expected.

more importantly, the nature of the crisis, the managing of which seemed to require smaller numbers than might have been expected.

Brezhnev's leadership (as well as Khrushchev's in the past) is thought to operate with a number of subgroups that have varying memberships depending on their functional area. Under Brezhnev the Soviet national security agencies (the Ministry of Defense and the Ministry of Foreign Affairs) appear to play an important role in debates on issues involving Soviet relations with Western countries, such as SALT negotiations with the United States.[25] Here, the role of leaders primarily responsible for domestic affairs appears to be less influential; their influence on an issue such as SALT is evident at the Politburo level only after the policy has been initiated and elaborated. One generalization seems safe: different types of foreign policy issues (e.g., crisis situations in Eastern Europe) could involve different sets of players, with a larger representation of decisionmakers in the departments supervising East European affairs, and perhaps even domestic politics. Issues of Soviet relations with Eastern Europe are much more likely to come before the full Politburo and the Central Committee departments dealing with internal affairs than are issues involving the West.

Czechoslovak Crisis, 1968

Czechoslovakia in 1968 experienced, over a period of about eight months, profound and revolutionary changes that have proven unique in the history of the communist movement. The peaceful revolution of 1968 was the natural outcome of de-Stalinization and of a mounting crisis in a developed country with predominantly democratic traditions deeply rooted in its political culture.[26] The process of democratization in Czechoslovakia, which was prepared by the reformist-minded forces in the Czechoslovak Communist Party, had gone largely unnoticed for several years by most analysts and policymakers in the West and East, including the Soviet leaders. They misread the nature of the power conflict in the Czechoslovak Communist Party in late 1967, which led to the overthrow of the President and First Secretary Antonín Novotný in January 1968 and to the election of his successor Dubček. Knowing that Novotný's position was untenable, and perhaps misreading the situation, the Soviet leadership did not intervene on behalf of Novotný, who had sought their support before his ouster.

As H. Gordon Skilling's *Czechoslovakia's Interrupted Revolution* demonstrates, however, Novotný's fall was not simply an outcome of the power struggle at the top of Czechoslovak leadership, but was conditioned by several factors: the economic crisis of 1962–63 and the ensuing economic reformism, the unsolved Slovak question, the slow process of political rehabilitation, open dissent of writers and students, and the awakening of the reform-minded intellectual community of the Party and their struggle for freedom of thought and expression.[27] Thus, not surprisingly, the mounting crisis and discontent led not only to Novotný's personal defeat but also soon afterward to the defeat of his many conservative supporters and their repressive policies. Moreover, in several months it grew into a struggle for a democratization of Czechoslovak society. The protracted nature of the political crisis, the continued resistance of Novotný and his supporters to his successor Dubček, a series of affairs in 1968 (such as the dramatic escape to the United States of General Jan Šejna amid rumors of an unsuccessful army coup to prevent Novotný's fall), and the further relaxation of censorship mobilized public support. The reform-minded leaders of the Communist Party incorporated their pluralistic concept of socialism "with a human face" into the Action Program, which was accepted in April 1968, after an initial period of hesitation, as the Magna Charta of Dubček's new leadership. Its main features in domestic politics were to allow greater intraparty democracy, granting more autonomy to state bureaucracies, the other political parties, and the Parliament; the restoration of civil rights (e.g., freedom of assembly and association) and more vigorous continuation of political rehabilitation; the restoration of the national rights of ethnic minorities within a federally organized state; and economic reform. In addition, Dubček permitted the establishment of several new political clubs, and later on during the crisis, abolished censorship. In foreign affairs, the Dubček leadership pledged in the Action Program to pursue more independent policies—but only policies that followed the interests of the Warsaw Pact in general and those of the USSR in particular.[28]

Beginning in March and April 1968, free discussion of the reformist program and of ensuring its continuation was given increasing play in Czechoslovak politics. The Czechoslovak news media generated public support for the Dubček leadership and its reformist forces in their continuous struggle against Novotný, who retained his presidency until March 1968. The uninhibited news media demonstrated growing criticism not only toward the question of Novotný and his supporters and their past policies—particularly policies relating to human rights and unfavorable economic conditions—but also at times toward the internal policies of Czechoslovakia's neighboring Warsaw Pact allies.

The astonishing swiftness of developments in Czechoslovakia between January and April 1968 presented a dilemma to the Soviet leadership. The resignation of Novotný's Moscow-oriented supporters, and especially the reformist programs of Dubček's leadership and the revival of freedom of the press, had created, from the Soviet point of view, a dangerous political situation in one of the most important countries of Eastern Europe. The situation had the potential for affecting neighboring East European countries as well as the Soviet Union itself. The Czechoslovak slogan of "socialism with a human face" implied that the face of Soviet socialism was less than human.

Yet the Prague Spring was a different kind of revolt from that which Soviet leaders had experienced in Budapest in 1956. Dubček's leadership did not challenge the basic elements of Soviet national security interests; it did not recommend revising Czechoslovakia's foreign policy orientation. Czechoslovakia would retain its membership in the Warsaw Pact and the Council for Mutual Economic Assistance (CMEA, or COMECON). Neither did a limited pluralism signify loss of overall control by the Communist Party; power, although somewhat diffused, would remain in the hands of the reform-oriented Party leadership. Although the reforms were only gradually introduced, and their outcome at this point was not entirely clear, from the Soviet point of view, the developments in Czechoslovakia were problematic and potentially dangerous.

Still, any threat to the Soviet Union's dominant influence in Eastern Europe was only potential, not imminent, and it would have been incremental at that. For a long time, Soviet decisionmakers were unsure what policy option to choose with respect to Czechoslovakia. Should they reverse or merely limit the post-January changes in Czechoslovakia? What means should they use to influence Czechoslovakia? Should these means be restricted to political and economic countermeasures, or should the Soviet leaders resort to military intervention? To examine Soviet decisionmaking, we must analyze first the options available to the Soviet leadership and then the various interests of senior Soviet decisionmakers which eventually caused them to take the stands they did on the Czechoslovak crisis.

Soviet Options

Although Soviet leaders were undoubtedly united in their aversion to Czechoslovak reformism, they were for a long time reluctant to opt for military invasion. In fact, some of them engaged in a rather intensive search for a nonmilitary solution. This became obvious after March 1968, as the Soviet leaders began to exert a variety of pressures, political and psychological, aimed at persuading Dubček and his colleagues to slow down the momentum of the Prague Spring.

The Soviet leaders put political pressure on Dubček's leadership during various consultations and negotiations: at the Dresden multilateral conference in March, during bilateral negotiations in Moscow in May, and at an unparalleled Politburo-to-Politburo summit in Čierna in July 1968. The political pressures were accompanied by a psychological one: Soviet and other Warsaw Pact troops (mainly East German and Polish) conducting maneuvers on the Czechoslovak borders.[29] Another form of psychological pressure was used later in the crisis: the presence of Warsaw Pact troops on Czechoslovak territory during and after the maneuvers in June and July.

In addition, some Soviet decisionmakers may have toyed with the idea of using economic sanctions as a form of pressure against Czechoslovakia.

(Reportedly, some Czechoslovak officials hinted at possible Soviet cancella tion of the quarterly wheat shipment to Czechoslovakia in April 1968 Soviet leaders must soon have recognized, however, that large-sca economic pressure had often proved futile in international politics: witnes the League of Nations boycott of Italy in the 1930s, the U.S. boycott c Cuba and the U.N. boycott of Rhodesia in the 1960s, and the Soviets' ow experience with economic sanctions against Yugoslavia in 1948-49 an China and Albania in 1960-61. If the Soviet leadership had refused to ex port to Czechoslovakia, such sanctions would have provided the Dubče leadership with an excellent opportunity not only to ask for Wester economic assistance but perhaps even to retaliate by denying the Sovie Union some important commodities, such as uranium. The Soviet leader must have soon recognized that economic warfare would be self-defeating Thus, despite the reports of depleted grain supplies by the end of April there is no substantial evidence that economic pressure was used.[30]

The use of force was considered as a last alternative. Undoubtedly, mili tary intervention had been debated within the Soviet leadership all along Czechoslovak military intelligence reports estimated that preparations for a possible intervention began in February and March, about the time when Czech-speaking Slavic specialists from the Leningrad universities were said to be mobilized; and some Soviet officials hinted that they feared a military action against Czechoslovakia.[31]

But, this may have been, as Michel Tatu suggests, a "technical prepara-tion" for intervention in case of an emergency—some unexpected develop-ment such as an anti-Communist coup or Czechoslovak withdrawal from the Warsaw Pact. Although the majority in the Politburo was slow to order a military invasion, sometime in May, as Brezhnev later admitted, it began to contemplate military intervention as one of its viable options, but only in the worst-case scenario.[32] Consequently, it decided to proceed apace with the military buildup around Czechoslovakia. Such a buildup served two purposes: logistic preparation or rehearsal for the worst possible op-tion—invasion, and further psychological pressure on and dire warning to the reformists to keep events more tightly in hand. Thus, the military buildup at the Czechoslovak borders (primarily in Poland and East Ger-many) started in the early spring of 1968 and continued for several months during the crisis. Reportedly, by late May and early June the Soviet divi-sions in East Germany and Poland had moved from their regular garrison locations and had camped on the Czechoslovak borders. In East Germany, twelve tank and motorized rifle divisions of the Soviet Army and two East German divisions were stationed in the Erzgebirge, north of the East Ger-man—Czechoslovak borders.[33]

Again it should be stressed that military intervention was contemplated only as a last option, after all other instruments of pressure— political and economic coercion, covert operations, and military maneuvers—had failed. The ultimate decision on the use of military force in Czechoslovakia depended on the changing perceptions of the Soviet ruling elite of the developments in Czechoslovakia and the estimated risks involved in such an action, and on the process of consensus-building within this elite and among their East European allies.

Parochial Priorities, Perceptions, and Stands

All senior Soviet decisionmakers were disturbed by the Czechoslovak reformism. They all agreed that the political situation in Czechoslovakia had to be stabilized, and they recognized that military force might be required. Thus, covert preparations for military action and possible intervention probably began as early as February – March 1968, in the early stages of the crisis. (Later on, in May, military intervention began to be seriously considered as an option.) The intracrisis military buildup, as noted, served not only as logistic preparation for an invasion but also as an instrument of psychological pressure against Czechoslovakia. In fact, the buildup had been accomplished by June – July, but the political decision to invade Czechoslovakia was taken only in August after much pulling and hauling among senior decisionmakers. Each player, depending on his bureaucratic position, domestic interests, and personal background and idiosyncrasies, gave a somewhat different reading (or several readings) of the Czechoslovak issue. Consequently, the players took contrasting stands on the crisis and disagreed on the means to be used in its stabilization.[34]

The decisionmakers responsible for domestic affairs were especially concerned with the possible effect of Prague reformism on the Soviet Union. In the perception of Party bureaucrats in the USSR's non-Russian republics, such as P. E. Shelest, Politburo member and First Secretary of the Ukrainian Communist Party, and P. M. Masherov, candidate Politburo member and First Secretary of the Belorussian Communist Party, "deviate" ideas of reformism and federalism could spill over from Czechoslovakia to encourage nationalism in their own non-Russian republics.[35] Shelest was perhaps also alarmed because of Dubček's federalization of Czechoslovakia, the restoration of national rights of the Ukrainian minority living in Slovakia, and the revival of the forbidden Greek–Catholic Church with consequent far-reaching repercussions in the Western Ukraine, some of which, in the interwar period, formed part of the Czechoslovak province of Ruthenia. To the Central Committee bureaucrats charged with ideological supervision and indoctrination, such as A. Ia. Pel'she, Politburo member and head of the Party Control Committee, P. N. Demichev, candidate Politburo member and Central Committee secretary responsible for the Ideological Committee, S. P. Trapeznikov, head of the Department of

Science and Education, and the middle-level officials such as G. M. Markov and N. M. Gribachev of the Board of Soviet Writers' Union,[36] the Czechoslovak "revisionist disease" posed a threat to the containment o: dissidence in domestic affairs, especially among the intellectual, scientific and literary communities. Czechoslovak revisionism was also seen as rein forcing reformist ideas among liberal-minded members of the Soviet estab lishment (such as Academician A. D. Sakharov and General P. G. Gri gorenko), who hoped to see in their own society the conditions then materi alizing in Czechoslovakia.

Another group of decisionmakers with strong organizational ties feared that Czechoslovak reformism would galvanize Soviet dissidents and reform ists. Reformism was a threat to the KGB's mission and authority in Eastern Europe.[37] To General A. A. Epishev's Department of Political Administra tion of the Soviet armed forces (MPA) (concerned with ideological and political supervision of the Soviet armed forces), Prague reformism and the weakening of morale observed in the Czechoslovak armed forces were a threat to discipline in the Warsaw Pact.

On the other hand, some decisionmakers with responsibilities for foreign affairs appeared to read the Czechoslovak issue somewhat differently, con cluding that intervention would be too costly. What was primarily a domes tic issue to officials responsible for affairs at home was rather an issue of external relations to officials mainly responsible for foreign affairs. M. A. Suslov, Politburo member, leading theoretician and Central Committee secretary responsible for coordination of Soviet policies in the international communist movement, and B. N. Ponomarev, Central Committee secretary overseeing the International Department, and Ponomarev's deputy V. V. Zagladin were concerned with the impact of the events in Czechoslovakia *per se.* A military intervention would undermine their organizational mis sion, their personal prestige, and the maintenance of good ties with their constituencies, i.e., the Communist parties and trade organizations in the West and the "progressive" forces in the Third World in general. More over, it would threaten the coming World Communist Conference sched uled for November 1968.[38] These officials also feared that Soviet action against Czechoslovakia would jeopardize Soviet *Westpolitik* and the stra tegy of a united front with West European Social Democrats, in turn en hancing the latter's interest in NATO. (Indeed, Soviet – West German dip lomatic dialogue ceased at the peak of the Czechoslovak crisis.)[39] And they probably warned that intervention would weaken the USSR in its struggle with China and push the Chinese into the American camp.[40]

Politburo member and Chairman of the Council of Ministers A. N. Kosy gin, who at that time was responsible for governmental diplomacy and ap peared to be an advocate of the Non-Proliferation Treaty (NPT) and an early start to SALT negotiations also seemed to fear the detrimental effects of intervention.[41] Bureaucrats in the International Department and the Ministry of Foreign Affairs who were charged with relations with Western countries seemed to feel that intervention would be detrimental to their ongoing foreign policy strategies, would weaken American opponents of the MIRV and ABM systems, and would enhance the electoral prospects of the U.S. presidential candidate who was perceived at the time as particularly anti-Communist and as favoring U.S. "superiority"—Richard M. Nixon.[42]

Coalitions in Soviet Politics

In the Soviet decisionmaking process under the conditions of collective leadership, coalition politics is an important strategy, aimed at creating a consensus for a certain policy or political course. In the words of Soviet leader N. I. Bukharin, "people must struggle for a majority if they want to guarantee the execution of their policies, which they consider to be correct."[43]

To create consensus for a policy, the participants in Soviet decisionmaking need, if not active cooperation, at least the approval or acquiescence of a majority within the ruling elite. In almost all political systems, the building of a majority requires compromise. In the Soviet political system, it requires, in addition, engagement in various kinds of maneuvers: trading, internal bargaining, and persuading wavering or uncommitted leaders. It also calls for appealing to various pressure groups (important segments of the Party apparatus) and to a broader forum of supporters (at the Central Committee level), and changing the composition of participants in a debate on a controversial policy.

In Soviet politics, coalitions (also known as "blocs" or "factions") seem to be loose, issue-oriented, heterogeneous alliances of convenience among different subgroups for a temporary common purpose. In a sense, despite repeated official insistence on unity, Soviet politics in the first decade after the Bolshevik Revolution—as well as in the post-Stalin era, when collective leadership was restored—can be characterized as coalition politics. It should be borne in mind that, despite Lenin's charismatic authority, even the first important decision of his leadership (to assume power in October 1917) was taken only after he had secured a winning coalition for such an action, and despite opposition from his oldest associates, L. B. Kamenev and G. E. Zinoviev. Perhaps the Brest Litovsk debate can serve as a prime illustration of the importance of coalitions in decisionmaking and coalition-building strategy within the Soviet leadership in the pre-Stalin era (1917 – 29). In January – February 1918, a coalition of Soviet leaders led by Lenin advocated making peace with Germany and terminating Soviet involvement in World War I. This coalition was able to muster a "winning majority" only after weeks of bitter debate, several defeats by Politburo voting, and internal bargaining and maneuvering. The vote (6:4) which finally brought victory to Lenin's coalition against advocates of continuing the war (led by Bukharin) came only with the abstention of several leaders, such as Leon Trotsky, who had originally voted against Lenin's coalition. The importance of the various coalitions (Stalin, Zinoviev, and Kamenev versus Trotsky; Stalin, Bukharin, A. I. Rykov, and M. P. Tomskii versus Zinoviev and Kamenev: and the Stalin-led coalition versus Bukharin, Rykov, and Tomskii) and of coalition-building in Soviet politics in the 1920s for various foreign and domestic policies has been demonstrated by Stephen Cohen in his work on Bukharin.[44]

With Stalin's usurpation of absolute power, and his replacement of the collective leadership with a dictatorship in the 1930s, coalition politics lost some of its importance for two decades. Yet we have scraps of evidence indicating that, even during the Stalin era, coalition strategy had some importance in prepolicy dialogue.

As Max Jakobson has pointed out, there seems to have been an ongoing dialogue within the Soviet leadership prior to the Soviet-Finnish War in 1940. While the final decision to intervene in Finland was obviously reached by Stalin, in prepolicy debate the invasion was apparently advocated by a coalition of three leaders: Party boss of Leningrad Andrei Zhdanov (responsible for Party work and the defense of the city of Leningrad close to the Finnish borders), Soviet Comintern official and Finnish Communist exile Otto Kuusinen, who had a personal stake in the Soviet intervention, and the commander-in-chief of the Baltic Fleet, Admiral V. F. Tributs.[45] Jakobson suggests that this coalition was a major propellant in the drive for military intervention that apparently succeeded in convincing the more hesitant and cautious Stalin—who was the final arbiter in the decisionmaking process—to go along.

With the restoration of collective leadership after Stalin's death, coalition politics reemerged as an important instrument in the Soviet decisionmaking process. The most crucial decisions of the post-Stalin era have been made by coalitions of senior Soviet leaders. The decision to restore relations with Yugoslavia in 1955 was taken by a coalition of Soviet leaders led by Nikita Khrushchev, despite the resistance of V. M. Molotov and his supporters.[46]

Soviet management of the crises in Poland and Hungary in October – November 1956 perhaps also illustrates the exercise of coalition politics within the Soviet leadership. The available evidence regarding the Polish issue suggests that the advocates of military intervention (such as minister of defense General G. K. Zhukov, who was apparently concerned about the cohesion of the Warsaw Pact and the dismissal of Soviet military personnel in Poland) did not succeed in creating a "winning majority" within the Politburo in favor of intervention.[47]

In dealing with the Hungarian issue in October – November 1956, Soviet

cisionmakers appear to have been divided into two coalitions—interven-
nist and noninterventionist. The interventionist coalition seems to have
en more successful in creating a winning consensus. This consensus,
wever, was reached only after some unsuccessful attempts at reconcilia-
n by the Soviet leaders A. I. Mikoian and Suslov, and after Hungary's
thdrawal from the Warsaw Pact, which undoubtedly strengthened the
se of the interventionist coalition.[48]

Coalition politics also played an important role during two political crises
nd power struggles) in the post-Stalin era. A coalition of several
aders—a so-called anti-party group—tried unsuccessfully to oust
hrushchev in 1957.[49] This coalition was not orthodox or conservative in
licy orientation, yet, as Robert Tucker has pointed out, neither was it "a
lid bloc with a single coherent policy line, but an *ad hoc* coalition of men
ho had come to oppose Khrushchev's positions" on several policy issues
at different times and in a different degree."[50]

Reexamination of the 1957 case provides valuable suggestions regarding
e role of coalitions in Soviet politics. The anti-Khrushchev faction, which
characterized by Wolfgang Leonhard as "a strange coalition,"[51] was
otivated by various perceptions of payoffs in foreign and domestic
olicies and by organizational and personal interests: Molotov and G. M.
1alenkov opposed Khrushchev primarily for past foreign and domestic
olicy disagreements; Bulganin, for his own personal idiosyncrasies and op-
ortunism; Kaganovich, because of the bitter feelings existing between him
nd Khrushchev since the 1940s; K. E. Voroshilov, out of fear of Khrush-
hev; and M. G. Pervukhin and M. Z. Saburov, because of their disagree-
1ent over Khrushchev's program of economic decentralization. The issue
hat united them was Khrushchev's removal.

The pro-Khrushchev coalition (Suslov, Mikoian, and E. A. Furtseva) had
pparently concluded that support for Khrushchev was essential to achieve
heir perceived payoffs.[52] Similarly, the anti-Khrushchev coalition of 1964
vas also composed of Soviet leaders with various interests and stakes, and
vithout a coherent political line. They were united by their concern about
organizational issues and Khrushchev's decisionmaking style, e.g., the
mall, unofficial "kitchen cabinet" which neglected the principle of collec-
ive leadership.[53]

From the scattered evidence, we can draw tentative conclusions regarding
he role of coalition politics and coalition-building in the Soviet decisionmaking process. It seems that under the conditions of collective leadership,
Soviet decisionmakers tend to create issue-oriented coalitions of a size that
they believe large enough to carry their policies. At a minimum, a winning
coalition in Soviet politics should be composed of a majority of senior decisionmakers; but it must also find support among influential Central Committee bureaucrats. As the political crisis of June 1957 demonstrated, the

anti-Khrushchev "arithmetic majority" coalition in the Politburo failed
become a winning coalition because it was not able to secure sufficient su
port from key CC members in the face of Khrushchev's maneuverings.

Coalitions in Soviet politics seem to be temporary, heterogeneous, int
institutional alignments loosely built around a single issue. Yet perceiv
payoffs on related issues can also apparently influence the motivations
participants in coalition-building. The composition of such coalitions c
change unexpectedly and dramatically. Not ideological considerations, b
calculations of costs and benefits are prime motivating factors in t
buildup of Soviet coalitions. In other words, Soviet decisionmakers,
entering into coalitions, are moved by political expectations (payoffs)
well as by threats of reprisal if they refuse to join. Here, we are concern
primarily with the expected political payoffs, which can be described
William Riker's terms as a hypothetical comparison of the political gai
and losses of potential coalition members.[54] The payoff to participants m
or may not be directly related to other foreign policy, domestic, or person
issues.

Coalition-Building and the Czechoslovak Issue

In the post-Khrushchev collective leadership, coalition politics ar
coalition-building seem to have played an equally prominent role. The pre
ent collective leadership seems to preserve its political stability despite ser
ous disagreements among the various coalitions on issues of foreign an
domestic policies (rapprochement with West Germany, détente with th
United States and the SALT negotiations, dispute with China, econom
reform). The continuous debate within the Politburo (and among key Cer
tral Committee bureaucrats) during the Czechoslovak crisis illustrate
coalition-building under the conditions of collective leadership in the pos
Khrushchev era. The first steps toward mobilizing support, and the
coalition-building, evidently began in late March 1968 and continued unt
the decision to intervene was taken in August 1968. During the early sprin
the Soviet leadership pursued a cautious, wait-and-see policy towar
Czechoslovakia. The internal debate among the Soviet decisionmakers an
their advisers, and the tacit disagreement on strategy during this period, ac
tually provided Dubček's leadership with an unusual opportunity to con
solidate internally and to legitimize domestic reform policy through th
Central Committee's acceptance of the Action Program. The first un
mistakable indications of coalition-building against Dubček occurred at th
April session of the Soviet Central Committee.

As stressed earlier, there was a diversity of opinion among senior Sovie
decisionmakers regarding the "Czechoslovak threat." They differed mainl
over the question of how to cope with reformist Communism in Czechoslo
vakia. Their varying perceptions on this issue led them to take differen

:ands, and consequently to build or to join two opposing coalitions: those
ı favor of and those against military intervention.

Obviously, the polarization of the Soviet ruling elite was a complicated
rocess; to portray it as a division into only two camps is something of an
·versimplification. There were those who wavered and shifted their stands,
nd those who for a long time remained undecided as to what coalition they
hould join. Considerable differences also existed within each coalition. As
he crisis mounted during the spring and summer, however, Dubček and his
eformist supporters began winning ground in spite of the coercive actions
·f the Soviets. With this development, the options of the Soviets became
ewer, and the idea of military invasion attracted increasing numbers of
upporters. Finally, in June – July the ruling elite seems to have become
)olarized into two basic camps: advocates of and skeptics of the invasion,
vith some leaders shifting their stands. Despite its obvious oversimplifica-
ion, this assumption may be plausibly advanced to characterize the gradual
livision of opinion in the Soviet leadership.

Coalition of the Advocates of Military Intervention

The advocates of a hard-line policy toward Czechoslovakia mistrusted
Dubček's leadership and apparently conceptualized the Soviet decisionmaking with respect to Czechoslovakia as a *zero-sum* political game, where one
side's gain equals the other side's loss. They viewed the situation in Czechoslovakia as "counterrevolutionary," and clearly aimed at military conflict
with and the defeat of Dubček and his supporters. Although the members
of this coalition must have had some differences of opinion about the
implementation of military intervention, they probably perceived intervention as the only option available. Ukrainian Party leader Shelest (responsible for Ukrainian domestic affairs and, from the beginning, one of the
toughest critics of the Prague Spring) appears to have been the most vocal
member of this coalition. The representatives of the Party bureaucracies in
the national republics of the Western part of the Soviet Union (such as the
Belorussian Communist Party leader Masherov and Party leaders in the
Baltic republics of Estonia, Latvia, and Lithuania) also seem to have
visualized the payoff from a military solution as the removal of the threat of
Czechoslovak liberalism and experiments with federalism. Perhaps some of
them, such as Shelest, believed that joining the interventionist coalition
would in the end bring some added flexibility in supporting local interests.[55]

The other members of the interventionist coalition were Central Committee officials—chiefs of the bureaucracies charged with Party organization,
indoctrination, administrative affairs, and ideological watchdog functions
—such as Trapeznikov,[56] and officials from the large cities of the Russian
Soviet Federated Socialist Republic (RSFSR) (for example, candidate Politburo member and First Secretary of the Moscow Party Committee Grishin).

We can hypothesize that these Soviet officials expected a similar payoff fc advocating force against Czechoslovakia—the removal of the "cancer" c Czechoslovak reformism, which seemed to be affecting Soviet literary an intellectual communities through uncensored Czechoslovak public media.

Perhaps they also expected to gain leverage in future bargaining on di ferent issues. In particular, ideological watchdogs such as Trapeznikov whose position by 1967 seemed to have weakened as a result of obvious ar tagonisms in Soviet scientific circles over his orthodox orientation, migh have expected that a crackdown on Czechoslovak liberalism could be use as a weapon against Soviet dissidents and reformists and consequently as means of improving their position.[57] It was probably Trapeznikov's Centra Committee Department of Science and Education that distributed, prior tc the April session of the CPSU Central Committee, an alleged secret lette containing a "very sharp critical position" on the Czechoslovak issue. Th letter, which was sent to the regional bureaucracies, was designed for the in struction of teachers of social disciplines.[58]

The regional Party bureaucrats, some key Central Committee members and other opponents of Soviet economic reform (including some Sovie economists) probably hoped that by rejection of the Czechoslovak "heretical" economic reforms associated with the name Ota Šik (and by assertions that the Czechoslovak economic reform was leading to a "resto ration of capitalism"), they could provide additional ammunition against supporters of E. G. Liberman's proposed economic reform in the USSR (more conservative than the Czechoslovak one, but still unacceptable to them).[59]

In April 1968 there were signs that the interventionist coalition was gaining support among some segments of the Soviet national security bureaucracies, particularly the Main Political Administration of the Soviet armed forces, the Warsaw Pact Command, and the KGB. At the April Plenum of the Central Committee of the CPSU, one of the speakers, Army General Epishev, made the first reported interventionist appeal. He suggested that if the "healthy forces" (in the Soviet lexicon, pro-Soviet elements in Czechoslovakia) called on the Soviet Army for "fraternal assistance" against the "counterrevolution," it would do its duty.[60]

General Epishev, chief of the Main Political Administration of the Soviet armed forces (responsible for political work, ideological orientation of military personnel, and selection of officers for command positions), was probably afraid that the lack of discipline in the Czechoslovak Army would spread to the Warsaw Pact forces in neighboring countries, and ultimately to the Soviet armed forces. The Soviet generals who were responsible for the Warsaw Pact forces also seemed to be deeply concerned about the effect of the reform movement on the organizational mission of the Warsaw Pact forces in general, and the Czechoslovak armed forces in particular. After the April session of the Central Committee of the CPSU, Warsaw Pact commander-in-chief General I. I. Iakubovskii allegedly pressured the Dubček leadership (unsuccessfully) to accept a joint Warsaw Pact maneuver that would involve stationing Soviet troops on Czechoslovak territory, and publicly referred to the increased danger of war and the necessity of joint military exercises.[61] At this time the Czechoslovak leadership was apparently still able to delay or reject Iakubovskii's pressure, on the ground that the presence of foreign troops might create a dangerous situation during a period of revolutionary ferment in Czechoslovakia. While touring Czechoslovakia in early May, another Soviet General, First Deputy Chief Inspector of the Soviet General Staff A. S. Zhadov (whose responsibilities seemed to be related to the activities of the Warsaw Pact forces), also reportedly stated that "the negative" forces are manifesting themselves in Czechoslovakia, but good Czechoslovak communists "have nothing to fear, because a simple call will suffice—the entire Soviet Army as well as the armies of friendly nations will be ready."[62]

One must also count some high officials of the KGB and their representatives in the Central Committee among the advocates of armed intervention. Of all bureaucratic organizations, the Soviet secret police, particularly its services in East European countries, must have been the most frustrated by later developments in Czechoslovakia, for many of their most trusted men had begun to be dismissed or recalled by Czechoslovak Minister of Interior Josef Pavel. Thus, the KGB organizational mission in Czechoslovakia was gradually put in jeopardy. The KGB also probably tried to halt the investigations of its activities during the 1950s, which involved two *causes célèbres,* the Jan Masaryk[63] and Rudolf Slánský affairs. It also feared the impact of Prague reformism on the efficiency of the Czechoslovak intelligence service—the second largest producer of disinformation among the Socialist countries.

The Advocates of Military Intervention in Eastern Europe

The Soviet interventionist coalition found supporters in some East European countries, particularly in East Germany and Poland and belatedly in Bulgaria. Polish leader Władysław Gomułka and East German leader Walter Ulbricht feared that the "infection of liberalism" would spread to their countries and undermine their positions. Thus, in East Germany as in the Ukraine, Czechoslovak newspapers (e.g., the German-language newspaper *Volkszeitung*) began to be confiscated in the spring of 1968.[64] In the Ukraine, subscriptions to the Ukrainian-language publications *Nove Zhyttia* and *Duklia* were forbidden. Both Ulbricht and Shelest were concerned about Czechoslovak radio broadcasts. Radio Prague's broadcasts in German were reportedly jammed.[65]

In Poland, the first signs of the influence of the Prague Spring began to appear during the March student demonstrations. Demonstrators carried placards reading "Bravo Czechs" and "*Polska czeka na swego Dubczeka*" (Poland is waiting for its own Dubček).[66] Polish leader Gomułka, himself already under pressure from his opponents in the Polish leadership, later admitted that the Prague Spring evoked an emotional echo among Polish students.[67] He had personal reasons for animosity toward the new Czechoslovak leadership, and toward Dubček in particular. According to his interpreter Erwin Weit (who is now living in the West), Gomułka "hated the Czech leader because of his popularity within Czechoslovakia, and envied him for it. Naturally these ambivalent feelings were the result of the memory, which he tried in vain to suppress, of the time, twelve years earlier in October 1956, when he, like Dubček, was the hero of his own people . . . thus his attitude to Dubček was negative from the start."[68] In the spring of 1968, Czechoslovak newspapers were confiscated and Czechoslovak students and newspapermen were expelled from Poland.[69] According to Dubček, Poland in 1968 began to "boil with unsatisfied people" (i.e., unsatisfied with Gomułka's policies), and the Polish leaders began to push the Czech leadership into "absurd actions," perhaps because, as Dubček believed, they felt that pressure against the Czechoslovak leadership would help "solve their own internal conflicts."[70]

Czechoslovakia began to acquire a certain symbolic importance in the internal and bureaucratic politics of both Poland and East Germany. Gomułka and Ulbricht used the developments in Czechoslovakia to define their own internal positions; they became outspoken critics of the Prague reformers and persistent advocates of a hard-line policy toward Czechoslovakia in the early stages of the crisis, as demonstrated by their performance at the Dresden Conference in March 1968. At Dresden, Ulbricht passed a definitive judgment about the Prague Spring, arguing that "if Czechoslovakia continues to follow the January line, all of us here will run a very serious risk which may well lead to our downfall."[71] Polish and East German diplomatic notes in early May also expressed sharp resentment at the Czechoslovak media's treatment of Polish events and West Berlin issues.

Moreover, Ulbricht and his supporters feared that the new Dubček regime would take a softer line toward West Germany. They were also intimidated by the Action Program of the Czechoslovak Party, which advocated support for the West German Social Democrats. Thus, the East German leadership exerted pressure on the Czechoslovak leadership, and, as Dubček pointed out, tried to "prescribe" policy with respect to West Germany. Ulbricht's actions reflected his "unclear attitude toward the politics of W. Brandt."[72] Attacks in the press by the East German leaders on Czechoslovak reformers such as Josef Smrkovský, and Czechoslovak reports about a secret East German document asserting that Ulbricht's leadership had lost confidence in Dubček and had begun to think about a collective military intervention in the early stage of the crisis, reflected the stand of the East German leadership on the Czechoslovak issue.[73]

In advocating policies to crush Czechoslovak "revisionism," Ulbricht may have expected a payoff from a military solution to the Czechoslovak crisis—the prevention (or at least the delay) of the rapprochement between the Soviet Union and West Germany. Perhaps the events in Czechoslovakia were not entirely unwelcome to Ulbricht, however, as they could be used as a warning to those East European—and perhaps even those Soviet—leaders seeking West German–Soviet rapprochement.

Developments in Czechoslovakia had perceptible effects in Bulgaria only late in the crisis. Perhaps because of geography and a different political situation Bulgarian concern with Czechoslovak reforms was not comparable to that of the East German and Polish leaderships.

Coalition of the Skeptics of Military Intervention

In Soviet politics the building of a strong coalition advocating a controversial policy seems to lead inevitably to the building of a countercoalition questioning the wisdom of such a policy. The Czechoslovak issue is a case in point. Skeptics of the wisdom of military intervention in Czechoslovakia hesitated to commit themselves to a policy leading toward a military conflict with the Dubček leadership. Having addressed themselves to the possible gains and losses of joining the interventionist coalition, they preferred nonalignment; later, when pressure from the interventionist coaltion grew and General Epishev first threatened intervention, they began to form a noninterventionist coalition.

Undoubtedly, a diversity of opinion existed among those Soviet officials who questioned the wisdom of military intervention, some advocating political bargaining, others, political and perhaps economic coercion or even actions aimed at the destabilization of Dubček's regime. For example, in April 1968 Zagladin, one of the skeptics of the invasion, was reported by M. Voslensky, an eyewitness and adviser to the Central Committee of the CPSU, to have implied that the situation in Czechoslovakia should not be dramatized since "it cannot be compared with Hungary" in 1956, but rather with Poland in 1956 after Gomułka's election as first secretary of the Polish Party. Then too, voices of "panic" were heard, but "nothing happened." Zagladin agreed with Voslensky that the USSR's policy should be politically supportive of Dubček against both extremes in Czechoslovak politics: the discredited supporters of Novotný as well as the anti-Soviet forces.[74] What united these policymakers were the high risks of military intervention. Overall they conceptualized the Czechoslovak crisis in terms of a *non-zero sum* political game and recommended resolution of the crisis by a variety of means *short of invasion, and at considerably less political cost.* Suslov, the main overseer and coordinator of Soviet policy in the international communist movement, began to emerge as spokesman for this coalition. Also belonging to the noninterventionist coalition were the high officials of the International Department, Central Committee secretary Ponomarev and Ponomarev's deputy Zagladin, both of whom appeared to believe that nonintervention would pay off through uninterrupted Soviet *Westpolitik* (including rapprochement with West Germany) and, in particular, in the success of the anti-Chinese World Communist Conference scheduled for November 1968. After all, it was Suslov who, at the Budapest preparatory conference of Communist parties in February 1968, promised to "do everything necessary to create the most favorable conditions for the conference." The resolution of the April 1968 session of the Central Committee of the CPSU described the conference as a "central element" in the activities of the CPSU for the near future.[75] These promises and tasks apparently were instrumental in shaping Suslov's and Ponomarev's position on Czechoslovakia. The two leaders' interest and personal stake in the success of the upcoming conference served to ensure that their stand on the Czechoslovak issue would be moderate.

Prime Minister Kosygin, then mainly responsible for diplomacy with Western countries, probably also expressed doubts about a hard-line policy toward Czechoslovakia. He apparently joined the noninterventionist coalition because of the possible repercussions of military action on U.S.–Soviet relations—particularly, on the prospects of beginning the SALT and NPT talks. It should also be noted that because of developments in Czechoslovakia, Kosygin's domestic policy, which was said somewhat to favor Liberman's economic reform, seems to have come under heavy criticism from opponents in the spring and summer of 1968.[76] After the intervention, economic reform was called a "revisionist heresy," occupying an important place in the attacks against Dubček's leadership. Soviet economic reform was shelved after the invasion of Czechoslovakia.

The skeptics of the wisdom of military intervention were also probably supported by certain government bureaucracies, such as several subdivisions of the Ministry of Foreign Affairs responsible for diplomacy with the West,[77] and perhaps by some segments of the armed forces, such as the Strategic Rocket Forces. (The commander of this service, the late Marshal N. I. Krylov,[78] probably did not share the fear felt by his colleagues in the Warsaw Pact Command or in the Soviet Ground Forces that in an age of intercontinental missiles Czechoslovak reformism would seriously endanger the strategic position of the Soviet Union.)

The Skeptics of Military Intervention in Eastern Europe and Dubček Supporters in West European Communist Parties

Among the ruling parties in Eastern Europe, two openly adopted supportive attitudes toward the Prague Spring: Rumania and, a bit more discretely, Yugoslavia. This support was demonstrated particularly during the Ceauşescu and Tito visits to Prague in August, shortly before the invasion. However, both parties' representatives were excluded from the crucial meetings of the Soviet and East European leaders dealing with the Czechoslovak issue. Thus, a more significant role would have been played by the Hungarian Party, whose representatives became directly involved in management of the crisis in apparent efforts to achieve a political solution.[79] Hungarian leader János Kádár, who favored a moderate domestic policy of limited pluralism, and who backed Hungarian economic reform, probably feared that an intervention would have repercussions on Hungarian internal politics. Thus, Hungarian policy toward Czechoslovakia during the crisis could at first be characterized as benign neutrality. Kádár was playing the role of honest broker in resolving the conflict through bargaining with Dubček's leadership. Kádár and his supporters in the Hungarian leadership perceived a nonmilitary resolution of the conflict as beneficial both to the successful continuation of the Hungarian New Economic Mechanism (NEM) of economic reform and to limited, cautious political reforms—e.g., strengthening the role of the trade unions, which began in 1968. As Kádár pointed out to Czechoslovak leaders Dubček and Z. Mlynář, "Success of the Czechoslovak reforms would undoubtedly mean new hope for developments in Hungary."[80]

Dubček and his reformist supporters were also supported in varying degrees during the crisis by several West European Communist parties, particularly the Italian and Spanish parties, and to a lesser degree the French Communist Party. Italian Party leader Luigi Longo, engaged in elections in May, expressed his approval of Prague reformism at the Central Committee session at the end of March and during his visit to Prague in early May.[81] So did exiled Spanish leader Santiago Carrillo. In July French Communist leader Waldeck-Rochet, as shown below, acted as a "mediator," in the manner of Kádár, between the Soviet and Czechoslovak leaderships.

The Secretary General

Compared with such chief executives in Western political systems as the American president, the Soviet secretary general probably has somewhat more limited decisionmaking power and enjoys fewer prerogatives. Although the office of Party secretary general theoretically constitutes a base of enormous personal authority and power, the reemergence of the collective leadership as the normal pattern of Soviet decisionmaking in the post-Stalin era restrains the incumbent from becoming a personal ruler. It has been demonstrated that American presidential decisions are influenced and shaped by bureaucratic and domestic politics, notably the presidential elections. While an American president may see a connection between his stand on foreign policy issues and the outcome of the next presidential election, the Soviet secretary general sees a possible link between his stand on domestic and foreign policy issues and the possibility of removal from office.

Although events have shown that an American president can be removed from office by the threat of impeachment, he cannot be deposed by a mere coalition of National Security Council (NSC) or cabinet members. In Soviet politics, this possibility is quite real, as Khrushchev's fall in 1964 demonstrates. As the office has evolved, the secretary general does not assume Stalin's role of *vozhd* (supreme leader) but rather acts as *primus inter pares*. He cannot afford to ignore entirely the other members of the ruling oligarchy. Neither can he ignore the group of Soviet officials who constitute the "Moscow community," composed primarily of key Central Committee officials and leaders of various bureaucracies. In like manner, an American president cannot scorn the Congress and the "President-watching" group of government-related professionals which Richard Neustadt refers to as the "Washington community."

In contrast to an American president, who has the power to accept or reject the views of the NSC and to alter the composition of the government (a power shared by a British prime minister with respect to his cabinet), the secretary general of the CPSU functions under the constraint that his decisions must have the support of his colleagues in the ruling elite. Whereas the American president has come to exercise, to borrow from Neustadt again, "the power to persuade," the Soviet secretary general is required not only to persuade but also to identify himself with, or even better, to create a "winning" coalition in the Politburo. (This was especially true in the late 1960s, when the influence of Brezhnev's personal secretariat was minor compared with its important role in the 1970s, particularly before Brezhnev became Chairman of the Presidium of the Supreme Soviet in 1977.)

It is not an accident that Brezhnev has often been called the Kremlin's "great compromiser" and "consensus leader," mediating amidst the conflicting interests of other decisionmakers and preserving the delicate balance of power in the Politburo. In this respect, he seems to be more successful in forging a winning consensus within the Soviet decisionmaking collectivity than his predecessor, whose style in the last years of his leadership antagonized his colleagues and ultimately led them to unite against him.

These constraints of office and the consensus style of his leadership could be observed in Secretary General Brezhnev's behavior during the Czechoslovak crisis. In trying to play the game according to the rule of *primus inter pares,* he vacillated during the several stages of the crisis. At the very beginning of the Prague Spring, he seemed to support Dubček's appointment as first secretary of the Czechoslovak Communist Party. During his first diplomatic mission of December 8, 1967 (reportedly at the invitation of President Novotný), and without the knowledge of the Central Committee of the Czechoslovak Party, Brezhnev did not try to bolster Novotný, as he had four years earlier on Khrushchev's behalf.[82]

In fact, Brezhnev surprised the Czechoslovak leaders with his flexible attitude. After he became aware of Novotný's weak position, he reportedly told the Czechoslovak leaders, *Eto vashe delo* [That is your own affair], and left.[83] Undoubtedly, Brezhnev was unwilling to back a sure loser, probably being convinced that Dubček, who had spent part of his youth in the USSR and was an experienced party official, was a reliable successor.

Although Brezhnev complained privately to Dubček about the latter's February speech in Prague, in early 1968 he was "in no hurry to express his views" in public on the Czechoslovak issue (which, as Soviet writer B. Polevoi observed at the time, "would have been done immediately by Khrushchev").[84] Only after March–April 1968, when segments of the Soviet bureaucracies, particularly the Ukrainian Party apparatus, had expressed apprehension and concern over possible repercussions of the Prague Spring on domestic Soviet policies, did Brezhnev take a hard line on the Czechoslovak issue—in his public speeches and during negotiations with Dubček's leadership in Dresden in March, and in Moscow in May 1968.[85]

Brezhnev's cautiousness and vacillation became more obvious when he apologized in June 1968 to the Chairman of the National Assembly, reformist J. Smrkovský. Although Smrkovský had been publicly attacked by East German leader K. Hager in March 1968, privately attacked by Brezhnev in the same month (at the Dresden summit) as being "not a promising political figure," and considered a public enemy by the East German leaders and press, he encountered a surprising degree of flexibility during his negotiations with Brezhnev in June 1968. In fact, at that time, during private discussions with Smrkovský, Brezhnev went so far as to apologize for the Soviet "propaganda" attacks against Smrkovský, explaining that this had happened "because of a lack of information."[86] At this point, the "flexible" Brezhnev appeared to believe in the political future of the reformist Smrkovský. He even suggested that Smrkovský take over the post of the inexperienced Dubček. In discussions with Smrkovský's delegation, Brezhnev expressed regret over "certain mistakes committed on the Soviet side" with respect to policies vis-à-vis Czechoslovakia, and pledged the willingness of the Soviet Union to defend its good intentions, even at the International Court in the Hague concerning the "unjust accusation that appeared in connection with events in Czechoslovakia." Brezhnev, defending himself, stressed that "*he* had never given instructions that something should be done this way or another."[87]

Interestingly, in the discussions with Smrkovský's delegation, Brezhnev compared Czechoslovakia's development with the scenario in Poland in 1956, as Zagladin of the International Department had done earlier, and not with that in Hungary in 1956, as the Soviet interventionists did during the crisis. Brezhnev argued that the Soviets had never "forced Poland into socialization," so why should they force Czechoslovakia into something?[88] Although Brezhnev had several times expressed a hard line toward developments in Czechoslovakia, he wavered between the two coalitions—advocates and skeptics of intervention—until the very day of the decision to intervene, acting as a broker while still attempting to identify himself with the prevailing coalition. Other players probably also shifted their stands during the protracted crisis, particularly those with no organizational commitments. The continual changes in Soviet decisions, especially (as will be shown) during the last strenuous phase of the crisis, suggest that other decisionmakers besides Brezhnev might have altered their positions several times.

Consensus-Building and Maneuvering

During the crisis, both a deadline and the requirements of consensus-building had their impact on coalition formation. The decision of the Czechoslovak Central Committee on June 1 to convene an Extraordinary Fourteenth Party Congress on September 9 projected an important deadline for the interventionist coalition. At this Congress most of the pro-Soviet Central Committee members would be expelled and a new pro-Dubček slate would be elected, thus legitimizing Dubček's program. The interventionists argued that the date of the Party congress amounted to a deadline for the Warsaw Pact as well as for Czechoslovakia. Thus, the Warsaw Pact commander-in-chief Marshal Iakubovskii insisted on deploying Warsaw Pact troops in Czechoslovakia until September 20[89]—the closing day of the Party congress—and was reluctant to order their withdrawal in spite of earlier assurances. According to one witness, Ulbricht stated that the date of the Czechoslovak congress set a deadline for the Warsaw Pact countries. Afterward "they would be faced with a completely new situation. For then there would be a new Central Committee and a new Presidium of the Central Committee; all the good communists would lose their posts." Thus, the Warsaw Pact "must react before this Party Congress can take place."[90] In short, the planned Czechoslovak congress provided the occasion for resolving the issue.

Various maneuvers occurred in the effort to create a consensus on policy. The interventionist coalition evidently tried to enlarge the decisionmaking circle by bringing new participants to the Central Committee meetings during the crisis. For example, in April, Konstantin F. Katushev, a regional party official with no previous experience in foreign affairs, replaced an experienced but perhaps not "hard enough" foreign policy bureaucrat, Konstantin V. Rusakov, to the important post of party secretary in charge of the Department of Liaison with Communist and Workers Parties.[91] At this point Shelest and Katushev, officials with no prior serious experience in foreign affairs, were included in a Soviet team participating with representatives of ruling parties in Eastern Europe at the meetings dealing with the Czechoslovak problem. Shelest's and Katushev's prominent roles in the Czechoslovak crisis are reflected in their presence at the major meetings of the Warsaw Pact devoted to Czechoslovak affairs.

During the crisis the interventionists also appeared to be expanding the decisionmaking circle to include participants who could dramatize the danger of the situation in Czechoslovakia for the non-Russian republics in the Soviet West. In general, bureaucrats from this part of the Soviet Union belonged to the interventionist coalition, constituting one of its most important factions. At the April session several speakers and discussants were representatives of these republics: Shelest, Masherov, First Secretary of the Estonian Communist Party I. G. Kabin, and First Secretary of the Moldavian Communist Party I. I. Bodiul. These officials, because of the geographic proximity of their republics to the East European countries and the cultural and social affinities between them, seemed more concerned about "contamination" from the Czechoslovak "disease" than did bureaucrats from Soviet Central Asia and the Far East. Party representatives from major cities in the RSFSR and bureaucrats charged with ideological supervision and indoctrination also feared the repercussions of Czechoslovak reformism among Soviet intellectuals and writers. Two of them appeared as speakers or discussants at the April session of the Central Committee of the CPSU: First Secretary of the Moscow City Party Committee Grishin, and secretary of the board of the USSR Writers Union Markov. Both must have been upset by the reports that certain Moscovite intellectuals who knew some Czech language had translated the reports on the Dubček reformist Action Program from the Czechoslovak Party newspaper *Rudé právo* and had circulated them among their friends in Moscow.[92] The Soviet press generally ignored the controversial passages of the Action Program.[93] The only extensive Russian translation of the Action Program was printed in the *Information Bulletin* of the Czechoslovak Party. Even this publication, normally available at the Lenin Library in Moscow, was said to be relegated to the special archives of the library.[94]

Grishin's concern about the spillover of Czechoslovak reformism was reflected in his public speech shortly after the April session of the Central Committee of the CPSU. He attacked "revisionists" and "nationalist" elements and their program of "spontaneity, unlimited decentralization, and the reduction of the Party to the level of a politico-educational organization"—the very essence of the Czechoslovak Action Program. Grishin declared that the Soviet Union would provide "political, economic, and if necessary *military aid*" to countries threatened by imperialism.[95]

Because of the interventionists' apprehension at the April Central Committee session, things may have been said that called into question Soviet performance in the international Communist movement in general and in Czechoslovakia in particular. Probably also because of the interventionists' pressure, the resolution of the April session called for "vigilance" against ideological enemies at home and abroad and reaffirmed the "readiness to do everything necessary" in defense of the socialist commonwealth.[96]

Organizational Maneuvers

As noted, the maneuvering among Soviet decisionmakers with respect to Czechoslovakia took place within an organizational context. An illustration of this point is the performance of the Warsaw Pact Command and its commander-in-chief, Marshal Iakubovskii, during the June military exercises on Czechoslovak territory. According to an informal agreement between Kosygin and the Czechoslovak leaders Dubček and Premier O. Černík, units of the Warsaw Pact were originally not to participate in these exercises. Also in contradiction of the agreement, Warsaw Pact forces crossed the Czechoslovak borders at many points other than those agreed upon. Some units arrived in early June during the Czechoslovak Central Committee meeting. With them came such military equipment as armored units, tactical air units, and mobile radio station equipment designed to jam Czechoslovak radio and television—all of which had apparently not been agreed upon. The Warsaw Pact forces first entered several major military air fields capable of handling heavy Soviet air transports. Czechoslovak officers were apparently not informed about this development in advance; moreover, they were excluded from the post-exercise analysis held by Marshal Iakubovskii. Dubček sent a message to Kosygin complaining about the Warsaw Pact Command's performance, which contradicted their May agreement. Subsequently, it became known that the Warsaw Pact Command had introduced 16,000 troops into Czechoslovakia for the maneuvers between June 20 and 30. The troop withdrawal announced on July 1 was delayed until the Čierna-Bratislava negotiations in late July and early August. Rather than concessions, the continued presence of troops produced a stiffening of Czechoslovak public will and a growing anti-Soviet attitude.

Similarly, some departments of the KGB aligned themselves with those bureaucracies whose organizational mission was adversely affected by Prague reformism. As mentioned earlier, KGB operatives in Prague had been dismissed, their security surveillance system had been dismantled, and past KGB activities had been revealed. Therefore, it is not surprising to learn that the KGB engaged in various maneuvers to influence the decision-making process on Czechoslovakia. KGB intelligence reports and actions during the crisis, as shown below, were aimed at dramatizing the situation in Czechoslovakia and building support among Soviet bureaucracies and the public for intervention.

Playing Coalition Politics

Differences between the two principal coalitions among the Soviet leaders regarding Czechoslovakia were highlighted several times during the crisis. Whereas a Soviet military delegation, led by Minister of Defense Marshal A. A. Grechko and including the interventionist Epishev, used pressure and coercion during its May visit to Czechoslovakia, Premier Kosygin, visiting Czechoslovakia at the same time, used persuasion. In fact, Kosygin's visit to Czechoslovakia was not only a fact-finding mission, but probably also an effort aimed at defusing the crisis. The result of Kosygin's visit was a temporary *modus vivendi*.[97]

The Kosygin-Dubček compromise can be summarized in a few words. Czechoslovakia would remain a loyal member of the Warsaw Pact and COMECON; the Czechoslovak Communist Party would retain its monopoly of power, forbid anti-Soviet polemics in the press, reduce the scope of activities of various political clubs, and outlaw new political parties; and to prove its loyalty as an ally the Czechoslovak leadership would agree to staff exercises (without ground forces) on its territory in June. In return, Kosygin, in spite of his personal irritation with developments in Czechoslovakia, was said not to object to the Extraordinary Party Congress.[98]

Soviet coalition politics was also conditioned by the politics and players in Eastern Europe. As in the Soviet Union, two schools of thought apparently existed among the East European elites regarding the Czechoslovak situation. One was represented by East German leader Ulbricht and Polish leader Gomułka, the other by Hungarian leader Kádár. While Kádár was credited by Yugoslav and Czechoslovak sources with displaying a moderate stand during the conference of the Warsaw Pact leaders in Moscow in May 1968, Ulbricht argued for a hard-line policy vis-à-vis Czechoslovakia.[99] In addition, Soviet troop exercises carried out during the Moscow conference took place on Polish and East German, but not on Hungarian soil, although the Soviet Army maintained four divisions in Hungary and only two in Poland. Also, while Brezhnev displayed a degree of moderation in negotiations with Czechoslovak reformist Smrkovský, Ulbricht decided, on June 11, 1968, to introduce new passport and visa regulations for travel through East Germany to West Berlin—curiously, at a time when Soviet officials continued their diplomatic dialogue with West Germany. It is likely that Ulbricht's restrictions were meant to be a signal of disapproval of the continuation of secret West German–Soviet negotiations, as well as a bid for a tough Soviet stand on the Czechoslovak issue.[100]

Use of the Press

Disagreements between top senior decisionmakers rarely become public in the Soviet Union. A public rift is an admission of weakness in the political system and in the individuals involved, and could signal political death and disgrace. Political comebacks, possible in the open systems of the West and even in China, are rare in the Soviet Union. Decisionmakers try to avoid intense political conflict, particularly in public.

Thus, conflict in the Politburo often shifts downward to the Central Committee's bureaucracies and to the staff level. Since Soviet decisionmakers are severely limited in what they can say publicly, they pursue their bargaining and internal maneuvering through the cryptic language of Soviet politics, withholding position statements until a consensus has been reached. Still, despite institutionalized censorship and secrecy, the press can occasionally be used as an effective instrument in internal debate.

During the Czechoslovak crisis, in April 1968, the interventionists, making good use of the Soviet press, launched a hostile campaign against Dubček's leadership and in subsequent months thwarted the attempts of the noninterventionists to defuse the crisis. In fact, such periodicals as *Pravda Ukrainy, Radíans'ka Ukraina,* and *Kommunist Ukrainy* (all published by the Ukrainian Party bureaucracy in Kiev), *Sovetskaia Rossiia* (the newspaper of the Central Committee of the CPSU, reflecting the strong influence of RSFSR party officials and ideological watchdogs),[101] and *Literaturnaia gazeta* (published under the auspices of the Writers Union of the USSR, where ideological watchdogs like Markov and Gribachev had a strong influence) showed in the early stages of the crisis apprehension and hostility toward Dubček's leadership.

These periodicals first publicly condemned the idea of "democratic and national forms of Marxism"[102] and then began continuous attacks on "revisionist" and "nationalist" elements in Czechoslovakia. They did not cease their campaign even during the temporary truces in May and June, when the Soviet noninterventionists sought a compromise with the Czechoslovak leadership. Indeed, they registered their disapproval of any moderation of Soviet policy and advocated escalating the crisis, the most pointed example being the attack in *Sovetskaia Rossiia* accusing former Czechoslovak president Masaryk of having financed a plot to kill Lenin in 1918. Since Masaryk was already fully rehabilitated at this time and was viewed as a national hero, this incident, which provoked an emotional reaction in Czechoslovakia, was probably aimed at prejudicing Kosygin's May diplomatic mission to Prague.[103] Not surprisingly, these glaring affronts to Czechoslovak sensibilities seriously affected communications between Moscow and Prague; indeed, Smrkovský asserted that "responsible circles in the Soviet Union have not been very pleased with the article [in *Sovetskaia Rossiia*] but rather to the contrary."[104] All these attempts were obviously tailored to prejudice Soviet-Czechoslovak reconciliation and to undercut the noninterventionists.

On the other hand, some Soviet periodicals—*Izvestiia* (sometimes reflecting the views of Soviet governmental bureaucracy), and *Novoe vremia* (which appears in English as *New Times* and is published by the Soviet Trade Union publishing house)—adopted a more cautious attitude toward Czechoslovakia, particularly during the earlier stages of the crisis.[105] Here three other journals should also be mentioned: *Kommunist* (the theoretical magazine of the CPSU devoted to international communist and ideological problems), *Problemy mira i Sotsializma* (published in Prague under the auspices of Ponomarev's International Department and which appears in English as *World Marxist Review*,[106] and *Mirovaia ekonomika i mezhdunarodnye otnosheniia (MEMO)* (published at the Institute of World Economy and International Relations, or IMEMO). In April *Kommunist* launched a forceful anti-Chinese campaign, ignoring almost entirely the danger of "revisionism" in Czechoslovakia. A series of five such articles appeared, apparently prepared by the CPSU's International Department. They were supposed to be a theoretical explanation of the Soviet reassessment of developments in China, to be presented at the World Communist Conference in November 1968, prior to the Ninth Party Congress in China, which at that time was rumored to be scheduled for the fall of 1968.[107] Similarly, *Mirovaia ekonomika i mezhdunarodnye otnosheniia* did not criticize the Dubček leadership at all during the crisis. On the contrary, in one of its articles in April 1968 Iu. Zhilin—a Soviet official who is believed to work as a consultant to the International Department—pointed out, with obvious refererence to Czechoslovakia, that "it would be wrong to dramatize (*dramatizirovat'*) difficulties" in the world Communist movement and that they will be overcome.[108] As shown earlier, this view was also shared by Zagladin, a deputy head of the International Department.

Even the CPSU's most important periodical, *Pravda,* had for several months of the crisis adopted a cautious stand on Czechoslovakia, presenting the critical events in Prague in a selective but more or less calm manner until mid-June 1968.[109] The positions of these periodicals seemed to reflect the cautious attitude of some Soviet bureaucracies, particularly those concerned with the detrimental effects of the Soviet hard line toward Czechoslovakia.

As was evident at numerous junctures during the crisis, Soviet senior decisionmakers, under certain circumstances, used the press to promote their political maneuvering. For example, N. V. Podgorny, Politburo member and Presidium Chairman of the Supreme Soviet, decided to "go to the public" by issuing an unusual statement about "the intrigues of circle hostile to progress and socialism" in Czechoslovakia.[110] Podgorny's pronouncement, made shortly after the May negotiations between Czechoslovakia and the Soviet Union (in which he had participated), was probably a means of signaling to Soviet and East European elites his "tough" stand on the Czechoslovak issue.

In Eastern Europe as in the Soviet Union, periodicals were used to signal emerging positions on the critical Czechoslovak issue in 1968. East German and some Polish presses launched a vicious campaign against Dubček's leadership, even during the periods when the Soviet central press was silent or denied, in the authoritative comment of I. Alexandrov (a pseudonym) that the Warsaw Pact was interfering in Czechoslovak affairs.[111] This clearly demonstrated the disapproval of Polish and East German leaderships toward attempts of the noninterventionists to defuse the crisis.[112] On the other hand, Hungarian periodicals reflected the cautious attitudes of Hungarian officials in general and Kádár in particular, and tried to project a soft line in their reports on Czechoslovakia.[113]

Polarization of Political Forces in Czechoslovakia: Formation of an Antireformist Coalition

Contrary to conventional wisdom, the Czechoslovak leadership was not united during the crisis, particularly during the peak in July–August 1968. This should not come as a surprise. After all, the coalition that overthrew President Novotný in January 1968 was full of internal contradictions, being composed of heterogeneous elements: Slovak party leaders Dubček and V. Bilak; reform-minded figures such as Šik, F. Kriegel, Smrkovský, and J. Špaček; representatives of the so-called Ostrava faction (officials who came from an important industrial region in Moravia), Černík and D. Kolder; and cabinet ministers such as A. Indra, concerned with limitations on the actions of individual ministries.

Indeed, with Novotný's final defeat on March 28, when he resigned as president, the anti-Novotný coalition lost its *raison d'être*. Subsequently, under increasing Soviet and East European pressures—as well as pressures from domestic politics—various interest groups and news media began a fresh process of differentiation. Old coalitions were dissolved, and new ones emerged. The anti-Novotný coalition began to polarize into several distinct groups divided in their attitudes toward the continuous power struggle and the issue of reforms. Signs of this polarization first appeared during the debate at the Central Committee session of the Czechoslovak Communist Party in April, grew to size in May, and crystalized in late June.

It would be misleading to label the Soviet leaders as "doves" or "hawks" in their attitudes toward Czechoslovakia. Likewise, it would be an oversimplification to classify the Czechoslovak leaders into "conservative" and "progressive" factions, as the Czechoslovak and Western media often did during and after the crisis. (The Soviet oversimplification was a division in-to "healthy" and "revisionist," or "right wing," forces.) Such labels are meaningless. Czechoslovak leaders exhibited a wide range of views from antireformist to radical, which were based not only on different perceptions of reform but also on different evaluations of the forthcoming Party congress (particularly varying forecasts of the power struggle) and the extent of Soviet pressure, and on differing bureaucratic and personal interests (such as simple opportunism and fear about loss of privileges). Thus, the views of some leaders differed from issue to issue, and the various coalition affiliations altered during the crisis.[114]

Dubček himself was influenced by many conflicting pressures from various coalitions and groups, and often wavered. It was only during the May–June Party conferences at district and regional levels that he became an unreserved supporter of radical political change. Then the polarization of the Czechoslovak ruling elite (the Presidium and the Secretariat) crystalized into more distinct coalitions, becoming more and more divided in their attitudes toward continuing the reformist program. Very roughly, one may describe the contending coalitions in the Czechoslovak leadership from June to the day of the invasion as follows: a reformist coalition composed of vigorous reformers—J. Smrkovský, Kriegel, V. Slavík, C. Císař—and of moderate reformers—Dubček, Černík, Spaček, B. Šimon, Z. Mlynář; an antireformist coalition, including Kolder, Indra, Bilak, O. Švestka, A. Kapek, and M. Jakeš. In addition, there were several centrist, wavering or undecided leaders—J. Piller, E. Rigo, F. Barbírek, J. Lenárt, S. Sádovský.[115] Thus, from June to the very day of the Soviet invasion on August 20, an uneasy balance and division existed between competing coalitions and wavering members. It should be emphasized again that both coalitions—reformists and antireformists—were loose, heterogeneous groups (antireformists not opposing all reforms; reformists not favoring all reforms). The coalitions were not unified on a definitive political platform, but on their differing evaluations of the process of reform in general and on the outcome of the Extraordinary Party Congress on September 9 in particular.

The antireformist coalition was composed basically of the members who had differed in the past on a variety of issues. It included some of those who had actively helped to bring Novotný down (Kolder, Bilak, Švestka). Some of these leaders supported the reformist program and Dubček in the early stage of the crisis. (Kolder was chairman of the committee in charge of preparing the Action Program.) But, because of fear of reformist change—some being Soviet sympathizers (Bilak, Indra, Jakeš, Kapek), but, perhaps more important, all of them fearing that they would not, for a variety of reasons, be reelected at the forthcoming Party congress—they begar after April–May to sabotage the reformist course.

The antireformist coalition was relatively small and isolated. It could rely, nevertheless, on supporters in the Central Committee, in some high of fices in the bureaucracies of the security forces, in the defense and state bureaucracies, and in certain regional bureaucracies. All of these supporters were officials—many of them not elected as delegates for the Party congress—who also feared they would lose their positions. On the other hand, the reformists in the Czechoslovak leadership were supported by a majority of the newly elected Party regional secretaries, by the Party apparatus in important regions (Prague, Brno, Bratislava, and Ostrava), and by a majority of Party members.[116] As a result, they did not feel threatened by the upcoming Party congress.

The first signs of antireformist activities became obvious at the April session of the Central Committee, where certain antireformists (such as Indra) tried to prevent the election of the more vigorous reformers (such as Šik) to the Czechoslovak Presidium.[117] During the important session of the Czechoslovak Presidum on May 7–9, the antireformist elements attacked Dubček and his supporters and pressed for a halt to the reform. They likewise began publicly to deplore "activities of antisocialist forces"[118] and even manufactured the evidence of a "counterrevolution" in Czechoslovakia. They opposed the reformist pressure to convene a Party congress in September and later only reluctantly agreed to do so.

There is scattered evidence that the antireformists began as early as May and June to alert the Soviet leadership about the danger of "counterrevolution" in Czechoslovakia and to cultivate covert relations with potential allies, the advocates of a hard-line policy toward Czechoslovakia in the USSR and Eastern Europe. Indra became the main organizer of the People's Militia meeting in June, which delivered a letter to the Soviet Embassy in Prague deploring the irresponsible actions of the Czechoslovak public media. The letter was not published in the Czechoslovak press at that time, but it was immediately picked up by *Pravda* (Moscow) on June 21 and by other Soviet media and was used as a pretext for the widespread anti-Czechoslovak campaign. At that time Indra and Kolder had developed a special relationship with Soviet ambassador S. V. Chervonenko, while another antireformist, Bilak (himself of Ukrainian origin), cultivated a similar, but Ukrainian, connection with the spokesman of the Soviet interventionist coalition, Shelest.[119] The stands and intentions of some antireformists became obvious during the May bilateral negotiations in Moscow. There, Bilak was a member of the Czechoslovak delegation (the other members were the reformists Dubček, Smrkovský, and Černík) and was reported by Smrkovský to have argued for the Soviet positions, so that he acted as a "fifth member" of the Soviet delegation and "we were three against five, not four against four.''[120] As shown below in Chapter 5, the overt and covert activities of the antireformists, particularly their reports to the Soviet leadership about the "counterrevolution" in Czechoslovakia, played an important role in influencing Soviet decisionmaking. On the one hand, the interest of the antireformist coalition (to prevent the Party congress) coincided with the interests of transnational interventionist coalitions in the Warsaw Pact countries. On the other hand, antireformist reports and activities made it obviously more difficult for skeptics of the intervention in the Soviet leadership to succeed in their efforts to find a political solution to the crisis. This phenomenon was to become a significant factor in the debate on Czechoslovakia.

II *Today the key to a progressive restructuring of the system of government in the interests of mankind lies in intellectual freedom. This has been understood in particular by the Czechoslovaks, and there can be no doubt that we should support their bold initiative, which is so valuable for the future of socialism. . . . That support should be political, and in the early stages include increasing economic aid.—*A. D. Sakharov

*What does "socialism with a human face" mean? Socialism is itself the most human thing possible . . . . This kind of catch-phrase is used by the Western imperialists to cause confusion in the socialist camp and, eventually, to destroy it.—*W. Gomułka

The July Debate: Linkages and Pressures

The Two Thousand Words Manifesto

The Czechoslovak crisis was revived, and Soviet and East European pressures intensified, in early July 1968 with the controversy stirred up by the Two Thousand Words Manifesto, drafted by the Czech writer L. Vaculík. The dynamics of this development can be understood only against the background of the polarization of forces in the Czechoslovak leadership.[1]

There was no spectacular development in Czechoslovakia at that time. Dubček's leadership did not attempt either to modify its foreign policy orientation or to allow the establishment of a pluralistic system of the Western type. The reformists were determined, however, to continue their program. The Soviet leaders were alarmed by the advancing reform movement in Czechoslovakia as well as by the polarization of forces in the Czechoslovak ruling elite. It is likely that the emerging signs that the antireformist coalition would suffer defeat at the Party congress provided a strong impetus for Soviet advocates of intervention to intensify pressure upon the reformists.

The glamour surrounding publication of the Two Thousand Words Manifesto on June 27, as well as other peripheral phenomena of Prague reformism—premature formation of the Social Democratic Party and the existence of several clubs such as *Klub angažovaných nestraníků* (KAN, the Club of the Non-Party Engagés) and K231 (which offered membership to all those who had been sentenced to prison under the law for the defense of the republic, No. 231)—provided an excellent opportunity for advocates of intervention to renew their pressure. Shortly after publication of the manifesto, the temporary truce constructed in May by Kosygin and Dubček ended, and pressures from the Warsaw Pact countries began to mount. Actually, the manifesto pledged support to the Party's "progressive wing" and its Action Program. It also requested an acceleration of the reform process and the "resignation" of antireformist Party officials, and suggested that this process begin at the forthcoming district conferences to elect delegates to the extraordinary regional conferences, which would in turn choose delegates to the September 9 Extraordinary Party Congress.

In a way, the manifesto truly reflected the polarization within the Czechoslovak ruling elite, particularly that within the anti-Novotný coalition, which had begun after publication of the Action Program. The manifesto also reflected the internal political atmosphere in the summer of 1968. The authors, who seemed to be trying to influence the outcome of the regional Party conferences, were primarily concerned with the slowed momentum of Czechoslovak reform and with the activization of antireformist forces. The original purpose of the authors of the manifesto was to rouse public support for the reform movement and to combat growing antireformist resistance to the democratization process, found especially at the lower levels of government and Party during the summer prior to the congress. They feared an anti-Dubček coup d'état, perhaps backed by the Soviet troops still in Czechoslovakia. The antireformist forces in the Czechoslovak leadership exploited the publication of the Two Thousand Words. Antireformist Indra sent an urgent telex to the Party organizations (with the understanding of the Czechoslovak leadership, but formulated in his own militant way),[2] calling for a struggle against the "counterrevolutionary" plans. But the real reasons behind the fears of some antireformists, such as Indra and Kolder, concerning "counterrevolution" became obvious at the beginning of July at the regional conferences. While the reformist-minded coalition (Kriegel, Smrkovský, Špaček, Černík) in the Czechoslovak Presidium obtained a clear mandate for nomination at the congress, some of the antireformists, including Indra and Kolder, had at this stage not been elected as delegates: Indra had to be elected from a new region in Central Slovakia; Kolder had received a clear expression of no-confidence. Although, technically, Kolder could still have participated at the Party congress in September, he could hardly have hoped for reelection.[3]

While antireformists used the Two Thousand Words Manifesto as a convenient pretext for attacking Czechoslovak reforms, reformists assumed a more relaxed attitude toward it, seeking to control the excesses of the reformist movement by nonrepressive means. They were later criticized by the Soviet leaders, however, for this moderate attitude.

Although the manifesto failed to influence developments in Czechoslovakia significantly, it stirred up public opinion in favor of the reformist movement. It also became a crucial factor in the final stages of polarization of the Czechoslovak ruling elite into two coalitions, and in the balance struck between the external pressures of Czechoslovakia's allies and the internal demands of the Czechoslovak people. On the one hand, it strengthened the position of the Czechoslovak reformist coalition by adding popular support. On the other, it enabled the advocates of military intervention in the Soviet Union and Eastern Europe to intensify their pressure. The manifesto was almost certainly used in the Kremlin debate as "proof" that the political situation in Czechoslovakia was out of control. The Soviet reaction toward the manifesto in early July revived the crisis that seemed to have died in May. Obviously, internal and external enemies of the Prague Spring were concerned primarily with the outcome of the forthcoming Party congress. The regional conferences elected more than 50 new members of the regional Party committees and 1,359 delegates for the forthcoming congress, about 90 percent of whom were reformist supporters (mostly moderate, though some were radical).[4] In fact, many of the antireformist coalition members actually were defeated before the September congress met. The outcome of the regional and district Party conferences, which were held at about the time the manifesto was published, presaged the probable outcome of the September Party congress: defeat of a substantial number of antireformist-oriented leaders, and legitimization of Dubček's reformist program.

July Debate: Foreign Policy Linkages

There are signs that after publication of the Two Thousand Words Manifesto the Kremlin debate on the Czechoslovak issue grew stronger. The interventionist coalition tried to stack forces in the Soviet Politburo and Central Committee in its favor. Apparently, it used internal developments in Czechoslovakia as a powerful argument to gain the support of wavering colleagues. Curiously, the interventionist coalition intensified its pressure on Czechoslovakia at about the same time that the Soviet prime minister and the Soviet minister of foreign affairs were launching a series of moderate steps aimed at the United States. On May 4, the Presidium of the USSR Supreme Soviet unexpectedly ratified a consular convention between the Soviet Union and the United States that had been signed on June 1, 1964, and ratified by the United States in March 1967. The long-awaited convention was proclaimed by President Johnson on June 13 and put in force on July 13, 1968.[5] While Kosygin was trying to defuse the Czechoslovak crisis, the Soviet Union communicated to the White House its decision to resume negotiations on a new two-year cultural exchange agreement.[6] Senior Soviet officials in the Ministry of Foreign Affairs hinted to U.S. diplomats that the Soviet Union was willing to enter into SALT negotiations. These signals came after sixteen months of debate among Soviet decisionmakers, indicating that a consensus might finally have been reached in the Kremlin on this issue. On May 20, Minister of Foreign Affairs Andrei Gromyko's first deputy, V. V. Kuznetsov, said that the Soviet Union was "ready to reach an agreement on practical steps for the limitation and consequent reduction of the strategic means for delivering nuclear weaponry."[7] U.S. Secretary of State Rusk, who by that time had had several talks with Kuznetsov and Soviet Ambassador to the United States Anatoli Dobrynin, began to feel that the Soviet leadership was finally ready to open SALT negotiations.[8] (The Soviet delegation at SALT I was originally supposed to be headed by Kuznetsov. He was diverted from this role, however, to negotiate with the Czechoslovak leaders directly after the Soviet intervention, in September 1968; and in 1969 he led border talks with Chinese leaders. Another Soviet diplomat, Deputy Foreign Minister V. K. Semionov, was appointed in 1969 to head the Soviet delegation.)

Another important result of the Soviet diplomatic offensive of May through July came on June 12, when U.S.–Soviet accord induced the U.N. General Assembly to endorse the nuclear Non-Proliferation Treaty after years of hard bargaining and over the objections of China and some allies of both the United States (e.g., West Germany) and the Soviet Union (e.g., Rumania). Successful conclusion of the NPT was a kind of Soviet precondition for accord on SALT.[9]

There were also indications that the Soviet foreign policy establishment was still interested in continuing *Westpolitik*. The secret talks between West German Foreign Minister Willy Brandt and Soviet Ambassador to East Germany and Central Committee member Peter Abrasimov continued. These talks were suggested at the end of May, when the Soviets launched their diplomatic offensive toward the United States.[10] It appears, therefore, that in spite of the Czechoslovak crisis the Soviet foreign policy establishment was still interested in pursuing the dialogue on the renunciation-of-force issue with West Germany from May to July of 1968.

These steps were motivated by a variety of factors, two of the strongest being fear of China and the possibility of a U.S.–Chinese rapprochement. For some Soviet leaders, mainly those responsible for foreign policy affairs, détente with the United States must have seemed just as important as the struggle against China.

While Soviet-Czechoslovak relations reached disturbing proportions during the May crisis, signs began to emerge of a possible future reconciliation between the United States and the People's Republic of China. On May 2, the Johnson administration invited correspondents from China to cover the presidential election campaign, for the first time since 1949. While Soviet Premier Kosygin was still negotiating in Prague, on May 21, the U.S. under secretary of state, Nicholas Katzenbach, made a major speech on U.S. policy toward China, stressing that there was no U.S. threat to Chinese security and that the United States would welcome a change in Peking's position.

Although many Western analysts considered these steps to be the last overtures of a lame-duck administration, it appears that Soviet leaders and their advisers, particularly those responsible for managing external affairs, perceived them as a serious indication that their old fear of Sino-American rapprochement was becoming a reality.[11] Moreover, as the May issue of the CPSU magazine *Kommunist* asserted, in its continuing anti-Chinese campaign, "China strives to bring the USSR and the United States on a collision course to provoke a nuclear conflict and take this opportunity for establishing its domination in the international arena through, in the words of a Chinese proverb, 'sitting on the fence and watching two tigers fight.' "[12] The Russian fear of a struggle on two fronts perhaps became an important argument in the debate between the interventionist and noninterventionist coalitions on the Czechoslovak issue. Recalling Chinese behavior during the 1956 ferment in Eastern Europe, the noninterventionists may have argued that China would try to exploit the invasion politically.

On balance, the Soviet foreign policy offensive seems to have been a carefully elaborated response to changes in the external setting. The offensive came simultaneously with the temporary *modus vivendi* reached by Kosygin and Dubček in May–June. This point was spelled out by Soviet Minister of Foreign Affairs Gromyko in his address to the June 27 session of the Commission of Foreign Affairs of the Supreme Soviet's Chamber of the Union, which was chaired by Suslov, the commission's head.[13] In his presentation, Gromyko referred briefly to the decision taken at the April Central Committee session regarding the "subversive struggles" of imperialism against socialist countries and reemphasized a national security image shared by all Soviet decisionmakers: "The socialist countries will not permit a single link to be torn out of the socialist community."

Gromyko's speech was devoted mainly, however, to Soviet global policy questions and included a summary of long-term objectives of the Soviet foreign policy establishment: (1) continuous struggle with China, (2) im-

rovement of relations with the United States, and (3) continuation of
Vestpolitik—in particular the diplomatic dialogue with West Germany.
Jnlike the Soviet leaders, Shelest, Pel'she, and (since March) Brezhnev,
iromyko did not try to avoid the subject of Sino-Soviet relations. On the
ontrary, he described "hostile subversive activities of the Mao Tse-tung
roup" and "recent provocations," such as the April incident involving
oviet ships in the Port of Whampoa.

While attacking China, Gromyko took a moderate line toward the United
tates in the spirit of the Soviet diplomatic offensive of May and June. He
nade an historic statement, for which the U.S. government had waited
ighteen months, confirming that the Soviet Politburo had decided to enter
nto SALT talks: "The Soviet Government is ready for an exchange of
pinions on the mutual limitation and subsequent reduction of strategic
neans of delivery of nuclear weapons, both offensive and defensive, in-
luding antiballistic missiles."

Gromyko's speech also struck a moderate tone with respect to Soviet
politics vis-à-vis Western Europe: "The Soviet Union will continue to con-
ince all other states in Europe of the need to discuss and solve problems of
European security." Although Gromyko criticized West German Ostpoli-
ik, his speech struck a moderate tone in noting "a more sober approach to
he question of [Germany's] borders" mentioned "at the recent congress of
West German Social Democrats." Even more important, Gromyko announced that the Soviet leadership (despite objections from Ulbricht, and
perhaps from some Soviet decisionmakers) was interested in continuing the
West German–Soviet diplomatic dialogue: "The Soviet government is
ready for a continuation of the exchange of views with the German Federal
Republic."

It is reasonable to assume that this speech by the Soviet minister of
foreign affairs reflected several decisions taken by the Politburo before the
session of the Supreme Soviet. We do not know the details on how consensus was reached regarding the sudden series of foreign policy approaches
towards the United States, particularly concerning the SALT talks. Nevertheless, it should be noted that the offensive came at a time when some
Soviet decisionmakers were forming a noninterventionist coalition to ease
the tensions with Czechoslovakia. On June 21, several days before
Gromyko's speech to the Supreme Soviet, Kosygin wrote a letter to President Johnson stating that he hoped it would soon be possible "more con-
cretely to exchange views."[14] In other words, he envisioned an early repetition, in the Soviet Union, of the Glassboro summit with the president.
Several days later, just before the NPT was signed, Kosygin advised President Johnson that, on July 1, Soviet radio would broadcast a statement
confirming Gromyko's announcement of Soviet willingness to enter into
SALT negotiations.

Kosygin hailed the NPT as "a major success for the cause of peace," and

publicly expressed his view that conclusion of the treaty would create bett
conditions for the progress of arms control talks. As he put it, it would the
be "possible to achieve concrete results in the disarmament that all peop
of the world are waiting for."[15]

Available evidence suggests, however, that at the time of the politic
crisis in Czechoslovakia not all Soviet decisionmakers shared Kosygin's of
timism regarding détente with the United States. Since the time of th
Glassboro summit, relations with the United States, particularly regardin
the SALT talks, had been a subject of some controversy within the Sovie
ruling elite and various bureaucracies. Gromyko implied this in his histori
speech on June 27, when he alluded to what was apparently an argumen
among Soviet decisionmakers on SALT, by assailing "good-for-nothin
theoreticians who try to tell us . . . that disarmament is an illusion."
Some of the members of the Soviet ruling elite seem to have been unim
pressed by Kosygin's attempts at a U.S.–Soviet accommodation at a tim
of revolutionary ferment in Czechoslovakia. Only three days after Kosy
gin's speech, Shelest, as he had earlier in February, violently attacked "mili
tant imperialism, particularly in the United States." Entirely ignoring th
series of U.S.–Soviet agreements reached between May and July, Sheles
stated that the United States "is experiencing serious social upheavals" and
"intensifying its ideological diversion against the Soviet Union and many
other socialist countries."[17] In presenting a neo-Zhdanov thesis of intensifi
cation of the international class struggle, Shelest saw no hope for bette
relations between the Soviet Union and the United States. Again attacking
the "revisionist and nationalist elements," he made it clear that he mean
Dubček and his supporters in the Czechoslovak leadership:

Not a single Communist can or will agree with those *pseudo-theoreticians* who, for-
getting the class nature of the communist movement and socialist system, propagandize fictitious and improbable "*models of socialism*," abstract humanism, and ideas
of so-called "democratization" and "liberalization" of socialism. It is not hard to
see through to the social-democratic core in all these theses. For us communists of
the Ukraine who have passed through a stern school of class struggle with internal
and external counterrevolution it is extremely painful to see one of the individual
fraternal parties fall for the bait of opportunists of various colors.[18]

The policy implications of Shelest's speech seem to have been that (1) no
deals should be made with the United States during the time of revolutionary ferment in Czechoslovakia, and (2) the Soviet Union should stop
Czechoslovak reformism, even by the use of force.

Secretary General Brezhnev also seems not to have been a great supporter
of détente with the United States at that time. Three days after Kosygin's
announcement (while the Johnson administration was still rejoicing over
the U.S.–Soviet diplomatic deals), Brezhnev delivered one of the most

violently anti-American speeches of the post-Stalin period. Again playing the role of secretary general, Brezhnev did not completely dissociate himself (as Shelest did) from those in the Soviet leadership who advocated political accommodation with the United States. His speech did include brief references to the NPT and the agreement to begin SALT talks. On the other hand, he left no doubts regarding his true feelings about the current prospects for better Soviet-American understanding. Perhaps implying his personal disagreement with Kosygin's moderation, Brezhnev depicted U.S. willingness to negotiate with the Soviet Union as a sign of weakness. He described America, as Shelest had, as "shaken by social and racial conflicts" and used the hot U.S. summer of 1968 as evidence of "the manifestation of the general crisis of capitalist society." Moreover, he asserted, "the American leaders attempted to build the so-called great society, but suffered defeat. The universal prosperity promised to Americans has turned into violence, terror, and into a policy of military adventure. . . ."[19]

Two days after the U.S. and Soviet foreign policy establishments had achieved several diplomatic successes, Brezhnev called the United States "the rotting, the degrading and the decomposing society." He envisioned not a Soviet–U.S. accommodation, as Kosygin had, but a "monopolist America [that] will be inevitably replaced by another America, the America of the working class."[20]

Several days later, Brezhnev seemed to disagree even more explicitly with Kosygin's optimistic statements regarding the future of U.S.–Soviet relations. Brezhnev argued that ". . . we cannot, however, ignore the fact that exponents of aggression, or the hawks [in the U.S. government], as they are called, retain their position." As he put it, " . . . We must be ready for any serious turn of events."[21]

Brezhnev's violent anti-Americanism stands in sharp contrast to his more recent efforts to display appreciation of some aspects of the American way of life, as well as his personal commitment to limited détente with the United States. Obviously, one does not know what Brezhnev had in mind when he made these statements in July 1968, but one can make some safe guesses. Brezhnev's address should be considered in the context of the deepening Czechoslovak-Soviet crisis after the publication of the Two Thousand Words Manifesto. Brezhnev could have ignored neither the internal developments in Czechoslovakia nor the pressure of the interventionist coalition led by Shelest. While in mid-June Brezhnev was willing to admit "some mistakes" in Soviet behavior toward Czechoslovakia, by the beginning of July, in apparent response to developments in Soviet and Czechoslovak domestic politics, he violently attacked Bonn's *Ostpolitik* and argued for a new hard-line policy toward Czechoslovakia (which was later inaccurately called the "Brezhnev Doctrine"): " . . . we cannot and never will be indifferent to the fate of socialist construction in other countries. . . ."[22]

The question of how the United States would react to Soviet action against Czechoslovakia undoubtedly played an important role in the Kremlin debate on the Czechoslovak issue. It is quite possible that the skeptics of the wisdom of military intervention demanded that the interventionists demonstrate that, in the event of a Soviet assault upon Czechoslovakia, the United States and its NATO allies would not intervene or cause serious difficulties.

Thus, the anti-American sentiments expressed by both Shelest and Brezhnev contained important policy implications: to wit, the United States was caught up in its own troubles and would probably not interfere if the Soviet Union got tough in dealing with Czechoslovakia. Brezhnev's outburst might also have been influenced by Soviet bureaucratic politics. At that time (and until mid-1971), it was Premier Kosygin, not Secretary General Brezhnev, who was the recipient of confidential communications from the U.S. president. The primary responsibilities, and ultimately the stakes, in successful negotiations with the United States on such important matters as SALT rested with Kosygin. The planned summit of 1968 was to star Kosygin, not Brezhnev. Although Kosygin showed little political ambition, Brezhnev might have considered the image of Kosygin as a successful statesman, the one who would negotiate on Soviet soil with the American president, as a personal threat to his position of *primus inter pares* in the Politburo. This may have been one reason why Brezhnev took a position opposing that of Kosygin. In attacking the United States at a time when Kosygin apparently had a personal stake in continuing negotiations with the U.S. president, Brezhnev behaved as Khrushchev had when, for some time in the mid-1950s, he had opposed Premier Malenkov's policy of peaceful coexistence.

Like most Soviet decisions, the decision to mount a series of diplomatic approaches towards the United States was the product of internal bargaining. Advocates of SALT talks, such as Kosygin, may have given in to advocates of a hard-line policy toward Czechoslovakia by agreeing to a tougher campaign for conformity in Eastern Europe in return for easing relations with the United States. Yet, without completely disregarding this interpretation, the evidence suggests that the scenario in July 1968 was more complicated; whatever connection existed between these issues was overpowered by the dynamics of each. The Soviet June 1968 decision to opt for SALT cannot be traced to any single motive. Needless to say, the limited evidence prevents a detailed or conclusive analysis of contradictions in Soviet statements and behavior. It can only be said with certainty that while Shelest and Brezhnev were making strong anti-Czechoslovak and anti-American statements, unmistakable signs appeared that pressure from the interventionist coalition had succeeded in creating a consensus within the Politburo on a new hard-line policy toward Czechoslovakia.

July Pressures

As in May, in July Soviet pressures on Czechoslovakia combined both political and psychological elements. The Czechoslovak leadership was suddenly subjected to intense psychological warfare aimed at supporting the antireformist coalition. The Warsaw Pact Command delayed removing its troops from Czechoslovakia upon completion of military exercises. In fact, on July 1, when the Czechoslovak Press Agency (ČTK) announced the end of the exercises, the Soviet agency (Tass) withdrew its similar report. Under cover of a military exercise, the Warsaw Pact Command had deployed 16,000 men in Czechoslovak territory and was reluctant to lose this small, but important, strategic advantage. In keeping his troops on Czechoslovak soil, Marshal Iakubovskii, commander of the Warsaw Pact forces, used as an excuse the argument that current Czechoslovak forces would be unable to contain conventional NATO forces without the "assistance" of Warsaw Pact troops. Later it was reported that the delay in withdrawal was caused by the developing internal political situation.[23]

After strong arguments between Iakubovskii and the Czechoslovak leaders the Soviet troops did finally begin to withdraw. The pullback slowed after several days, however. (Actually, the behavior of the Soviet troops in Czechoslovakia in the summer of 1968 was reminiscent of their behavior in Hungary in October–November 1956, when despite earlier promises from the political leadership the troop commander had been reluctant to order withdrawal, either because he received new instructions or because of the ambiguity of his orders.) In fact, the continued presence of Soviet troops after completion of the military exercises was a kind of intervention—the first one—on a small scale.

While the Soviet generals toyed with psychological warfare, the Czechoslovak leadership was subjected to political pressure. Between July 4 and 6, when Shelest and Brezhnev made tough public statements, the Czechoslovak leadership received letters from its allies (the Soviet Union, East Germany, Poland, Hungary, and Bulgaria) criticizing political developments in Czechoslovakia and proposing a new joint conference of five Warsaw Pact members (originally scheduled for July 7) at which the Czechoslovak issue would be discussed. The letters reportedly revealed considerably differing viewpoints; for example, the letter from the East German leadership was markedly hostile (more hostile even than the Soviet letter), the one from the Hungarian Party markedly moderate.[24]

The intensification of pressure upon Czechoslovakia was accompanied by a new Soviet hard-line policy toward West Germany. This posture (previously advocated by Shelest and Brezhnev) was expressed in a Soviet *aide mémoire* claiming that the West German wish to renounce force was not trustworthy and referring to the obsolete "enemy state" article in the U.N. Charter. Without waiting for a reply, the Soviet government began to publish the texts of all confidential diplomatic notes on the renunciation of force during the 1966–68 negotiations.[25] The Soviet–West German dialogue was halted, and the two countries reached the lowest point in their relations in several years. These unexpected steps sharply contradicted the Soviet stand expressed in an *aide mémoire* of January 29, 1968,[26] and repeated by Foreign Minister Gromyko on June 28, that the Soviet Union was interested in continuing the diplomatic dialogue with West Germany. The sharp changes in Soviet policy toward West Germany were probably supported (if not urged) by critics of the Soviet–West German rapprochement in the Soviet leadership, such as Shelest, and by Ulbricht in Eastern Europe. (For both, it must have been significantly more difficult to cultivate an image of West German "revanchism" while the secret Soviet–West German diplomatic exchange was taking place.)

By the same token, the newspaper *Izvestiia* commenced publication of secret Soviet–West German diplomatic correspondence on the same day that *Pravda* published an authoritative article signed by I. Alexandrov that seemed to be a semiofficial analysis of the seriousness of the Czechoslovak situation. This article drew the first explicit Soviet analogy between events in Czechoslovakia in 1968 and those in Hungary in 1956. The article depicted the Two Thousand Words Manifesto as a "platform" for the "counterrevolution" in Czechoslovakia, and "evidence of the activation of the right wing and actually counterrevolutionary forces in Czechoslovakia which are evidently associated with imperialist reaction." Alexandrov assessed the polarization of the Czechoslovak ruling elite, which reached its peak with the publication of the manifesto. He pointed out that "healthy forces [Soviet terminology for the antireformist coalition] in the Party and the country regard this document as an open attack against the socialist system, against the leading role of the Czechoslovak Communist Party, and against Czechoslovakia's friendship with the Soviet Union and other socialist countries." On the other hand, Alexandrov's article criticized "certain leading figures in Czechoslovakia who have made ambiguous statements in which they try to minimize the danger inherent in the counterrevolutionary Two Thousand Words by insisting that the fact of its publication should not be overdramatized."[27] (Later, during negotiations at Čierna, Brezhnev demanded that those "leading figures"—Kriegel, Císař, and others who were among the most outspoken and radical reformers—be dismissed.)

Literaturnaia gazeta went even further in its description of the manifesto as "counterrevolutionary," criticizing Dubček's supporter Presidium member Kriegel, who "expressed solidarity with works of this kind. . . ."[28]

The policy implications of these articles seem clear: there was a serious threat to the political stability of Czechoslovakia; the Czechoslovak Presidium was divided into two coalitions; and the one composed of those who opposed the manifesto and (more important) continuation of the reform program should be given Soviet support and assistance, including military intervention.

The Warsaw Conference

Again in July 1968, as in March and May, the Czechoslovak leadership was subjected to the pressure of an unexpected multilateral disciplinary summit meeting of five Warsaw Pact members. This conference came as a surprise to the public in both East and West. To be sure, the Czechoslovak leadership seemed to sense that such a summit might take place. On July 8, Secretary General Brezhnev informed Dubček in a telephone conversation that it would convene on July 10 or 11, and requested Czechoslovak participation.[29] On July 11, the day *Pravda* published Alexandrov's article, the Czechoslovak Presidium received a letter from the Soviet Politburo again urgently requesting their presence in Warsaw. Apparently, the meeting was again postponed for several days, while Hungarian leader Kádár met secretly with Dubček at the Hungarian-Czechoslovak border on July 13, perhaps in an attempt to convince him to participate in a multilateral summit meeting of the Warsaw Pact. The Czechoslovak Presidium discussed the letter from the Soviet Politburo and decided, on July 12, to accept only bilateral negotiations—and only on Czechoslovak soil. This decision was made over objections from antireformist coalition members Kolder and Bilak, and perhaps others.[30]

Despite the Czechoslovak refusal to attend, the Warsaw Conference was hastily and secretly convened on July 14. On the afternoon of July 13, the Czechoslovak leaders learned through an extraordinary letter presented by Soviet Ambassador Chervonenko that representatives of the five Warsaw Pact countries were on their way to Warsaw.[31]

Soviet behavior at the conference followed the pattern seen in Dresden (March) and Moscow (May). It combined political pressure, secret diplomacy, and psychological warfare aimed at encouraging antireformist elements. Again Soviet troops moved to the Czechoslovak borders. Although the Warsaw Pact Command had agreed to begin troop withdrawals on July 13 (announced by a Czechoslovak government spokesman on July 11), the pullback had almost halted by July 14–15, when the Warsaw Summit meeting took place.

Surprisingly, the Soviet Tass agency had to delay its announcement of the Warsaw Conference for twenty-four hours, probably because Premier Kosygin (accompanied by First Deputy Minister of Foreign Affairs Kuznetsov) was on an official visit to Sweden. Kosygin arrived to join the delegation at the last minute (July 14).[32]

The Soviet delegation to Warsaw was similar to that at the previous meeting in Dresden. Besides Kosygin, it included Secretary General Brezhnev, who headed the delegation; First Secretary of the Ukrainian Communist Party Shelest; Chairman of the Supreme Soviet Podgorny; and the secretary of the CPSU responsible for relations with ruling Communist parties, Katushev. The main overseer of the international Communist movement, Suslov, and the head of the International Department, Ponomarev, were again absent.[33]

Because Kosygin was responsible for foreign policy and diplomacy, his absence on noncritical business in Sweden was highly peculiar—particularly at a time of drastic policy change, including the new hard line toward West Germany and the growing confrontation with Czechoslovakia. Even more intriguing were Kosygin's performance at a press conference and public remarks that he made in Sweden. He reportedly made a Freudian slip of the tongue several times, saying "Czechoslovakia" when he meant Sweden.[34] Kosygin did urge his questioners to read the article published recently in *Pravda* as representing "our appraisal of the events now taking place in Czechoslovakia,"[35] apparently referring to Alexandrov's article. Nevertheless, while some of his colleagues—Brezhnev, Shelest, Podgorny, and Katushev—were already leaving Moscow for the Warsaw Summit, Kosygin was expressing his personal confidence in the Czechoslovak Communist Party and its leadership: "We are confident that the Czechoslovak Communist Party will never yield its guiding role. The encroachment on Czechoslovakia's socialist foundation will be effectively rebuffed *by the Czechoslovak people and Communists.*"[36] This statement was the first of its type by a senior Soviet decisionmaker since publication of the Two Thousand Words Manifesto. It perhaps implied Kosygin's reluctance to identify himself with the policies advocated by the interventionist coalition.

While the Soviet and East European leaders were negotiating in Warsaw, the Czechoslovak leadership decided to send a cable to Brezhnev saying that "in the interests of the international relations which link our Communist Parties, no steps should be taken which might have an unfavorable impact on the complex situation in Czechoslovakia."[37]

The participants at the Warsaw Conference seemed to agree that the political situation in Czechoslovakia was serious and that something had to be done about it. Yet, as happened on previous occasions, e.g., the Moscow Conference in May, differences arose as to what. The delegations again represented opposing schools of thought regarding the crisis: advocates of military intervention and those who still doubted the wisdom of such a measure.

East German leader Ulbricht pressed strongly for intervention, as he reportedly had during the May summit meeting. According to the eyewitness Weit, Ulbricht stated that such an action was pertinent because, "willingly or unwillingly" a section of the Czechoslovak leadership has become the 'servants of world imperialism.'"[38] According to Weit's recollections, Ulbricht also argued that the West German imperialists had had time to realize that it was not so easy for them to subjugate the German Democratic Republic; so now they were trying a policy of encirclement so that they could also attack the GDR from its southern flank.[39] Ulbricht was strongly supported by the Bulgarian Party leader, T. Zhivkov, who, although at times giving a visibly sleepy impression, made one of the toughest speeches at the conference, suggesting that the Czechoslovak working class be given every assistance in its struggle against counterrevolution, "military assistance not excluded." The Warsaw Conference marked a transition in the Bulgarian attitude, and Bulgarian attacks on Czechoslovakia became as intense as those from East Germany and Poland.[40] Gomułka argued that " . . . in no circumstance can we allow the counterrevolution to be victorious"; but he maintained a certain degree of caution and deliberately omitted mentioning any type of assistance in his speech, waiting perhaps for the other delegations to make their proposals as to how to cope with the counterrevolution in Czechoslovakia.[41]

As at the Moscow Summit, Hungarian Party leader Kádár represented the noninterventionist position. He was, however, somewhat more receptive than he had been in May to the idea that the situation in Czechoslovakia represented a danger. Kádár's stand was possibly shaken by certain excesses of the Czechoslovak press, such as an article in the intellectual newspaper *Literární listy* dealing with the execution of the Hungarian Prime Minister Imre Nagy in 1957. Needless to say, freedom of the press in Czechoslovakia proved to be a double-edged sword. On the one hand, the press was able to apply pressure on the antireformist forces in the Czechoslovak Communist Party by arousing national support for reformist demands; on the other, some articles, such as the one on Nagy's execution, actually aided the cause of the interventionist coalition. Kádár considered its publication at a time when Dubček was heading for Budapest to renew the 1947 Czechoslovak-Hungarian Treaty of Friendship, Cooperation, and Mutual Aid as an interference into the internal affairs of the Hungarian Party and a personal insult. The affair caused some shift in the Hungarian attitude.[42]

Nevertheless, in Warsaw Kádár again expressed reservations about the wisdom of military intervention. Although he agreed with the proposal to send a joint letter to the Dubček leadership, according to Weit he argued in favor of a moderate policy, emphasizing that "any decisions over and above this could lead to serious consequences in the whole world communist movement, and also inside Czechoslovakia."[43]

At the Warsaw Summit meeting Ulbricht demonstrated impatience with his allies' hesitation in taking action against Czechoslovakia. His performance demonstrated convincingly his ability to manipulate and bring political pressure to bear on his East European colleagues. Kádár received a dose of abuse from Ulbricht: "If you think, Comrade Kádár, that you are helping the cause of socialism with your objections and reservations, then you are making a big mistake. And you have no idea what will happen next. Once the American-West German imperialists have got Czechoslovakia in their control then you will be the next to go, Comrade Kádár. But this is something you can't or won't understand!"[44] In an effort to influence Gomułka's stand on the Czechoslovak issue, Ulbricht informed him that the Polish-born scholar (and, in the 1970s, national security adviser to President Carter) Zbigniew Brzezinski, whom Gomułka hated intensely, was allowed to lecture in Prague and that the East German authorities had detailed information about this visit.[45] At Gomułka's request, Ulbricht promised to deliver documents concerning Brzezinski's visit to Prague. The contents of these documents were probably reflected in *Neues Deutschland*, which, with false pretensions, reported that Brzezinski sought to instigate intellectual ferment in Czechoslovakia in his "counterrevolutionary" lecture at the Prague Institute of International Relations and Economics. He was alleged to have declared: "Leninism has no relevance in an advanced modern society."[46] Ironically, Brzezinski had actually made that statement four years earlier, in 1964, when Novotný was still in power in Czechoslovakia.[47]

Secretary General Brezhnev was the only spokesman for the Soviet delegation at the Warsaw Conference. According to Weit, Prime Minister Kosygin gave the impression of being "very worried," apparently because "the role of judge, which he had adopted at this meeting, did not seem to suit him."[48] Brezhnev's speech at the meeting again illustrated the performance of a man who plays the precarious role of secretary general of the CPSU. He took a tough stand, as he had earlier, being unmoved by Kádár's reservations and the misgivings of the West European Communists. He argued that there are some general principles of socialist society formulated by the classics of Marxism-Leninism to which all socialist countries should adhere. Repeating the rationale of Alexandrov's article, Brezhnev maintained, according to Weit, that the latest developments in Czechoslovakia indicated clearly that the Party leadership was "no longer in control of the situation." The most convincing evidence of this was the Two Thousand Words Manifesto. Admittedly, the Czechoslovak Party leadership had immediately dissociated itself from the manifesto; disregarding "all the principles of democratic centralism," however, some of the Prague comrades [probably again a reference to Kriegel] had tried "publicly to defend the 'Two Thousand Words Manifesto'. . . ." Brezhnev interpreted their behavior as evidence that "counterrevolutionary ideas" were represented even in the highest circles of the Czechoslovak party, and that it was impossible for the fraternal parties "to take the dishonorable role of inactive spectators."[49]

On the other hand, as Weit recalled, Brezhnev avoided Ulbricht's extremism and showed some flexibility, stating that

the Soviet Union [did not wish] to impose its own opinions, attitudes and methods on any other socialist country. Such an attitude would be contrary to the whole history of the Soviet Union and the Soviet Communist party. The Soviet Union has always supported the view that every Party was in the best position to know conditions in its own country, and would apply the general principles of the socialist development of society creatively, and take account of national characteristics.[50]

Brezhnev also stated that "the criticisms of the shortcomings and errors in the pre-January period in Czechoslovakia were fully justified" and, apparently justifying the results of his diplomatic mission to Czechoslovakia in December 1967, that the Soviet Union was "in favor of any constructive criticism."[51] However, since this criticism was being used to undermine the leading role of the Czechoslovak Communist Party, it was the duty of the other socialist countries to assist the Czechoslovakian working class so that "the counterrevolution will not succeed in Czechoslovakia."[52] But he did not say (as Zhivkov and Ulbricht had) how it was going to be stopped. In fact, the obvious contradictions discernible in Brezhnev's speech demonstrate again that the decision to intervene militarily in Czechoslovakia had not yet been taken. Although Brezhnev took a hard line on this issue, he wavered not only between the views of Kádár and Ulbricht but, perhaps even more important, between the interventionist and noninterventionist coalitions in the Kremlin.

The Warsaw Summit resulted only in a decision to send a joint letter, a kind of ultimatum, to the Czechoslovak leadership. Skeptics of the wisdom of intervention (such as Kádár) were apparently relieved, while advocates of intervention (such as Ulbricht) were furious that no final decision had yet been made as to how to deal with the Czechoslovak "revisionists."[53] Ulbricht probably feared that the Soviets had agreed to negotiate with Dubček, and that a new, unhealthy compromise would be reached.

The Warsaw Letter to the Czechoslovak leadership was written by a drafting committee composed of representatives from each of the delegations. The Polish and Soviet drafts were used as a basis—they were similar in principle, but used different terminology. The committee members consulted other members of the delegations about practically every sentence. Hence, suggestions from all the delegations were reshaped through private bargaining and discussion among the delegation members.[54] The letter was, in fact, the product of a process whereby various individual interests were gradually transformed into one group interest.

The Warsaw Letter was in some ways reminiscent of Stalin's letter to Yugoslavia in 1948. Not surprisingly, the Yugoslav press published it under the headline "Cominform 1968." The Soviet dissident periodical *Politi cheskii dnevnik* [Political Diary] called it "another document that com promises the international communist movement; it contains a number o unacceptable and, in principle, incorrect propositions and thus openly inter feres in the affairs of a country and Communist Party friendly to us."[55]

The signers of the letter declared that they did "not have any intention of interfering in affairs that are purely internal affairs" of Czechoslovakia that they would not "hinder rectification of errors and shortcomings, including the violation of socialist legality" (under former Party leader Novotný) or "interfere with the methods of planning and administration of Czechoslovak socialist national economics" (economic reform), and that they would welcome "adjustment of the relations between Czechs and Slovaks."[56] In this part of the letter the Polish delegation insisted on a paragraph referring positively to the process of rehabilitation in Czechoslovakia and stating that this "should be continued."[57] The representatives of three other parties (the USSR, East Germany, and Bulgaria) were against this formulation.

There were no references in the letter to the forthcoming World Communist Conference. Only a few of the sections contained in the letter were related to foreign policy issues, but even these reflected the views of Shelest, Brezhnev, and especially Ulbricht rather than those of Kosygin. The letter stated that "international tension is not waning . . . American imperialism has not renounced its policy of force and open intervention against peoples fighting for freedom . . . . The arms race has by no means slowed down." There was no reference to the relaxation of tension between the United States and the Soviet Union, as evidenced by the NPT or the SALT negotiations, publicly praised by Kosygin and Gromyko only two weeks earlier.

A hard-line policy with respect to West Germany can also be found in some passages of the Warsaw Letter, such as those alleging that "FRG [Federal Republic of Germany] ruling circles . . . seek to make use of the events in Czechoslovakia to sow discord amongst the socialist countries, to isolate the GDR, and to implement their revanchist schemes. . . . [They] have been especially active in this." The letter also accused the Czechoslovak leaders by saying that "the attempts at flirtation by the Federal Republic authorities and revanchists have found a response in ruling circles of your country." According to Weit, Ulbricht's influence could be found in these passages. The East German delegation insisted on referring to the "machinations of the Kiesinger-Strauss government" in nearly every sentence—which was protested by some of the other delegations.[58]

The letter contained many charges against the Czechoslovak leadership, some of which could provide a rationale for future military action. Most of these charges were concerned with Czechoslovak domestic affairs, particularly political developments. The letter implied that Dubček had lost political control. It complained not only about "the social democrats persistently seeking to create their own party" and other "political organizations and clubs," but also about the "revisionist forces" *within* the Party, which "have taken over the press, radio and television." Dubček's reform-oriented supporters in the Czechoslovak Party and its leadership were accused of being "outright champions" of such antisocialist appeals as the Two Thousand Words Manifesto, which was an "organizational political platform of counterrevolution." The letter contained a thought reminiscent of one of the tenets of the future so-called Brezhnev doctrine, the obligation common to all socialist countries of "not allowing the loss of revolutionary gains already achieved." Thus the defense of Czechoslovakia's socialist gains was declared to be not only the "task" of Czechoslovakia but the mutual task of all Warsaw Pact countries. The letter expressed support for and promised "comprehensive assistance of the fraternal socialist countries for healthy forces . . . in Czechoslovakia . . . capable of upholding the socialist system and dealing a defeat to the antisocialist elements." It specified what the Czechoslovak antireformist coalition ("healthy forces") should do to satisfy its allies: reinstate censorship, ban political clubs, and, most important, repress so-called "rightist forces" within the Party.

Perhaps some of the participants at Warsaw hoped that the letter, combined with the psychological pressure of troop movements on the borders, would suffice to generate an internal coup d'état in Czechoslovakia, possibly at the forthcoming Central Committee meeting. Ignoring Ulbricht's objections, Brezhnev successfully argued against immediate release of the Warsaw Letter, thus giving the Czechoslovak leadership at least one or two days to have the letter from the Warsaw meeting translated and to review its contents.[59] Another reason for delay in publishing the letter was fear of the reaction from some Communist parties. As Gomułka, supporting Brezhnev, put it, "Unfortunately there are parties in our international Communist movement which are so undisciplined that they do not even agree with us in such an obvious fact as the existence of counterrevolution" in Czechoslovakia. Gomułka argued that immediate publication would give them time "to learn its contents" and "to organize themselves so that they can continue to support the revisionists" within the Czechoslovak Communist Party and back up their positions.[60]

The Warsaw Letter, formulated on July 15, was published in *Pravda* on July 19, the day when the Czechslovak Central Committee met to discuss its contents. The "healthy forces" in Czechoslovakia were called into action, while the Soviet Central Committee of the CPSU held another important session devoted exclusively to the Czechoslovak situation. The Soviet Politburo was preparing to make one of the most difficult decisions since Khrushchev's fall. Shall we, or shall we not intervene? This became the central issue for the next five weeks.

The Central Committee of the CPSU: July 1968 Session

The Central Committee of the Soviet Communist Party occupies a place along with the Politburo as an important participant in the decisionmaking process. It is a much broader political institution than the Politburo, and the interests of numerous important bureaucracies, lobbies, and pressure groups are represented at this level.[61] The committee has grown in stature since Stalin's time, when it was little more than a propaganda device, to become an important advisory and consultative body where the Soviet version of policy debate and discussion occurs.[62]

Sessions of the Central Committee can become, under certain circumstances, important meetings aimed at information-sharing, consultation, and communication among Soviet decisionmakers and various bureaucracies. Soviet leaders may use these sessions for consensus-building or for mobilizing support for a controversial policy outside the highest decision-making mechanism. Soviet Politburo members report to the Central Committee on various matters of foreign and domestic policy, and at the same meeting questions on these policy matters are discussed.

The top representatives of several bureaucracies are members of the Soviet Central Committee, and they often find themselves responsible for carrying out the decisions of the Politburo. Hence, their information on, and support for, certain policies are essential.

The importance of the Central Committee increases whenever there is serious disagreement among Politburo members. Such disagreements seldom occur at Central Committee meetings, and it is safe to assume that Soviet decisionmakers try hard to avoid them. Several standoffs have occurred, however, particularly during 1953–57, when Central Committee sessions assumed an important decisionmaking function. In such cases, the intensity of the Central Committee session is determined by the nature and scope of the disagreement within the Politburo. In 1955, for example, senior Soviet decisionmakers were divided on policy toward Yugoslavia. A coalition of Soviet Politburo members, led by Khrushchev, favored new, fairly flexible policies toward Yugoslavia; another Politburo member, Molotov, led an opposing coalition. According to S. Bialer, in a final resolution of the Soviet Politburo "the opposing points of view of Molotov and Khrushchev on the Yugoslav question were set out and it was decided to refer this question to the next full session of the Central Committee."[63] Thus, the Central Committee apparently served as arbitrator and had the final word in approving the Soviet-Yugoslav rapprochement.

In 1957, the Soviet Central Committee, albeit in a conspiratory manner, played a decisive role in resolving a political crisis. It rejected a decision adopted by a coalition of Soviet Politburo members—referred to later by Khrushchev as an "arithmetic majority"—who favored Khrushchev's dismissal. It was the plenum of the Central Committee meeting in October 1964 that endorsed (perhaps not unanimously, since no officials claimed as much)[64] and carried out through legal procedures the forced resignation of Khrushchev.

Unfortunately for students of Soviet politics, Central Committee meetings today lack the "semi-democratic" publicity they had during Khrushchev's era. To prevent leaks, publications of the proceedings of most of the important sessions are now kept secret; only brief official communiqués and final resolutions are published; and the Stalinist practice of informing the Party organization about Central Committee meetings through secret channels has been revived. Still, as during the Khrushchev era, the Central Committee of the CPSU today seems to serve as an important device for generating consensus and support of controversial policies among key bureaucratic elites. For example, shortly after the Soviet delegation—Brezhnev, Shelest, Podgorny, Kosygin, and Katushev—returned from the Warsaw Conference, the Central Committee of the CPSU held another session, this time devoted exclusively to the political situation in Czechoslovakia. While the April session of the Central Committee met only after several delays, the July session was convened hastily within two days of the Warsaw Conference. Apparently, members of the Soviet delegation to Warsaw—particularly the interventionists, Shelest and Podgorny—were anxious to create support and shared responsibility for their policy. They evidently aimed at obtaining formal approval from the Central Committee prior to the Czechoslovak Central Committee session, which was planned for July 19 to discuss the Warsaw Letter and at which it was hoped the antireformist coalition would attack Dubček's policies.

As in April, the main speaker at the Central Committee meeting was the head of the Soviet delegation to Warsaw, Secretary General Brezhnev. Because it was a secret session, we do not know what Brezhnev and the other speakers said. Nevertheless, from an analysis of available evidence it is possible to draw some tentative conclusions.

It is reasonable to assume that at the Central Committee session, Brezhnev reported on the Warsaw negotiations and the decision to send the Warsaw Letter. Probably, he again pressed for a hard-line policy toward Czechoslovakia, but without identifying himself fully with the interventionist coalition.

Careful examination of the list of speakers[65] and discussants at this session and of their public statements indicates that the interventionist coalition attempted to mobilize support at the Central Committee level for military action against Czechoslovakia. As in April, the only senior Soviet decisionmaker to speak besides Brezhnev was another member of the Soviet delegation to the Warsaw Conference, First Secretary of the Ukrainian Communist Party Shelest. As Richard Löwenthal has pointed out,

It was remarkable that Shelest who had publicly expressed his concern about the danger of "revisionist" demands for democratization in the Ukraine . . . should be the only other member of the Warsaw delegation to speak in the Central Committee discussion of Brezhnev's report . . . [while] both Suslov and B.N. Ponomarev, the secretary responsible for relations with nonruling Communist Parties, were silent—even though the resolution issuing from the session explicitly approved the Politburo's course "in relations with Communist and workers' parties of socialist and non-socialist countries. . . ."[66]

An intriguing pattern again emerged in Soviet decisionmaking regarding the Czechoslovak crisis: although the main subject of discussion was a foreign policy issue, most of the discussants were Party officials responsible for domestic affairs. Apparently, the interdependence of Soviet and Czechoslovak politics involved not only foreign policy but also domestic interests. This phenomenon could partly explain the enlargement of the decisionmaking circle to include more active participation from Central Committee bureaucrats responsible for domestic affairs.

The list of discussants for the July session of the Soviet Central Committee was similar to that for the April session. Almost half of these officials were from the non-Russian national republics of the western part of the Soviet Union; like Shelest, they were encountering a revival of nationalist sentiment in their own countries and saw danger in the Czechoslovak example. Although there is no record in the West of what he said at the July session, First Secretary of the Lithuanian Party A. Yu. Snechkus had a month earlier publicly expressed his fear that "Lithuania, together with other Baltic republics, has become an object of bitter attacks by imperialist propaganda." Snechkus also urged struggle against "nationalism and revisionism."[67]

Another discussant, the First Secretary of the Latvian Party, A. E. Voss, also publicly complained about the "ideological diversions from abroad." He implied that the situation in Latvia had become more dangerous, particularly during 1968, when "the revisionists and nationalists" were using a program of "democratic and humanist socialism" as a smoke screen for "the restoration of capitalist society."[68]

Besides Shelest, the Ukrainian Party bureaucracy was represented by two other regional officials—First Secretary of the Donetsk Regional Committee, V. I. Degtiarev, and First Secretary of the Transcarpathian Regional Committee, Yu. V. Il'nitskii. Il'nitskii's presence as a speaker at an important session of the highest Soviet decisionmaking body (where most senior Soviet decisionmakers were silent) is more than intriguing, since he, like Latvian Party leader Voss, was not a member of the Central Committee of the CPSU nor even an alternate member or a member of the Auditing Committee of the Central Committee. Because Il'nitskii represented a Ukrainian region that had been Czechoslovak territory before World War II and that contains the important Transcarpathian military district, his presence can be interpreted as a shrewd psychological attempt to highlight the urgency of the Czechoslovak "threat" to the Soviet West. As Hodnett and Potichnyj have pointed out, since it is unlikely

that a person of [Il'nitskii's] low political status would be called upon to oppose a decision of the CPSU Politburo or argue against the First Secretary of the Ukraine, we can say that it is most unlikely that he was invited to Moscow in order to urge caution. The obvious conclusion is that he must have been invited to dramatize the danger of Czechoslovak influences upon the Ukraine. This is an extremely important point, for it reveals better than almost anything else possibly could that the majority in the Politburo wanted or needed to convince the Central Committee of the seriousness of the Czechoslovak threat to the Soviet Union's south-western flank. Apparently Shelest's word on the matter did not carry conviction with everyone.[69]

Although we do not know what Il'nitskii said at the July session, we can safely guess. During and after the crisis he expressed his concern about the Czechoslovak influence on inhabitants of his region. Among other things, he attacked the traces of " 'democracy' and 'freedom' " remaining from the time of Masaryk and Beneš in the minds of the Transcarpathian population, and later he observed that Transcarpathia was vulnerable to "foreign radio stations and television studios"—probably referring to the Ukrainian language broadcasts from the Czechoslovak radio station in Prešov.[70] (Il'nitskii also participated in postintervention diplomacy; he accompanied Secretary Katushev's delegation to Prague in December 1968.)[71]

The presence of nonmembers of the Central Committee, such as Il'nitskii and Voss, may indicate that the interventionist coalition was trying to pack the session to create consensus and to push a policy that was probably being questioned even by some senior decisionmakers. In Khrushchev's era, such Central Committee sessions were said to be "enlarged," in order to justify the participation of nonmembers. (In fact, Dubček and his supporters used a similar tactic during the Prague Spring.) The presence of outsiders—a violation of Party rules—was criticized after Khrushchev's forced resignation and may have induced comment from some senior Soviet decisionmakers.

As in April, almost half of the speakers and discussants at the July Central Committee session were Party bureaucrats responsible for internal affairs, political stability in major Soviet cities, and ideological supervision of the intellectual community. This group included, again, Politburo candidate and First Secretary of the Moscow City Committee Grishin, who had also spoken at the April session; First Secretary of the Moscow Regional Committee V. I. Konotop; First Secretary of the Leningrad Regional Committee V. S. Tolstikov, who had also spoken in April;[72] President of the USSR Academy of Sciences M. V. Keldysh; and Secretary of the Board of the Union of USSR Writers Gribachev. First Secretary of the Volgograd Committee L. S. Kulichenko—who had accompanied Brezhnev and Shelest on their diplomatic mission to Czechoslovakia in February 1968 and had served as a discussant at the April session—also participated in the July session.

The content of the speeches at the crucial July Central Committee session is not available. Yet by knowing some of the speakers' concerns and responsibilities and by reading their public speeches during the crisis, one can surmise what facets of the Czechoslovak issue must have concerned them. For example, in the 1960s and 1970s, Academician Keldysh, who is also a Central Committee member, had been rather more occupied with bureaucratic and ideological supervision of the Soviet Academy of Sciences than with serious scholarly research at his Institute of Applied Mathematics. In March 1968, he argued that "imperialism tried to exploit vacillating and apolitical elements" among the intelligentsia, as happened in Poland at that time. Keldysh also threatened (in a speech at the Moscow Party Conference, which *Politicheskii dnevnik* called "tendentious") Soviet scholars and scientists who support Soviet reformists and dissidents in defiance of Party discipline, implying that science can march ahead without them.[73]

Undoubtedly, Keldysh was deeply concerned about the increasing interest among Soviet scientists and scholars in the Czechoslovak experiment. These intellectuals considered the Prague Spring a sign of hope for the reform of Soviet society. Academician Andrei Sakharov, the distinguished Soviet scientist (often called in the West the "father of the Soviet hydrogen bomb") and Nobel prize winner of 1975, referred hopefully to the Prague Spring in his famous June 1968 manifesto *Progress, Coexistence, and Intellectual Freedom,* which began to be widely circulated in the Soviet Union. (The manifesto was also broadcast by BBC, Voice of America, and Deutsche Welle, and was widely circulated in self-published *[samizdat]* sources among the Soviet intelligentsia.) Sakharov urged the Soviet leadership to support the "bold initiative" of the Czechoslovaks, "which is so valuable for the future of socialism and all mankind." He also called for Soviet political and economic support of Czechoslovakia.[74]

Gribachev, Secretary of the Board of the Union of Writers of the USSR, responsible for supervision and control of Soviet writers, also appeared to be concerned about the impact of Czechoslovak reformism on Soviet writers. In fact, several days after the July session, Gribachev seems to have complained about the influence of Czechoslovak reformism on Soviet youth.[75]

It can be surmised that both Keldysh and Gribachev took a tough stand on the Czechoslovak issue, emphasizing the disruptive echo of Czechoslovak reformism among Soviet scientists and writers.

There is no evidence that any of the discussants expressed doubts about the hard-line policy toward Czechoslovakia, or that they were skeptical of a policy of placing costly conformity to the bloc above the world Communist movement. On balance, the July session seems to have been stage-managed to give full support to the tough line against Czechoslovakia and to the results of the Warsaw Conference. As Frederick Barghoorn has put it, "Clearly, an attempt was made to create the impression that representatives of both non-Russian nationalities and of Soviet literary and scientific communities were supporting the Kremlin policy with respect to Czechoslovakia."[76]

The final resolution of the July session "unanimously" approved the activities of the CPSU delegation to Warsaw and its conclusion about "the necessity of a determined struggle for the cause of socialism in Czechoslovakia." It also expressed hope that the Warsaw Letter "will meet with the understanding of the Communist Party and people of Czechoslovakia."[77] In other words, Dubček and his supporters could either accept the Warsaw Letter ultimatum or be forced by an internal and/or external coup d'état to accept it.

In identifying the full Central Committee with the line of the Warsaw delegation, the Soviet leadership apparently aimed at demonstrating unity and dispelling signs of reluctance or indecisiveness. Although the approval was reportedly unanimous, the available evidence implies that consensus had not yet been reached as to how to resolve the Czech crisis.

Intensification of Pressure

A decision on a matter of such magnitude as launching a military intervention would probably not be made at a Central Committee session. Soviet decisionmakers would hardly wish to share such a sensitive national security secret with 360 persons. After the session of the Central Committee where the interventionist coalition tried to create consensus for a tough policy toward Czechoslovakia, the Soviet Politburo had to decide upon a course of action. All senior Soviet decisionmakers were certainly aware of the prevailing mood of the various groups of the Central Committee. There were also signs that bureaucratic groups favoring military intervention had intensified their pressure to change the balance of force within the Politburo between the two coalitions. On July 19, two days after the Central Committee session, *Pravda* reported the discovery of a "secret cache" of American-made weapons near the Czechoslovak–West German borders, allegedly brought to Czechoslovakia by "revenge seekers and champions of the old order."[78] By the same token, the same edition of *Pravda* reported that Soviet authorities had obtained a copy of an American "secret plan" for overthrowing the regime in Prague—implying that the United States was involved in a Czechoslovak counterrevolutionary movement.[79] Such accusations were denied by Secretary of State Rusk.[80] An investigation by Czechoslovak security officials found that the weapons "discovered" were of American,

World War II origins but packed in Soviet-made bags. As Smrkovský put it, this was clearly a "provocation (*provokace*)."[81] The KGB and their collaborators in Czechoslovakia almost certainly had a hand in this.

Pravda's evidence of July 19 regarding the discovery of arms in Czechoslovakia and the U.S. involvement in that country, fabricated by the KGB, exposed a new element of the Soviet decisionmaking game: psychological-political operations. Publication of these and similar materials at that time in the Soviet press could only be regarded as a form of political pressure on the Czechoslovak leadership, or possibly as preparation of Soviet public opinion for a military occupation of Czechoslovakia. Rumors began to spread in the Moscow community about the possibility of military intervention soon in Czechoslovakia.[82] Dramatizing the situation in Czechoslovakia probably provided the needed evidence for persons at the highest political level who were seeking a pretext for intervention.

On the day that *Pravda* tried to implicate the United States in Czechoslovak developments, another member of the Soviet delegation to the Warsaw Conference, Chairman of the Supreme Soviet of the USSR Podgorny, again, as in May, made a hard-line statement at an RSFSR Supreme Soviet session regarding developments in Czechoslovakia. Supporting Shelest's views, Podgorny strongly reemphasized the importance of the Warsaw Letter. He declared that "hostile forces in and outside the country are clearly trying to push Czechoslovakia off the socialist road and to force it away from the socialist commonwealth," and promised "all-around assistance" to the Czechoslovak fifth column.[83]

During the week following July 19, meetings were organized in various Soviet republics and regions to support the conclusions of the Warsaw Conference and the July session of the Central Committee, and to express confidence that the letter of the fraternal parties would meet with the understanding and support of the Czechoslovak Communists.[84]

Because of the urgency of the situation, Soviet Minister of Defense Marshal Grechko shortened his visit to Algeria and, like Warsaw Pact Commander Iakubovskii, headed for Moscow.[85] The armed forces newspaper *Krasnaia zvezda,* meanwhile, declared that the Soviet Army "is ready to fulfill its patriotic duty to crush any aggressor. . . . "[86] At this point the stage seemed to be set for intervention. On July 19, at the United Nations, Czechoslovak Press Agency (ČTK) reporter Karel Král directed world attention to the situation in Central Europe. Because ČTK is an official government organ, it was thought that Král's action was an unofficial Czechoslovak signal to the international forum of the threat of military action.[87]

Yet, some Soviet decisionmakers may still have calculated that the Warsaw Letter, combined with strong political pressure and psychological warfare, would split the Czechoslovak leadership and Central Committee, creating ideal conditions for an internal coup d'état. (Brezhnev, aware of the differences and coalitions in the Czechoslovak leadership, insisted during a telephone conversation with Dubček on July 11 that not only the Czechoslovak Presidium but also the Central Committee of the Czechoslovak Party, which contained many antireformists, should discuss the letters from the Warsaw Pact countries.)[88] On July 18, Moscow Radio increased its broadcasts to Czechoslovakia, carrying several unscheduled programs discussing the text of the Warsaw Letter.

As had happened several times before during the crisis, the increase in Soviet pressure backfired. The Warsaw Letter did not strengthen the hand of the antireformist coalition as intended by participants at Warsaw; on the contrary, it created a feeling of national unity, and it was used by reformist coalitions led by Dubček to strengthen their own positions. The members of the antireformist coalition were afraid to take political action. Soviet pressure played a decisive role in moving Dubček and some of his supporters, after several months of indecisiveness, to act like leaders of an independent state and to defy the Soviet leadership.

At the important July 19 session of the Czechoslovak Central Committee, Dubček's supporters achieved almost unanimous support for their policy of rejecting the anti-Czechoslovak charges in the Warsaw ultimatum. To be sure, the sense of unity shown at this meeting was partially the result of internal political maneuvering; but unlike that at the CPSU session, the maneuvering here was backed by popular pressure. The real differences between the two coalitions in the Czechoslovak leadership were not outwardly evident. In fact, on July 19, Dubček's supporters (using an old Khrushchev tactic, as the Soviet interventionist coalition had done two days earlier) invited several nonmembers to the session—pro-Dubček participants who had been elected only a few weeks earlier as delegates to the Extraordinary Party Congress. Only 88 of the full membership of approximately 120 attended. In addition, the antireformists were under strong pressure from Dubček's supporters, various pressure groups, and public opinion; few members had sufficient courage to oppose Dubček's anti-Warsaw line, finding it wiser to join the show of Party and national unity. Among the twenty-one speakers only one—Presidium member Kolder—stated that although he considered the Warsaw Letter true in some respects, the manner of the ultimatum forced him to support the viewpoint of the Party.[89] During a telephone conversation with Dubček on July 17, after the Czechoslovak Presidium had rejected the Warsaw Letter, Brezhnev reportedly indicated his awareness that not all Czechoslovak leaders agreed with the reformists when he asked Dubček, "Did Comrade Kolder also vote against it?"[90]

Dubček's skillful performance and his ability to manage the July 19 session,[91] supported by the reformist groups with the pressure of TV, radio, and the press, contributed to the defeat of the antireformist coalition, which was incapable of political resistance.

The Central Committee of the Czechoslovak Communist Party (except for Kolder, who abstained in the voting) had decided to support the earlier decision of the Czechoslovak Presidium not to go to the Warsaw disciplinary summit and had voted to endorse the Presidium's reply rejecting the accusations in the Warsaw Letter. Soviet attempts to divide and conquer had failed, at least for the time being. Dubček's reformists had won support not only from the Czechoslovak ruling elite, but also from the majority of the Czechoslovak people, at least until September 9—the day of the Extraordinary Party Congress.

After the defeat of the Czechoslovak fifth column, the Soviet decisionmakers became aware that an internal coup d'état was not feasible without military intervention. The choices available to the Soviet Politburo after July 19 were limited. It could decide either to live with Dubček's leadership and try to influence Czechoslovak developments by political and economic instruments (as in Poland after October 1956), or to back a *putsch* with pure military force (as in Hungary in 1956).

July Decision

Although the sharp debate within the Soviet Politburo on the Czechoslovak issue cannot be shown fully, the available evidence suggests that it intensified substantially during the July crisis. In fact, some public remarks made by Soviet interventionist leader Shelest on July 5 may well have been aimed at his cautious colleagues in the Politburo: "It is impossible to agree with those who reduce the principle of proletarian internationalism to nothing but the slogan of *independence and equality of nations*. It is not difficult to understand that if one emphasizes only this aspect of internationalism and ignores another, no less important aspect of it—the necessity for the association, alliance and *mutual assistance* of socialist nations—this can lead to separatism and self-isolation. . . ." Furthermore, Shelest complained about "some people who try to reduce the principles of proletarian internationalism to the provision of *unilateral material* and other assistance, at the same time ignoring *mutual aid* and evading responsibility for the common cause of the developing and strengthening of forces of socialism and the revolutionary movement. It is not difficult to understand that such a position has nothing in common with the Leninist concept of the question."[92]

There were signs during the July crisis that not all Soviet leaders were enthusiastic about the maneuverings of Shelest and his supporters to involve the Ukrainian factor, as had happened at the July Central Committee session, in the Soviet decisionmaking game. Although *Pravda's* editorial on July 19 described developments in Czechoslovakia as dangerous attempts to "undermine the foundations of socialist statehood," it also echoed Kosygin's expression of confidence in the Czechoslovak leadership: "Needless to say, the forces of socialism in Czechoslovakia, objectively measured, are far greater than those now striking at the revolutionary gains of the Czechoslovak people. The rightist elements, despite all their noise and attack, lack support among the broad masses of working people."[93] The policy implications of this comment in *Pravda* are similar to those of Kosygin's remarks in Stockholm: the dangers in Czechoslovakia exist but are not mortal; the Czechoslovak leadership is capable of solving its own problems; and military intervention is unnecessary. Such a reference to confidence in the forces of socialism in Czechoslovakia contradicted Podgorny's speech, which implied that "assistance of fraternal countries" was necessary.

Perhaps it was no accident that on July 18 Premier Kosygin again signaled that he favored a continuation of friendly relations with Dubček's leadership, by reassuring Czechoslovak Deputy Prime Minister Hamouz that "the Soviet side is sincerely interested in extending existing cooperation with Czechoslovakia," adding that he personally was "aware of no obstacles which would hamper such an extension."[94]

At this important juncture of the Soviet-Czechoslovak conflict, the other members of the Soviet noninterventionist coalition—Suslov and the head of the International Department, Ponomarev—appeared to prefer a political compromise. While Brezhnev was in Warsaw, the leaders of the French and Italian Communist parties, Waldeck Rochet and G. Pajetta and C. Galuzzi, went to Moscow to speak on behalf of embattled Czechoslovakia. This action was the first joint anti-Soviet venture of the French and Italian parties. Soviet pressure and intervention in Hungary in 1956 received almost unanimous support from Communist parties all over the world, but the pressure on Czechoslovakia was denounced by a good majority. Suslov, main overseer of Soviet policy in the international Communist movement, and Ponomarev's deputy, Zagladin, met with Waldeck Rochet as the main negotiators on the Soviet side.[95]

The evidence suggests that Waldeck Rochet, Pajetta and Galuzzi—the representatives of the two strongest Western European Communist parties—used the long-planned World Communist Conference, scheduled by Suslov and Ponomarev to open in Moscow on November 25, as a lever for restraining Soviet advocates of military intervention. Having reportedly mobilized seventeen Communist parties which considered the Warsaw Letter and Soviet pressure as unjust, and which expressed support for Dubček's leadership, they also apparently hinted to Soviet negotiators that, in the event of a military intervention, they would not only boycott the forthcoming conference, but would convene their own conference of European Communist parties. The possibility of using such a conference as a political weapon in support of Czechoslovakia had been considered since April by some reform-minded Western European Communist officials—such as Franz Marek, a former Politburo member of the Austrian Communist Party. Apparently realizing that a conference of most of the European parties would jeopardize the plans that he and Suslov had made for a World Communist Conference, Ponomarev sent confidential letters in July to all West European parties, arguing that such a conference would be considered a hostile act against the CPSU.[96]

To be sure, the pressure of the West European Communist parties might not have impressed all Soviet decisionmakers, particularly those like Shelest who were mainly responsible for internal affairs and so were unwilling to put internationalist ambitions and world Communist unity above domestic concerns and conformity within the socialist commonwealth. Suslov, however, reportedly appeared to be "shaken."[97]

As argued earlier, the anti-Chinese-oriented World Communist Conference and its opening date, November 25, were of enormous importance to Suslov and Ponomarev. *Kommunist* published an editorial in June 1968 which seems to reflect the Suslov-Ponomarev view of the debate on the Czechoslovak issue. The editorial argues with those who, perhaps like Shelest, did not seem to care about either the conference or its opening date: "Of course the setting of the exact date for the beginning of the Conference is by no means a technicality but a matter of principle. . . . Having selected a date for the Conference which was convenient for all and having devoted sufficient, although comparatively short time for its preparation, the fraternal parties have proved indeed that they consider a new international conference as *absolutely timely, and that it would bear no postponing.*"[98]

At another meeting, held in Budapest in June 1968 to prepare for the conference, Ponomarev (as head of the Soviet delegation) skillfully succeeded in bringing back the Rumanian Party as an "observer" to the group preparing documents for the conference.[99] The Rumanian return was apparently an important step in the forthcoming negotiations with other hesitant parties to convince them to participate. It is not surprising that Suslov and Ponomarev were reluctant to forfeit their project, and therefore were skeptical about the use of military force in Czechoslovakia, as advocated by Shelest.

Although there is no hard evidence, it is likely that the Suslov-Ponomarev argument reminding the interventionists of the costs of military action, particularly with regard to the international Communist movement, combined with the defeat of the anti-Dubček coalition, was successful in convincing most of the wavering Politburo members to try to negotiate again with the Czechoslovak leadership. Indeed, the leader of the French Party, Waldeck Rochet, journeyed to Prague, perhaps with the approval of some Soviet decisionmakers, to act as a "mediator." On July 19 Dubček and Rochet agreed that the dispute should not be discussed at the European Communist

Conference, but resolved in bilateral negotiations between the Czechoslovak Presidium and the Soviet Politburo.[100] In conversations with Dubček, Rochet presented the main anxieties of the Soviet leadership concerning developments in Czechoslovakia, some of which he shared. He also explained that his initiative was aimed at preventing the rupture of Czechoslovak-Soviet relations.[101] After it became obvious that the Soviet leadership had again decided to seek a political solution to the crisis, the West European Communist parties withdrew their proposal for a separate conference of European Communist Parties.[102]

At that time, between July 19 and July 22, Soviet politics seemed to be in a state of flux—as it had been during the Hungarian crisis—full of confusion and hesitation between compromise and intervention. On July 19, the Soviet Politburo proposed a bilateral meeting of the Soviet and Czechoslovak ruling bodies "in Moscow on July 22 or 23," or if "more convenient for the Czechoslovak comrades, in Kiev or Lvov."[103] This offer, however, was unacceptable to the Czechoslovak Presidium, which refused to travel to the Soviet Union and insisted that the meeting be held on Czechoslovak territory after the departure of the last Soviet troops. Then, on July 21, Soviet Ambassador Chervonenko reportedly delivered to the Czechoslovak government a diplomatic note expressing concern about the security of the Czechoslovak borders in connection with the alleged discovery of arms, and demanding the dismissal of several high Czechoslovak officials, particularly General Václav Prchlík.[104]

But surprisingly, only a day later (July 22), after three hot days for Czechoslovakia, the Soviet Politburo made another concession: it accepted the Czechoslovak proposal to negotiate on Czechoslovak soil in Čierna nad Tisou, a small town near the Czechoslovak-Soviet frontier (instead of Košice, a large city in Eastern Slovakia proposed by the Czechoslovaks). This decision, apparently an *ad hoc* measure, surprised even some Soviet allies.[105]

On the same day, after several days delay, *Pravda* published an official editorial explaining the Soviet position on the Czechoslovak reply to the Warsaw Letter. (The text of the Czechoslovak reply was issued in Russian by Tass for a limited readership only.)[106] The editorial reflected the final decision taken by the Politburo majority in July 1968 regarding the resolution of the Czechoslovak crisis. While *Pravda* said that the Czechoslovak leaders still underestimated the danger of "counterrevolution" in their country, it stressed that they had nevertheless shown some desire to improve relations with their allies, and that bilateral talks between the ruling bodies could be constructive.[107]

In July, as in earlier stages of the crisis, skeptics of the wisdom of military intervention, albeit under more difficult circumstances, were still able to create a consensus for nonintervention, and again tried to resolve the

Czechoslovak crisis by political means. Political pressure, secret diplomacy at bilateral and multilateral levels, and even psychological warfare were the means preferred by noninterventionists for dealing with the Czechoslovak reformists. (The intervention was rumored to take place by the end of July—just at the time when the Soviet Politburo decided to negotiate.)[108]

The July decision for nonintervention cannot be reduced to simple motives. The noninterventionist coalition seemed to prefer to live with Dubček's leadership and to try to resolve the crisis by political instruments —negotiations. External considerations—particularly those regarding the world Communist movement and the unexpected internal developments in Czechoslovakia (especially the almost total defeat of the antireformist coalition)—apparently contributed to the shift in the balance of forces between the advocates of and the skeptics of military intervention, and, after several days of hesitation, to an eleventh-hour decision against intervention.

III *A Soviet journalist from the Novosti Agency:*
"Do you know that passage in the second volume of
Hašek's Good Soldier Schweik *where Schweik literally drives*
an Austrian railwayman crazy by explaining to him for
hours on end how the railways of the Hapsburg Monarchy
ought to run? The pretentionsness of the Czechs in teaching
us what socialism is, is unbearable. They may still be
Schweiks, but we aren't Hapsburgs. They'll find out soon
enough."—M. Salomon

Negotiations

The Conference at Čierna nad Tisou

The decision of the Soviet Politburo to negotiate bilaterally with the Czechoslovak Politburo on the latter's territory at Čierna nad Tisou was unprecedented in Soviet history. The implications of this decision and the resulting negotiations at Čierna nad Tisou and Bratislava are crucial in reexamining Soviet decisionmaking during the crisis.[1] During the Hungarian crisis of 1956, negotiations were conducted by only two senior Soviet decisionmakers: Suslov and Mikoian. During the Polish crisis of the same year, Khrushchev and three other Politburo members went to Warsaw to negoiate with the Polish leadership. During the Sino-Soviet dispute in the early 1960s, only a small Soviet delegation was sent to deal with the Chinese leaders. As we have seen, the Soviet delegations to earlier negotiations with Czechoslovak leaders had been composed of Brezhnev, Shelest, Podgorny, Kosygin, and Katushev.

Why, this time, did nearly the full Politburo become engaged in the negotiations? Almost certainly, at Čierna the Soviet leaders were anxious to test the equilibrium of forces between the two coalitions (reformist and antireformist) within the Czechoslovak Presidium. They may also have thought of playing the coalitions against each other, using the tactic of *divide et impera* while testing reformist willingness to use armed resistance against a Soviet intervention. More to the point, the negotiations in Čierna showed some division of opinion among Soviet leaders as to how to resolve the crisis, suggesting that the crucial element in their decision to bring most of the Politburo to Čierna was distrust among themselves, and hence a reluctance to let a small delegation (like the ones sent to the Dresden and Warsaw conferences) negotiate on behalf of the entire Politburo. The decision, then, symbolized the collective nature of post-Khrushchev top-level decisionmaking. As Löwenthal puts it:

> The Soviets were conscious [that] a new decision would have to be made at the end of the talks—the decision whether to regard their demands as satisfied, or whether to implement the ultimatum by giving marching orders to the allied armies, kept in a state of readiness all around Czechoslovakia. Moreover, the members of the collective knew that some of them would apply more exacting standards of compliance than others, and they evidently could not agree on trusting a single leader, or even a *troika,* with deciding in their name.[2]

The very composition of the Soviet delegation to Čierna indicates that this meeting was not a political bluff, or a smoke screen for military intervention, but a last attempt, at least by some Soviet leaders, to reach an agreement.[3] The delegation included secretaries of the Central Committee of the CPSU Ponomarev and Katushev (who were reportedly not originally supposed to participate in the negotiations).[4] Only two Politburo members, Kirilenko and D. S. Polianskii, stayed in Moscow to run the Party and government business. The Soviet delegation, led by Secretary General Brezhnev, was made up both of the advocates of military intervention and of its skeptics, apparently to strike a kind of bureaucratic equilibrium. Some advocates of military intervention were Shelest and apparently also Pel'she, Podgorny, Masherov, and Demichev; some of those who seemed to question its wisdom, Suslov, Kosygin, and Ponomarev. Unfortunately, we do not know what stands were taken by the remaining Soviet bargainers present at Čierna—A. N. Shelepin, Voronov, K. T. Mazurov, and Katushev. Suslov and Ponomarev apparently had the first opportunity to negotiate seriously with most of the Czechoslovak leaders.

The list of Soviet bargainers and their performance at Čierna seem to support the hypothesis stated earlier about Soviet management of a crisis with a socialist country. In essence, because of the interdependence of the domestic politics of the various socialist countries, the Czechoslovak crisis concerned not only the decisionmakers mainly responsible for national security and foreign policy affairs, but also some officials concerned with domestic affairs: Ukrainian Party leader Shelest, Chairman of the Council of Ministers of the RSFSR Voronov, Chairman of the Party Control Committee Pel'she, Party Secretary and candidate Politburo member in charge of ideology Demichev, and First Secretary of the Belorussian Party and candidate Politburo member Masherov. This group, then, was included in the negotiations on Czechoslovak internal affairs. Perhaps because of their presence, most of the negotiations focused on Czechoslovak domestic developments; questions regarding Czechoslovak foreign policy and the security of the Warsaw Pact alliance were not discussed in great detail.

Indeed, it was clear to the Soviet leaders even prior to the negotiations that there was little threat to Czechoslovakia from the West. The governments of the United States and West Germany had taken steps signaling clearly to the Soviets that they did not wish to exacerbate internal developments in Czechoslovakia. Thus, in early July the U.S. army in West Germany received orders to avoid excessive land or air patrolling and any incidents at the Czechoslovak borders.[5] Shortly before the negotiations began, the West German government, in an effort to avoid further accusations of provocation, decided to shift the military exercises of the Bundeswehr (code-named Black Lion) away from the Czechoslovak borders to the southwestern part of West Germany.[6]

The bargaining position of the Soviet delegation to the Čierna Conference was again strengthened—as it had been before and during the negotiations at Dresden, Moscow, and Warsaw—by psychological pressure from the Warsaw Pact forces on the Czechoslovak borders. Although the Soviet travel bureau had unexpectedly cancelled all Soviet tours to Czechoslovakia,[7] an unprecedented number of Soviet "tourists" of another type, KGB men, began to arrive. In a manner reminiscent of classic nineteenth-century diplomacy, secret diplomatic negotiations were combined with military maneuvers at the Czechoslovak frontiers.

The decision to use military force again as a form of pressure was related to, and perhaps taken at the same time as, the decision to negotiate. On July 23, when it became known that the Soviet Politburo had decided to compromise again and to negotiate with the Czechoslovak leadership, the Soviet media announced the largest logistic exercise ever held by the Soviet Ground Forces, under the command of Grechko's deputy and chief of Rear Services (Logistics), General S. S. Mariakhin. The exercise was nicknamed *Nemen*. During the maneuvers, thousands of Soviet reservists were called up and civilian transports requisitioned in a large logistic rehearsal. The maneuvers took place in the Soviet West extending from the Baltic to the Black Sea (the Ukraine, Belorussia, Latvia and the western part of the RSFSR).[8] During the negotiations they were extended to East Germany and Poland. In addition, prior to the Čierna Conference, a large-scale maneuver (nicknamed *Sever*) involving the Soviet Northeast and Baltic fleets and the navies of East Germany and Poland was begun in the Baltic Sea area.

While at least some of the Soviet political leaders were again trying to resolve the Czechoslovak crisis through political bargaining, Soviet military leaders—Minister of Defense Grechko, "interventionist" Epishev, Army General M. I. Kazakov (commander-in-chief of the Warsaw Pact forces during the June–July maneuvers), and Army General Shtemenko (who would soon replace Kazakov as chief of staff of the Warsaw Pact)—met with East German Minister of Defense H. Hoffman, apparently to assess the results of the military exercises around Czechoslovakia.[9] In addition to the new military presence, there remained approximately 8,000 Soviet soldiers inside Czechoslovakia, still "withdrawing" slowly from the June Warsaw Pact maneuvers.

The threat of military intervention was apparent, should negotiations fail. The movements of the Warsaw Pact forces were still aimed at intensifying the psychological pressure, intimidating the Czechoslovak leadership, and giving the Soviet delegation at the Čierna Conference a maximum bargaining position. Thus, at the time of the negotiations, the crews of the tanks and armored vehicles stationed on the Czechoslovak borders were noted at one point to have turned on their motors and then after a short while to have turned them off again.[10] At this juncture, however, the movements were also aimed at preparing for an actual military intervention in case agreement could not be reached and the Soviet Politburo opted for that alternative.

Dubček's bargaining power was considerably weakened by a political concession to the Soviets: the dismissal of Czechoslovak General Václav Prchlík, a Dubček supporter and head of the important Department of Defense and Security of the Central Committee. The official Soviet reason for demanding Prchlík's dismissal came after his critical public statements regarding the "unsatisfactory Warsaw Pact structure" at the press conference on July 15, which led to accusations that he had engaged in antisocialist, counterrevolutionary "distortion of the Warsaw Pact" and, after the intervention, had revealed "secret information" to the enemy.[11] The real reason for Prchlík's dismissal was quite different. His staff and that of Minister of the Interior Pavel had discovered during June and early July that the Warsaw Pact maneuvers had been aimed against "internal enemies" in Czechoslovakia and at controlling the Czechoslovak communications systems. Prchlík, fearing the possibility of a Soviet intervention, had objected to the use of Warsaw Pact forces as an instrument of pressure on Dubček's leadership. Moreover, under his guidance the officials in his department prepared a "memorandum" which evaluated the results of the Warsaw Pact maneuvers, discussed the possibility of military intervention in Czechoslovakia, and made tentative suggestions as to preventive measures and contingency plans that might be put into effect should this take place. This memo was presented to the Czechoslovak Presidium but was rejected without discussion at the insistence of antireformists such as Bilak, who was said to have revealed its contents to the Soviet embassy in Prague and to his ally in the Soviet Politburo Shelest.[12]

The sacrifice of Prchlík was rumored to have been supported by pressure from the antireformist coalition.[13] It was an unnecessary appeasing gesture toward the Soviet leadership at a time when they were willing to compromise. Very likely, it had the opposite effect to the one intended, in that it provided an important precedent for future Soviet "salami tactics"—i.e., for further demands for the removal of reformists in the Czechoslovak leadership. In an interesting parallel situation during the Soviet-Yugoslav crisis in 1948, Tito and his supporters refused even to discuss with Stalin his demands for the removal of Politburo member Milovan Djilas on similar grounds.

Much more important, however, was the fact that Prchlík's dismissal made the Czechoslovak bargaining position at Čierna less credible. It signaled rather convincingly that the Czechoslovak reformists did not consider military resistance even a hypothetical option. True, the defense of Czechoslovakia—a small power, which Franz Kafka used to call "a little anomaly within the living space of the great powers"—would have been extremely difficult because of the military orientation of the Warsaw Pact and the existence of a fifth column in the Czechoslovak leadership, which informed the Soviets about everything. David Vital convincingly argues that the leaders of small powers with inferior defense capabilities might have an important chance of safeguarding their independence and deterring a military invasion by great powers if they can escalate the potential cost of such an action to a would-be aggressor.[14] This is not to suggest that a credible Czechoslovak defense, or even its serious consideration, would have prevented the intervention; however, it might have been an important factor in the Kremlin debate, as it was during the Soviet-Yugoslav crisis of 1948, or the Soviet-Polish crisis of 1956. It might have provided a powerful argument for those in the Soviet leadership who thought that a military intervention would be too costly. One can never be sure of the effects of a policy. But it is possible that if the Czechoslovak leadership had decided to make credible the possibility of military resistance, the debate between the coalitions in the Soviet leadership would have been dramatically altered. Certain signs of division within the Soviet leadership, as demonstrated during the negotiations in Čierna, lead one to believe that preparations for military resistance might have tipped the scales in the Soviet Politburo in favor of those who were skeptical about intervention.

On the whole, the negotiations in Čierna revealed the naïveté and inexperience of Dubček's leadership in the managing of international affairs. Despite their many differences, Dubček was in many ways like Hungarian leader Nagy in 1956—a man of honesty and integrity, but a romantic Communist incapable of pursuing policies according to the dicta of Machiavelli's Prince. Dubček knew the necessity of seeking Soviet approval of reforms. He was able to identify himself with the demands of the majority of the people in Czechoslovakia. Although he was a skillful tactician in internal Party politics, he was a less perceptive foreign policy strategist and diplomatic bargainer. In his conflict with the Soviets, he failed to draw on Tito's experience of 1948. In contrast, he was willing to discuss Czechoslovak internal developments, apparently believing that he could answer the *realpolitik*-oriented Soviet leaders with the ideology of democratic socialism.

The Soviet delegation arrived at the Čierna Conference with a large staff of experts, their own radio linkup, and massive documentation; the Dubček leadership came with few advisers and no documentation. (Hence, for example, Soviet quotations from the Czechoslovak press could not be verified.)[15] The Soviet leadership had had a special group of experts studying Czechoslovak internal developments for several months; Dubček finally agreed to create a small group of Czechoslovak "Soviet experts" only a few days before the Čierna Conference.[16] Most of Dubček's advisers—the "brain trust" of the Czechoslovak Communist Party—were reform intellectuals and experts in Czechoslovak history, economics, and politics; there were few specialists in international affairs. Even more important, as Czechoslovak leader Mlynář frankly admitted, "none of the leading Czechoslovak reformists had any experience in the field of foreign policy, let alone practical experience with usual mutual relations among socialist countries. . . ."[17] The failure of the Czechoslovak leadership to elaborate a sophisticated foreign policy strategy and to do serious foreign policy research was a mistake. This, and the lack of a creative, active policy toward their allies, at least partially explains why the Czechoslovaks were not equal partners with the Soviet bargainers at Čierna and were often surprised by the positions taken by various Soviet decisionmakers, such as Suslov.

The negotiations at Čierna were conducted at the railway station and inside the private train of the Soviet Politburo. In a somewhat Kafkaesque manner, there would appear at Čierna every morning a special train carrying the members of the Soviet Politburo, who, presumably afraid to sleep in Czechoslovakia, would return each evening on the same train to Soviet territory only a short distance away. This conference began, like the one in Warsaw, with a long speech by Secretary General Brezhnev. He basically defended the wording of the Warsaw Letter, again accusing the Czechoslovak leaders of losing political control in Czechoslovakia, endangering political stability in neighboring countries, and trying to subject the negotiations to the pressure of a "nationalized public."[18] Brezhnev's speech was full of tendentious quotations from the Czechoslovak press. The Two Thousand Words Manifesto was again mentioned. As another proof of "counterrevolutionary danger," Brezhnev disclosed an action that was probably sponsored by the KGB in Prague: a single letter approving the presence of Soviet troops in Czechoslovakia, signed by 99 Prague workers of the 4,500 workers from the Auto-Prague factory.[19] (It was later revealed that some of the signatories were family members.) In a manner similar to Khrushchev's treatment of Gomułka and his supporters during the Soviet-Polish negotiations in October 1956, Brezhnev attacked as "revisionists" in the Dubček leadership Šik and Císař (who was put in charge of the business of the Czechoslovak Party in the absence of the Presidium).

Dubček answered Brezhnev in the name of the Czechoslovak delegation, defending the program of the reformist wing of the Czechoslovak Party, while pledging obligation to the Warsaw Pact and COMECON and rejecting the charges of the Warsaw Letter. Dubček's speech was skillful and moderate; nevertheless, he learned during the discussion following the next day's negotiations that it is difficult, if not impossible, to convince the Machiavellian Soviet bargainers with the force of ideas about one's own version of socialism—as Yugoslavia had learned in the late 1940s, and the Chinese in the early 1960s.

A good illustration of Dubček's naïve, ideologically oriented approach to the negotiations was his attempt to convince bureaucrat Brezhnev that the nationwide signature campaign prior to the Čierna Conference, in which roughly four million Czechoslovak citizens had signed resolutions supporting his policies, proved that the Czechoslovak leadership had political control firmly in its hands. Brezhnev, drawing from his own experience as a Soviet bureaucrat, apparently could not understand that a Communist leader had managed to identify himself with the will of the majority of his nation, and not primarily with that of the ruling bureaucratic elites. Thus, he replied in kind, arguing that he knew how such resolutions could be produced. Dubček tried to assure Brezhnev that these resolutions were different, that they had been initiated directly by the people. But for Brezhnev, this showed that Dubček's leadership was not in firm control of the Czechoslovak reform movement. In Brezhnev's words, "How can you claim that you are in control of the situation if the people sign a resolution without your prior knowledge.?"[20] And a Moscow Radio commentator reminded the Czechoslovak leaders on the second day of the negotiations: "Prior to this meeting we did not gather signatures in support of the CPSU and its leading representatives in our towns; there simply was no need for that, because the support of our people for our party was expressed by the largest and longest reference— the history of our state."[21]

As at the earlier Warsaw Conference, where he had not been impressed by Kádár's arguments, Brezhnev did not seem to be moved by Dubček's similar arguments in Čierna that the success of the Czechoslovak experiment was of importance for the Western Communist parties. Nor did he heed warnings about the irreparable damage that the Soviet hard-line policy vis-à-vis Czechoslovakia would cause to the international Communist movement. According to the French Marxist philosopher and ex-Politburo member of the French Communist Party Roger Garaudy, Brezhnev brushed off Dubček with the words, "We have the necessary means for dealing with those who dare to do that, by reducing them in the future to meaningless grouplets."[22]

The negotiations at Čierna demonstrated that, under a façade of unity, there were divergent interests in both delegations. The hard bargaining, which was originally scheduled to last only one or one-and-a-half days, lasted four days; and the scheduled visits of Yugoslav President Josip Broz Tito and Rumanian Party leader Nicolae Ceausescu had to be postponed several times. The activity of the conference can be characterized as a classical bargaining process in which the "payoffs" to various participants and the four coalitions represented were maximized.

On the Czechoslovak side, the members of the antireformist coalition perceived their payoff in terms of keeping their bureaucratic positions with Soviet assistance. They were uninterested in convincing the Soviet decision-makers of Dubček's ability to control developments in Czechoslovakia. *Pravda's* postintervention (August 22, 1968) narrative took an exaggerated stance, arguing that at Čierna right-wing opportunists (Dubček and his supporters) were in the minority and that "most of the members [of the Czechoslovak Presidium] took a principled line and stressed the need for vigorous struggle against the antisocialist forces."[23] This was only partly true. Even more than the Soviet leaders, the Czechoslovaks at Čierna failed to present a common front. This became clear during the discussions when the Soviet delegation, which had only a few speakers, insisted that all members of the Czechoslovak delegation explain their views. According to the late Czechoslovak leader Smrkovský, he, Černík, and Kriegel supported Dubček, while the antireformist coalition—Bilak, Kolder, and Švestka—spoke "from the position of Soviet argumentation" and "criticized everything" that Dubček and his supporters said.[24]

That the Czechoslovak Presidium was divided into two coalitions, as demonstrated clearly at Čierna, almost certainly influenced the management and final resolution of the Czechoslovak crisis. Perhaps Dubček's greatest error lay in not trying to neutralize at least the outspoken members of the antireformist coalition, Kolder and Bilak—not necessarily in a physical sense, as other Communist leaders (Tito, Mao, E. Hoxha, and Ceauşescu) did, but politically, through an immediate convocation of the Party Congress[25] to expel them from the Central Committee after the Warsaw Conference, as was suggested by some of his supporters. Probably the most compelling historical example of such an action was the decisiveness of Tito and his supporters in getting rid of representatives of the pro-Soviet fifth column and their potential collaborators, Yugoslav Politburo members S. Žujović and A. Hebrang. Kolder and Bilak, who during the Central Committee discussion (as well as several times earlier) had expressed serious disagreement with Dubček's defense against the Warsaw Letter charges, were not expelled from the Czechoslovak ruling body, as was their Yugoslav counterpart Žujović, who in 1948 had disagreed in a similar manner with Tito's defense against Stalin's charges.

So the pro-Soviet Czechoslovak leaders stayed in the Presidium, undermined the reformist position during the negotiations, and on the very day of the Soviet intervention tried to establish an anti-Dubček government. Prague Spring reformism was not the authoritarian Yugoslav Communism of 1948, and Dubček was not Tito but an "irresolute Prince," who did not grasp the Machiavellian notion of "how not to be good." Following a path of neutrality and tolerance in dealing with his enemies in the Czechoslovak leadership would prove disastrous to his political life.

Although the Soviet delegation was not so sharply divided as the Czechoslovak one, some differences nonetheless existed among the Soviet bargainers at the Čierna Conference. Smrkovský's impression was that the Soviet leaders had not yet decided at Čierna in favor of intervention. In his words, "There was not full unity among them."[26] Seeing different facets of the Czechoslovak issue, the Soviet negotiators tried to maximize their individual payoffs. Again, as in the earlier stages of the crisis, interventionist coalition spokesman Shelest was the sharpest and most outspoken in his attacks on the Czechoslovak leadership. His behavior in Čierna clearly indicated that he (as much as the antireformist Czechoslovak bargainers Kolder and Bilak) was not much interested in reaching a meaningful compromise.

On the contrary, Shelest, according to several accounts, was clearly interested in destroying the negotiations; he initiated vicious, vulgar attacks against Dubček and his supporters. His performance left no doubt as to whom he was referring to as "demagogues" and "pseudo-theoreticians who propagandize fictitious models of socialism" in his earlier speeches in February and July, and as to why he had brought the party official from Transcarpathia, Il'nitskii, as a speaker to an important CPSU Central Committee meeting in July. Involving the "Ukrainian factor" in the negotiations (as he apparently had at the Soviet Central Committee sessions in April and July), Shelest accused Dubček of wanting to take back the Transcarpathian Ukraine.[27] According to Czechoslovak leader Smrkovský, Shelest went so far as to accuse the Czechoslovaks of printing leaflets that "were distributed in Transcarpathia demanding the separation of Transcarpathia from the Soviet Union." Shelest held the Czechoslovak leaders who were present responsible for this.[28] Shelest also abused and insulted another Czechoslovak reformist, in the anti-Semitic spirit of the Ukrainian Party's "politics of Zionism," by calling the old Communist Kriegel "*Evrei i Galitsii*" [that Galician Jew][29] and not a partner in the negotiations. (Only a week after the intervention, on August 28, another Ukrainian Party of ficial, V. Kozachenko, would denounce "militant Zionists" as "enemies o Czechoslovakia" at an emergency session of the Union of Ukrainia writers.) After Shelest made his accusation, Dubček and his supporters in the Czech delegation told the Soviet leaders in Russian, "*Khvatit*" [That is enough],[30] and left. The negotiations broke down completely, and some o the Czechoslovak leaders thought of leaving the conference.

At Čierna, the Czechoslovak bargainers did not receive support or eve understanding from Premier Kosygin, as they had seemed to during th May crisis. Kosygin was a very tough and hard bargainer, certainly not th "dove" depicted by some Kremlinologists at the time. Kosygin's toughness however, does not necessarily suggest a drastic change in his stand on th Czechoslovak issue. It is conceivable that Kosygin, like others skeptical o intervention, was under heavy pressure in July from the interventionists, and perhaps even criticized for his attempts at moderation. (For example on the third day of negotiations, a Moscow Radio commentator reported the opinion of a Soviet worker, who complained that he"cannot understand why these [antisocialist] elements still have not been rebuffed in a serious way."[31] After the intervention Kosygin was said to be criticized within Party circles for "understanding the danger of counterrevolution in Prague."[3] Perhaps Kosygin's hard bargaining approach at Čierna was aimed at countering the criticism after his May visit to Czechoslovakia that he was "soft on revisionism" and was an attempt to achieve compromise through hard and tough bargaining.

The fragmented evidence suggests that Suslov, spokesman for those who were skeptical about military intervention, tried hard to arrive at a compromise with the Czechoslovak bargainers at Čierna. He reminded Secretary General Brezhnev during the negotiations on July 31 that the Soviet Politburo several weeks earlier had rejected the forceful approach toward Czechoslovakia advocated by East Germany's Ulbricht.[33]

Suslov's moderation was certainly not part of a deceptive game. To be sure, Suslov, like Brezhnev, had not been impressed by the force of Dubček's ideas about "socialism with a human face"; rather, he was concerned about the unpleasant developments among "his" constituencies—the West European and some East European Communist parties—during the negotiations. On July 30, the Soviet Politburo again received warning letters from the leaders of two ruling Communist parties (Tito and Ceauşescu). As before, during the Warsaw Conference, the majority of Western Communist leaders supported their Czechoslovak comrades. On the same day, two representatives of the exiled Spanish Communist Party reportedly delivered a new letter, signed by the representatives of eighteen European Communist parties, to CPSU Secretary Kirilenko in Moscow, which was transmitted to the Soviet Politburo in Čierna. The letter demanded an end to Soviet interference in Czechoslovak internal affairs; otherwise, the parties threatened, they would convene a conference of Western European Communist parties that would deal with the issue and probably condemn the Soviet Union.[34] The World Communist Conference planned by Suslov and Ponomarev again seemed to be placed in jeopardy.

Suslov, who had different bureaucratic responsibilities from Shelest, apparently again feared disastrous consequences for the cohesion of the international Communist movement and tried to maximize his payoff (or cut his losses) by finding a mutually acceptable political solution. Seeing a different facet of the Czechoslovak issue, he probably could not disregard the demands of the West European Communist parties in Shelest's or Brezhnev's manner. "If we go in," Suslov was quoted as saying, "we might as well abandon the conferences here and now."[35] Apparently, even the other skeptics of military intervention, such as Kosygin, realized the value of a peaceful solution to the Czechoslovak crisis. When the conference seemed on the verge of breaking up, Kosygin reportedly came to the Czechoslovak train to apologize personally for the Soviet insults, arguing that it was "necessary to act in a comradely manner. A breakdown of talks might have unpredictable consequences."[36] In a private discussion, the Soviet team of four (Brezhnev, Suslov, Kosygin, and Podgorny) also apologized to Dubček and Smrkovský for Shelest's insults, stating, as Smrkovský reported, that Shelest "overdid it [to přehnal]."[37]

On August 1, negotiations were resumed. This step resulted from personal talks between Dubček and Brezhnev (who had miraculously recovered from a vague illness). They decided to seek a political compromise through bargaining between two limited teams composed of four negotiators from either side. According to former Czechoslovak leader Zdeněk Mlynář, Dubček believed Brezhnev had a sincere interest in seeking compromise and thus avoiding the intervention advocated by Shelest, Ulbricht, Gomułka, and others.[38] The decision to compromise was reportedly confirmed at the Soviet Politburo session on the morning of August 1,[39] when the Soviet Politburo held a private discussion to map a strategy for political compromise. The bargaining that followed between the two teams of four is important in understanding the nature and scope of the compromise later reached at Čierna. The format worked to the advantage of the Czechoslovak reformers. In contrast to the earlier negotiations at Warsaw, the Soviet bargaining team now included two senior Soviet decisionmakers, Suslov and Kosygin, who were responsible mainly for foreign policy matters and who were skeptical of military intervention and did *not* include the interventionist Shelest nor any other Soviet decisionmaker responsible solely for internal affairs. The Soviet interventionists were represented only by Podgorny, and the team was headed by the again wavering Brezhnev.

The Czechoslovak bargaining team included only those who perceived their largest payoffs in reaching a compromise with the Soviet team: Dubček, Smrkovský, Černík, and President Svoboda. Svoboda had entered the talks at Soviet insistence even though he was not a member of the Czechoslovak Presidium. Contrary to Soviet expectations, however, he did not side with the antireformist coalition. Even more important, such representatives of the antireformist coalition as Kolder and Bilak had been excluded from the negotiations in this small circle. Thus, most of the bargainers on both sides seemed to be interested in reaching a compromise.

During the discussions, Brezhnev, Kosygin, and particularly Suslov adopted a conciliatory tone.[40] Suslov stated that "the Czechoslovak question must be settled by agreement if great harm is not to ensue for the international movement and its unity."[41] Interestingly, the wavering Secretary General Brezhnev again seemed to modify his stand, now identifying with the noninterventionists. He had apparently changed his stand after private talks with Dubček, recovery from his brief "illness" (which may have been of a political nature), and discussions in the Soviet Politburo.

The Czechoslovak team provided a new assurance of loyalty to the Warsaw Pact and COMECON, and again verbally promised to curb "antisocialist tendencies" (i.e., activities of the various political clubs, KAN and K-231) and to prevent revival of the Social Democratic Party. In fact, this was not difficult for the Czechoslovak negotiators to promise, for at about that time, some of the political clubs suspended their activities and practically ceased to exist. The reformist coalition had stressed repeatedly during the Prague Spring that reform did not mean return to a pluralist system involving several parties, as in the pre-World War II Czechoslovak Republic or even in the brief period of 1945–48. Traditional Western-type democracy was not going to be permitted. As Kriegel, one of the most radical of Dubček's supporters, put it: the Social Democratic Party will not exist, "even if we have to call up the militia against it." Furthermore, several days before the Čierna Conference, the Preparatory Committee of the Social Democratic Party gave written assurance to the Czechoslovak Presidium—an assurance which was presented to the Soviet leaders during negotiations—that they would suspend their activities until further notice.[42]

The Czechoslovak negotiators also seemed to be determined to control the press more effectively. On July 29, the first day of negotiations at Čierna, the Czechoslovak minister of the interior, Pavel, issued a provisional "list of secret facts of Czechoslovakia" to editors and publishers,[43] and Dubček presented the Soviet negotiators with a report on "methods of control of information media."[44] In return, the Soviet bargaining team promised that most of the charges of the Warsaw Letter would be forgotten. (For some of them, like Suslov, this was probably not difficult, because they neither participated at Warsaw nor signed the letter.) The Soviet bargaining team also promised that all Soviet troops would be withdrawn from

Czechoslovak territory, and, most important, that the September congress of the Czechoslovak Party would be approved. Furthermore, there were hints that the Soviet negotiators would agree to use economic instruments to resolve the crisis, as advocated earlier by Premier Kosygin. Secretary General Brezhnev suggested that the Soviet Union could award to Czechoslovakia a requested loan, perhaps not in hard currency but in rubles and grain.[45] On August 1, the Ministries of Foreign Trade of both countries had set up for the middle of August 1968 the first stage of preparations for negotiations on a Czechoslovak-Soviet trade agreement to go into effect in 1969.)[46] Finally, the Czechoslovaks reiterated their earlier condition that bilateral meetings with all Warsaw Pact members precede a multilateral summit. Their Soviet counterparts agreed that such a meeting would take place on Czechoslovak soil and would not include discussion of internal Czechoslovak affairs. Both delegations pledged to cease polemics, and they agreed to hold another multilateral summit of six Warsaw Pact countries in Bratislava, the capital of Slovakia, in two days.

On balance, the outcome of the negotiations in Čierna was a compromise, although a vague and ambiguous one. No official record of the Čierna negotiations is available; and both sides made only verbal promises, which were not included in either the Čierna Communiqué or the Bratislava Declaration. Hence, it is difficult, if not impossible, for historians and political scientists to prove whether it was the Soviets or the Czechoslovaks who broke the Čierna accord.

Perhaps Dubček, in the private conversation with Brezhnev already referred to, had made verbal concessions. He was said to promise to control the Czechoslovak press; to prevent the organization of any political groups outside the National Front; to strengthen the People's Militia and other security forces; to assure the protection of antireformist Communists opposed to the liberalization program; to end the published polemics against the Soviet Union; and to remove at least two reformists, Kriegel and Císař.[47] If it is true that Dubček promised to deliver on most, if not all, of these promises, then some of the postintervention Soviet complaints were justified. According to Czechoslovak leader Smrkovský, however, the Czechoslovaks made only very general promises. He stated that the final Soviet demands at Čierna were reduced solely to matters of Czechoslovak internal politics: (1) Kriegel should not be the chairman of the Czechoslovak National Front; (2) Císař should be dismissed as a secretary of the Czechoslovak Party; (3) the existence of a Social Democratic Party should not be allowed; (4) clubs such as KAN and K-231 should be forbidden; and (5) control should be established over the news media.[48]

Smrkovský indicated that the Czechoslovak bargaining team promised the Soviet negotiators that most of these measures to stabilize the domestic situation would be taken by the end of August, at the session of the Czechoslovak Central Committee and at the Party congress, and that the Sovi leaders noted it.[49] But the Czechoslovak team of four did not really make firm commitment to protect the antireformist coalition, or to dismis Kriegel and Císař at the Party congress. Yet perhaps during their privat discussions, Dubček (though a Slovak) tried to outfox Brezhnev like a typ cal Czech "Schweik"; and perhaps he made some ambiguous promises re garding the composition of the Czechoslovak leadership.[50] This may hav been a great tactical error. Another Czechoslovak leader, Šik, believes tha a more experienced Czechoslovak statesman, thinking more in terms o *realpolitik,* would have tried to conclude a less ambiguous (although per haps more conceding) *written* agreement. Perhaps even the personne changes in the Czechoslovak leadership would have been accepted, becaus at the congress the dismissed reformers might have been replaced by othe Dubček supporters (as happened for a short period after the interventio and the Moscow negotiations). The main goal of Dubček's team shoul have been to compromise in order to obtain a firm license from the Sovie Politburo to continue the reform program, and to save its major goal—th Fourteenth Party Congress. But the inexperienced Dubček was under con flicting pressures from the Soviet leadership, the Czechoslovak public various interest groups, the press, reformist and antireformist coalitions and reformist intellectuals and advisers of the Czechoslovak Communis Party. In such a situation he was incapable of combining open, populist in ternal politics with Machiavellian secret diplomacy.

But Brezhnev too must be held responsible for the ambiguity of the Či erna truce. He, as well as other wavering senior Soviet decisionmakers, may have preferred a general agreement to a specific one, one that would enabl him to change his stand later.[51]

Hence, only a brief communiqué was issued about the Čierna negotia tions. Yet even the drafting of this short, meaningless joint communiqué was enormously difficult and delayed the end of the conference for anothe day.[52] Both delegations had prepared their own drafts: the Czechoslovaks produced a long one, defending various features of the Prague Spring; the Soviets produced one twice as long and filled with rhetoric[53] (like the Bratis lava Declaration), which was signed two days later. Finally, after hard bar gaining and much consultation with other members of the delegations, the drafting committee—comprising Czechoslovaks Spaček (reformist) and Bilak (antireformist) and the Soviet representative, Secretary Katushev— produced the text of the communiqué. It said that "a broad comradely ex change of opinions on questions of interest to both sides took place," and that "the participants in the meeting exchanged detailed information about the situations in their countries." (There were no words about the interna tional situation, again indicating that the negotiations were almost entirely devoted to the Czechoslovak internal situation.) The communiqué stressed

hat the negotiations were conducted in "an atmosphere of complete frank-
ness, sincerity, and mutual understanding."[54] The absence of any mention
of unity implied that an agreement had been reached, but that many dif-
erences persisted. The only officially announced agreement was the decision to hold a multilateral summit of the six Warsaw Pact countries in
Bratislava on August 3.

The Bratislava Conference

The Bratislava Conference of six Warsaw Pact countries (the USSR, East
Germany, Poland, Hungary, Bulgaria, and Czechoslovakia attended;
Rumania again did not) followed the Čierna Conference within forty-eight
hours, on August 3, 1968. Like the previous multilateral summits during the
Czechoslovak crisis, it was more than an attempt to bolster the bilateral
Soviet-Czechoslovak negotiations. It signaled a final attempt by the Soviet
noninterventionists to find a political solution to the crisis by convincing interventionist elements in East Germany and Poland to abandon (at least
temporarily) their belligerent attitude. The Soviet delegation to Bratislava
included two members of the team of four which at Čierna concluded the
tentative agreement with the Czechoslovaks (Suslov and Kosygin), but also
interventionists Shelest and Podgorny, and the wavering Secretary General
Brezhnev. In addition, two Party secretaries were present—Katushev and
Ponomarev, who was skeptical about intervention. It seemed that equilibrium would be restored between the coalitions at the Bratislava Conference. The interventionists were represented, but they did not have a majority, as they had had at the Warsaw Summit, where Suslov and Ponomarev,
the senior Soviet decisionmakers in charge of international party affairs,
were absent.

At Bratislava, Hungarian leader Kádár—in a sense an ally of the Soviet
noninterventionist coalition—seemed to be satisfied with the Čierna compromise. After his arrival, Kádár said that he was "glad to come in a good
cause, with good intentions, and confidence."[55] On the other hand, the East
European interventionists, Ulbricht and Gomułka, who at Bratislava were
unable to put demands upon the Czechoslovak reformers and had instead to
agree with the Soviet reconciliatory line, were deeply disappointed with the
results of the Čierna Conference. Gomułka demanded to know why it was
"necessary to meet again when all that needed to be said had already been
said in the Warsaw Letter."[56]

Dubček had a different desire: to convince the Soviet negotiators that his
leadership would keep the promises made at Čierna. Thus, when he saw his
interpreters with the latest issue of the Czechoslovak journal *Reportér,* the
cover of which carried a reproduction of an old Russian woodcut of a
mounted Cossack being seen off to the wars by a girl in braids and a Rus-

sian robe, with the legend "Don't grieve at the long parting, Dunyasha; I'n off to maneuvers," he asked them to put it away with these words: "Jus don't let Brezhnev see it. I've promised him that everything would be in order with the press."[57]

At the beginning of the Bratislava Conference, Brezhnev briefly informed the other delegations that by an agreement made at the Čierna conferenc all signatories of the Warsaw Letter should consult with the Czechoslovak leaders to produce a joint document.[58] Thus, the Bratislava Conference was devoted entirely to drafting such a document, which became known as the Bratislava Declaration. First, the members of the Soviet delegation presented a preliminary version. Then several groups of Czechoslovak ad visers formulated changes and amendments to this initial document (Naturally, the Czechoslovak delegation had more objections to the Soviet text than any of the other delegations.) Finally, a drafting committee, com prising two or three representatives from each delegation—the delegation leader (the first secretary), the prime minister, and/or one advisory assistant or translator—worked jointly to draw up the definitive version of the declaration. On the Soviet side were Brezhnev and Kosygin; on the Czecho-slovak side, Dubček, Černík, and Mlynář. The Soviet working draft was taken as a basis for the negotiations, and worked over sentence by sentence and paragraph by paragraph. Thus, although the text of the Bratislava Declaration was a product of bargaining and compromise, it did not differ significantly from the original Soviet draft. Again, like the processes that led to the Warsaw Letter and the Čierna Communiqué, the bargaining process at Bratislava, which lasted several hours, transformed the various positions of individual participants into a group-negotiated compromise agreement.

This fact explains the ambiguity of the declaration. For example, at the insistence of the Czechoslovak negotiators, the text made no direct reference to Czechoslovakia. The result was a loosely worded document written in ideological language in some ways reminiscent of the Warsaw Letter. The declaration pledged that "unshakable fidelity to Marxism-Leninism, education of the popular masses in the spirit of the ideas of socialism and proletarian internationalism, and an implacable struggle against bourgeois ideology and all antisocialist forces constitute the guarantee of success in strengthening the position of socialism and rebuff-ing the intrigues of imperialism." It stressed that the internal policy of socialist countries should "firmly and resolutely oppose, with great vigilance and unshakable solidarity, all attempts of imperialism and all other anticommunist forces to weaken the guiding role of the working class and the Communist Parties." The socialist countries "will never allow anyone to drive a wedge between the socialist states or undermine the foun-dations of the socialist system."[59]

These ideological clichés failed to provide a framework for meaningful compromise or to answer the central question of how to resolve the Czechoslovak crisis. These passages of the Bratislava Declaration can best be explained in terms of the "images of national security" shared by all senior Soviet decisionmakers (see Chapter 1). The Soviet Union would intervene in a Warsaw Pact country if a "bourgeois" system (i.e., a pluralist system of several parties) were established. Yet, as I have demonstrated, under the cover of "shared images" there is plenty of room for disagreement among senior decisionmakers on when the Soviet Union should intervene in a socialist country (such as Czechoslovakia) if there is only a *potential* threat. In this case, the real issue for foreign policy decisionmaking was, What kind of instruments should be used to contain reformism in Czechoslovakia: peaceful (i.e., political and economic) or military? In this respect, the Bratislava Declaration did not provide a definitive answer. The presence of advocates of both schools of thought on the negotiating teams at Čierna and Bratislava may explain many seeming ambiguities in the final draft of the declaration. Its wording implies two answers: peaceful as well as military resolution of the Czechoslovak crisis. During the hard bargaining over the text of the declaration, Czechoslovak sources reported the following pattern: "the Czechoslovaks constantly suggested amendments" to the original Soviet draft, then "Ulbricht and Gomułka would support the original Soviet version," while Kádár "echoed the Czechoslovak view fairly consistently."[60] Bulgarian leader Zhivkov also tried occasionally to support Brezhnev's point of view. Zhivkov had already impressed the conferees as not being an exceptionally bright man; thus, it was not surprising that his "assistance" actually made the role of Brezhnev, who was willing to compromise on some points, more difficult. Although he had good intentions, he did not understand that Brezhnev changed his tactics from time to time and therefore relentlessly supported the original hard line, much to the visible irritation of Brezhnev, who, after ignoring Zhivkov's intrusions two or three times, began to signal with hand gestures that Zhivkov should not enter into the discussion.[61]

Regarding internal Czechoslovak affairs, the Bratislava Declaration stressed that the Communist parties should "advance firmly along the path of socialism by *strictly and consistently following the general laws governing the construction of a socialist society.*" This formulation may be interpreted as Czechoslovak consent to follow strictly the Soviet model of socialism. On the other hand, another portion of the declaration (suggested by the Czechoslovak bargainers and accepted by their counterparts) stressed that "in so doing, every fraternal party, while creatively deciding questions of further socialist development, takes into account *specific national features and conditions.*" This formulation may be interpreted as being a limited approval of Dubček's program of domestic reform.

Even the usual formulations regarding principles of cooperation among the Warsaw Pact countries were transformed through negotiation into a compromise formula, allowing two interpretations. The declaration spoke about the principles of "equality, respect for sovereignty and national independence and territorial integrity," but it also added the formula about "fraternal, mutual assistance and solidarity"—the word "assistance" often meaning, in Soviet political language, "military intervention."

Perhaps the most controversial and longest-discussed sentence in the Bratislava Declaration was the following, which referred to the successes of the Soviet Union and other socialist countries in constructing of socialism and Communism: "It is the *common* international duty of *all* socialist countries to support, strengthen and defend these gains, which have been achieved at the cost of every people's heroic efforts and selfless labor." This wording and that of the sentence immediately following—"This is the unanimous opinion of all the participants in the conference, who express unswerving determination to develop and defend the socialist gains in their countries"—and Brezhnev's stubborn rejection of the attempt by the Czechoslovaks to amend the text by including a phrase ensuring "full respect for the sovereignty and national independence of each individual state" were viewed with suspicion by the Czechoslovaks, especially Mlynář.[62] In the ensuing argument, Brezhnev was vehemently supported by Ulbricht, Gomułka, and Zhivkov; Kádár seems to have been receptive to the changes suggested by the Czechoslovak delegation. The Czechoslovak leaders could not, of course, have foreseen that the phrases referring to "fraternal assistance" and "the common international duty" to defend the socialist gains would be used repeatedly in the future to provide an *ex post facto* ideological justification for the invasion, and that they would become a part of the so-called Brezhnev doctrine of "limited sovereignty" of socialist states.[63] Inclusion of the phrases in the document does not imply, however, that Brezhnev had already decided in favor of invasion, but rather that he was still undecided at this point and probably saw them as a kind of "escape clause," should intervention subsequently be deemed necessary. According to the observation of the eyewitness Mlynář, Brezhnev certainly did not give the impression during the negotiations that he had decided on the action, taken only seventeen days later, to intervene militarily in Czechoslovakia.[64]

The declaration did not specifically give approval either to Czechoslovak reformism or to the September Party Congress. Regarding Czechoslovak domestic affairs, the ambiguous, contradictory text of the Bratislava Declaration, like the verbal agreements made at Čierna, obligated the Czechoslovak leadership only to vague tenets on maintaining political stability. On the other hand, Czechoslovak obligations in the realm of foreign policy matters were elaborated in a clear and unambiguous way. The Czechoslovaks

greed to "coordinate their actions in the international arena," in particu-
ar their policy vis-à-vis West Germany, Vietnam, and Israel, and to strictly
ollow their obligations to the Warsaw Pact and COMECON. But it should
e stressed again that it was not difficult for the Czechoslovak bargainers to
gree to the alliance obligations. Knowing the seriousness of the situation,
ney were determined (perhaps more than ever) to fulfill these obligations,
oping to get in return Soviet approval for the continuation of their reform-
st program and freedom from interference in their internal affairs.

Perhaps reflecting the results of the negotiations at Čierna, where the
Czechoslovaks were verbally promised economic assistance, and perhaps
eflecting noninterventionist attempts to resolve the crisis through economic
neans, the Bratislava Declaration (contrary to the Warsaw Letter) urged
"holding an economic conference at the highest level, and in the very near
uture." (The conference never took place.)

Also in the realm of foreign policy and international Communist affairs,
he Bratislava Declaration, probably reflecting the views of Suslov and
Ponomarev, hailed the World Communist Conference in advance as "an
mportant contribution to the cause of consolidating all the revolutionary
orces of the present time." (According to Mlynář, Dubček argued during
he discussions at Bratislava that the declaration would have more interna-
ional significance if the representatives of Rumania and Yugoslavia, and
perhaps even Albania, were to sign it. His suggestion that he act as mediator
n this respect during his forthcoming meeting with Tito and Ceauşescu was
ejected by the other participants, however.)[65] The declaration also reaf-
irmed the goals of Soviet *Westpolitik*. On June 27, Soviet Minister of
Foreign Affairs Gromyko had referred to the principles of the 1966
Bucharest and 1967 Karlovy Vary conferences, as did Premier Kosygin on
July 11. Following this pattern, the declaration referred to doing "every-
hing necessary to convoke" the European Security Conference. Finally,
egarding another important aspect of Soviet *Westpolitik*—relations with
West Germany—the Bratislava Declaration repeated the critical, militant
portions of the Dresden Communiqué and the Warsaw Letter about "West
German revanchism." But it also called for the support of "all forces
fighting against imperialism and revanchism and for democratic progress"
n West Germany—unmistakably including West German Social Democrats.
This formula, which was (in a similar version) included in the Czechoslovak
Action Program, was apparently added at the request of the Czechoslovak
negotiators. Since the Czechoslovaks had agreed to coordinate their policy
with the Warsaw Pact, the Soviet negotiators agreed to it.

East German leader Ulbricht, who had objected for years to a rapprochement with West Germany, reportedly objected vigorously to this formulation, requesting a clear definition of "all those forces" in West Germany.
Ulbricht also complained that it was no secret that in Bucharest, in Bel-

grade, and now in Prague, Brandt—in his view "the most dangerous Wes
German politician"—was considered a "progressive man." (Perhap
Ulbricht also had in mind some people in Moscow in the Soviet Interna
tional Department; in April 1969, he would have his first public disagree
ment with Suslov and Ponomarev regarding policy toward the West Germar
Social Democrats, and because of his obstructions to Soviet–West Germar
rapprochement, he would be forced to "retire" in April 1971.) Ulbricht re
minded his allies that this was a bad policy because "social democrats ar€
led by traitors of socialism [perhaps a reference to Ulbricht's persona
enemy, ex-Communist West German Social Democrat H. Wehner] anc
servants of imperialism," and because their policy is as dangerous for th€
European peace as that of the revanchists.[66]

Finally, the Bratislava Declaration was completed. But the gloomy mooc
of some participants persisted. Even Brezhnev did not seem to be overly en
thusiastic. When Dubček was about to read the declaration, Brezhnev
lumbered to his feet and stated that a great deal of fruitful work had beer
done and agreement had been reached. He then read out the text of the
declaration himself.[67]

On balance, the Bratislava Declaration of August 3, 1968, did not repre
sent complete reversal of previous policies. The declaration was neither a
Czechoslovak victory, as some Czechoslovak leaders (e.g., Smrkovský)[68]
and the Western press thought at the time; nor merely a smoke screen, as
some Czechoslovak leaders began to believe after the intervention; nor only
a simple ideological reproduction of the Warsaw Letter in a different form,
as some of the Czechoslovak postintervention historians would like us to
believe.[69] Another Czechoslovak leader, Kriegel, was perhaps closer to the
truth when he stated that the Bratislava agreement was a compromise, but
"loosely worded" and "provisional," and complained that the Czechoslo
vak Party "had not prepared any alternative," should the situation sud
denly change for the worse.[70]

In broader terms, the Bratislava Declaration seems to have been a com
promise not only between the Czechoslovaks and other Warsaw Pact dele
gations, but also between the two schools of thought within the Soviet lead
ership. The Čierna and Bratislava conferences were also last attempts by the
advocates of nonintervention (responsible for foreign policy matters, and
led by Suslov) to avoid a military action. The Bratislava Declaration, as
Löwenthal puts it,

showed the handwriting of Suslov—who was as conspicuous by his activity at Čierna
and Bratislava as he had been by his absence at Warsaw—and reflected his belief in
the magic power of ideological formulations to mold the policy of Communist par
ties in any situation. For the moment, it served to paper over the differences not
merely between Russians and Czechoslovaks, but within the Russian delegation: for
while Suslov and the 'conciliators' presumably hoped that it would help to avoid the
odium of military action, the hard-liners were certainly more skeptical.[71]

In a way, the Bratislava Declaration of August 3, 1968, was a confirmation of the moderate, noninterventionist approach taken at the Čierna negotiations by Suslov and several other Soviet leaders. In this respect, it was similar to the Declaration of the Soviet government of October 30, 1956 (which was unexpectedly brought to Budapest by Suslov and Mikoian).

Indeed, it would be a mistake to consider the Bratislava Declaration (like the Soviet Statement of October 30, 1956) a purely tactical or deceptive maneuver. Despite all differences, both agreements were temporary compromises between two schools of thought regarding resolution of a crisis. It is true that on August 3, 1968, Czechoslovakia was in a better position than Hungary had been on October 30, 1956. In Hungary, the Soviet leadership had committed itself only to a limited withdrawal; the withdrawal of the Soviet Army from Czechoslovak territory was total. The last Soviet units left Czechoslovakia on August 3, 1968, the day the Bratislava Declaration was signed. After months of hesitation, uncertainty, and confusion, the Soviet decisionmakers were at last willing to take their troops out, a move that undoubtedly strengthened the diplomatic position of the Czechoslovak leadership. The fact that the Soviet decisionmakers did not act while their troops were still on maneuvers in Czechoslovakia, the moderate behavior of at least some of them during the negotiations at Čierna and Bratislava, and, finally, their decision to agree to an unconditional troop withdrawal indicated not only their indecisiveness, but also that at least some of them were interested in resolving the crisis without military force. At the Bratislava Conference, the Czechoslovak leaders showed a readiness to help the Soviet decisionmakers save face and to persuade at least some of them of the benefits of a bargained solution. But the Czechoslovak leaders, as well as most Western leaders and observers, did not see (or were unable to see) the precarious nature of the compromise, which depended mainly upon the balance of forces between the coalitions in the Kremlin.

It has generally been overlooked that the Soviet leadership decided to withdraw the Warsaw Pact units from Czechoslovak *territory,* but not from the Czechoslovak *borders.* These units did not return to home stations but remained in encampment at the boundaries of the country.[72] This fact underscores the ambiguous nature of the compromise reached at Čierna and Bratislava. The Soviet Politburo did not decide to dismantle the military buildup around Czechoslovakia. In other words, the Soviet leaders perceived Čierna and Bratislava only as provisional settlements that preserved the option of intervention in the event the Czechoslovak reformers failed to implement the agreements.

The outcome of the Čierna and Bratislava negotiations suggests that the Soviet leadership had not accepted the doctrine of "unity in diversity." The leadership decided not to drop the pressure on Czechoslovakia, but, for the time being, to withhold military force as an instrument in resolving the crisis. They did not dismiss military intervention as an option if the situation were to deteriorate. The outcome of the negotiations brought only a temporary and ambiguous Soviet approval of the continuation of Czechoslovak reformism and of the September deadline for the Extraordinary Party Congress in Czechoslovakia. The real resolution of the crisis was to come later, after the Soviet leadership had evaluated the results of the Čierna-Bratislava negotiations. It would depend on Soviet assessments not only of the dynamics of Czechoslovak internal developments, but also of the dynamics of the external setting—the international response to the Bratislava truce. Perhaps even more important, however, the final resolution depended on the dynamics of the balance between the noninterventionists and interventionists and a number of wavering men in the Soviet Politburo and in the crucial Central Committee bureaucracies.

Despite all differences, Czechoslovakia between August 3 and August 20, 1968, like Hungary between October 30 and November 4, 1956, lived under conditions of extremely precarious independence.

IV

I also think that the Czechoslovaks have made gains on all levels and that other socialist countries will follow this path. I even think that internal changes in the Soviet Union can be expected.—Milovan Djilas, after the Bratislava Conference

The Bureaucratic Tug-of-War

The Čierna and Bratislava negotiations seemed to dissolve the imminent danger of military force in the resolution of the Czechoslovak crisis. Yet only seventeen days later—to the surprise of most students and observers of Soviet politics—the agreements reached at the negotiations were swept away by military intervention. The very fact that pure military force was used so soon after the climax in tension had passed, and that no dramatic postconference changes had occurred either in Czechoslovakia or in the external international setting, cast doubts on the predictability of Soviet behavior in the management of a crisis. We are led back to the essential question asked in the first chapter: Why did Soviet decisionmakers decide to intervene in Czechoslovakia so soon after agreement had been reached?

In seeking an answer, we should recall the real meaning of the Čierna-Bratislava agreement, particularly as revealed in its ambiguities. The Soviet decisionmakers indicated by their behavior that the negotiations were not merely a smoke screen for military intervention. Unless one accepts the thesis that Soviet leaders typically act in a cruel and perfidious manner, one is compelled to believe that the Čierna-Bratislava negotiations were aimed, at least on the part of some Soviet decisionmakers, at achieving a political solution of the crisis.

The Soviets would certainly not have bargained so hard for four days with the Czechoslovak leadership to conclude a *modus vivendi* if they had perceived it as merely a kind of political preparation for intervention. In fact, if that had been the case, it would have made more sense from their point of view to send Minister of Foreign Affairs Gromyko (or a small, select delegation), let the negotiations break down, and simply hold the Czechoslovak leaders responsible. The Soviet leaders would hardly have asked the leaders of the other Warsaw Pact countries to come to Bratislava to ratify an ambiguous and sketchy declaration that omitted any reference to the situation in Czechoslovakia. The military buildup before and during both conferences served as a logistic preparation for intervention in case the negotiations were broken off, but it still functioned as a warning—an instrument of psychological pressure on the divided Czechoslovak leadership. In fact, the Soviet decision at Čierna was again in favor of nonintervention, although it was perhaps taken by only a slight margin in the Politburo.

As I have demonstrated, the Čierna-Bratislava agreement was a compromise not only between the Czechoslovak and Soviet leaderships, but also between the coalitions within the Soviet Politburo. To understand why an unprovoked military intervention followed, it is appropriate to examine the impact of the Bratislava agreement upon the equilibrium of power between the coalitions in the Soviet Politburo, and the perceptions of various elites at the Central Committee level. Immediately after Bratislava, there were signs that these meetings and their ambiguous results had greatly intensified the tug-of-war among the various bureaucracies of the Central Committee of the CPSU.

The Relief and the Apprehensions of the Skeptics of Military Intervention

Skeptics of the wisdom of military intervention among the various segments of the foreign policy establishment were satisfied with the results of the bilateral negotiations. This seems to have been true of Suslov and the International Department, supervised by Ponomarev; of Prime Minister Kosygin; and probably of several divisions of the Ministry of Foreign Affairs and the Ministry of Foreign Trade that dealt with Western countries. They had good reason to honor the Čierna-Bratislava compromise, at least until November, when the World Communist Conference and the American presidential elections were scheduled to take place. Advocates of the SALT talks at the highest level apparently saw an opportunity to speed up preparations for an early start to the negotiations. Leading bureaucrats in the International Department probably envisioned, as an important payoff of the Bratislava truce, the removal of the threat to the forthcoming World Communist Conference.

Pravda's post-Bratislava editorial on August 5, probably reflecting noninterventionist views, reminded the advocates of intervention why the negotiations had succeeded: "The meetings at Čierna and Bratislava have reconfirmed the premise that wise, calm, thoughtful and patient discussion of complex questions on a principled basis permeated with profound concern for the vital interests of world socialism and the international communist movement is a norm that has justified itself in relations among the socialist countries and communist and workers' parties."[1]

This unusual statement raises some questions. Did *Pravda's* editorial imply that the previous negotiations (i.e., Dresden and Warsaw, in which Suslov and Ponomarev did not participate) were not "calm and wise," and were not conducted in the spirit of the "international communist movement"? This may have been an implicit criticism of the forceful approach of the advocates of intervention—primarily Shelest, whose words and actions at Čierna cannot be described as wise, calm, or thoughtful, and hardly as patient. *Pravda's* editorial probably reflected the views of bureaucrats in the International Department, who placed emphasis on Soviet interest in the international Communist movement, its "unity" and "cohesion," rather than on domestic considerations. It stressed again the part of the April resolution of the CPSU Central Committee that acknowledged, as a major goal, the preparation and convocation of a World Communist Conference as a "central element" in the Party's activities for the near future (i.e., until late November 1968). By the same token, *Pravda's* editorial repeated two important features of the Bratislava Declaration—the notion of "the common laws of building socialist society," and the notion of the rights of each party to "creatively solve the questions of further socialist development by taking national features and conditions into account."[2]

At the same time, *Pravda* had for several days carried letters from Soviet readers expressing enormous satisfaction with the Bratislava agreement, as well as positive comments from the Yugoslav, Rumanian, and West European Communist presses, which had not appeared for months in the Soviet media. On August 6, *Pravda* even reprinted parts of Dubček's speech, in which he expressed his desire for "strengthening the unity of the international communist movement." A similar assessment of the results of the Čierna-Bratislava negotiations appeared in the editorials of several other Soviet periodicals (some of which tried to avoid the hysterical tone of the campaign against Czechoslovakia pursued by *Sovetskaia Rossiia,* and *Literaturnaia gazeta).*[3]

The policy implications of these comments—apparently reflecting to some degree the views of those leaning toward nonintervention, and conforming with shared images of the Soviet leadership—were that unless the situation in Czechoslovakia deteriorated drastically (e.g., the one-party system was abolished, or Czechoslovakia withdrew from the Warsaw Pact or COMECON—in other words, the Hungarian scenario after November 1, 1956), intervention should be avoided, at least until November 1968, or perhaps indefinitely. There were indications that senior decisionmakers in the noninterventionist coalition were still able to convince their more hesitant colleagues of the benefits of a conciliatory approach. This seemed to be implied in the communiqué from the Soviet Politburo session of August 6, where the results of the Čierna and Bratislava conferences were discussed. It was unusual for the Politburo to discuss the results of both conferences, for at Čierna nine of the eleven Politburo members were represented, and at Bratislava five of the eleven. Yet perhaps reservations had already been expressed about the outcome of the negotiations. The seriousness of the situation was probably indicated in the wording of the communiqué, which called the negotiations "timely" and "of great importance for the further development and strengthening of relations between the CPSU and the Czechoslovak Communist Party, and between the USSR and the Czechoslovak Socialist Republic." Yet, the communiqué also stated that the Politburo "approves" and "highly appreciates" the activities of the selected Politburo team and the results of the negotiations.[4]

Skeptics of the wisdom of intervention must have known that the compromises concluded at Čierna and Bratislava were tentative and ambiguous —a kind of temporary *modus vivendi*. Hungarian leader Kádár—who had a stake in a nonmilitary solution of the conflict, perceived a payoff in continuation of the Hungarian policy of domestic reforms, and thus supported the Soviet noninterventionist coalition—made this clear in an interview only two days after the Bratislava agreement was concluded. He frankly admitted that there were differences of opinions "between the leadership of the Czechoslovak Communist Party and the leaderships of the other five parties judging certain questions," and that at Čierna and Bratislava it had been possible only "partly to clear up the misunderstandings and differences and partly to concentrate the six parties' attention on what is common" among them, even if "certain differences in assessment may possibly have remained."[5]

Kádár expressed his personal belief that the remaining differences would be overcome, and that the Bratislava participants would in the future concentrate their policies upon "what is common" to them—as agreed.[6] Yet Kádár indicated that the final resolution of the crisis would be decisive, and might come in the very near future (prior to the September Party Congress in Czechoslovakia). The Soviet Politburo had to make an important decision: either to live up to the Čierna-Bratislava truce and allow Czechoslovak reformism to continue, or to intervene militarily. Kádár, who apparently was aware of the significance of the precarious balance between the two coalitions in the Kremlin, pointed out that the Bratislava Declaration "is a document of historical significance," yet "it is not quite certain that it is being precisely understood by everybody"; however, "it will be understood in *a week, or in a month's time or later.*"[7]

Kádár's uncertainties and reservations seem to have been justified. The satisfaction with the results of the negotiations felt at least temporarily by segments of the Soviet foreign policy establishment was not shared by several bureaucratic elites. Shortly after the agreement was concluded, these bureaucracies and their representatives at the Central Committee and Politburo level began to signal disapproval of the *modus vivendi,* and to press for reconsideration of the Politburo decision.

The Pressure of the Bureaucrats Responsible for Ideological Affairs

The conclusion of the Čierna-Bratislava negotiations probably caused confusion and dissatisfaction within the Party apparatus at the middle level in regional and city committees, and in the Central Committee among bureaucrats responsible for ideological affairs. (Reportedly, while reading the text of the Bratislava Declaration in *Pravda,* a Party official threw the newspaper on the floor and spat on it in the presence of an official of one of the influential West European Communist parties, who observed that it was the first time in his life that he had seen a Soviet *apparatchik* behave in such a manner.)[8] It is plausible that the hostile attitude and the uneasiness generated among regional Party bureaucrats by the Bratislava truce was shared by their representatives at the Central Committee level. The regional bureaucrats constitute a heterogeneous but important elite with immense power and considerable autonomy. Secretary General Brezhnev seemed to intensify his efforts to cultivate their support and identify himself with their demands during the Prague Spring. Two regional Party bureaucrats— Katushev (who was promoted in April 1968 to head of the department dealing with ruling Communist parties [DLCWP]) and Il'nitskii—were involved in preintervention and postintervention diplomacy, and were included in the Soviet delegation that negotiated with the Czechoslovak leadership.

Understandably, the dissatisfaction of the regional bureaucrats was very likely shared by bureaucrats in the Politburo and the Central Committee who were responsible for ideological supervision and indoctrination—such as Trapeznikov of the Department of Science and Education. Some of these officials, regional bureaucrats and ideological supervisors with very conservative views, whom the Soviet historian Roy Medvedev has called "neo-Stalinists," were those "who most actively supported armed intervention in Czechoslovakia in 1968." According to Medvedev, "They presented a very distorted picture of the situation there, putting extraordinary pressure on the leadership of the party."[9]

A leading Soviet commentator, Yurii Zhukov, who had served during the Czechoslovak crisis as a mouthpiece for the interventionists, cautioned his Soviet readers (and probably some of his too enthusiastic colleagues) immediately after the Bratislava agreement: "It would be naïve to believe that the collapse of these plans [of the imperialists] will completely discourage those whose aim is to weaken the socialist community." According to Zhukov, "Imperialists intend to continue their undermining activities by appealing to the antisocialist forces" in Czechoslovakia.[10]

The hostile views of the bureaucrats responsible for ideological supervision appeared, as before during the early stages of the crisis, mainly on the pages of two Soviet newspapers, *Sovetskaia Rossiia* and *Literaturnaia gazeta*. Both again adopted an uncompromising attitude toward the Prague reformism. At a time when most Moscow newspapers were expressing joy over the outcome of the Čierna-Bratislava negotiations, *Sovetskaia Rossiia* launched a new polemic against external enemies by reprinting extensive material devoted to the problems of "ideological war against the socialist countries" conducted by such "subversive" foreign radio broadcasts as the Voice of America, the BBC, Deutsche Welle, and Radio Free Europe. The material in *Sovetskaia Rossiia* implicitly admitted that these broadcasts were influencing "politically immature" Soviet people and "unstable elements" of the population (here meaning the Soviet intelligentsia).[11] *Sovetskaia Rossiia* did not include Czechoslovak radio stations among its list of "subversive stations" because a day earlier (August 1) the Soviet and Czechoslovak bargainers had decided to stop the polemics between the two countries. Yet it is likely that the editors of *Sovetskaia Rossiia* and their supporters in the Central Committee used this campaign to signal their dissatisfaction with the ambiguous agreements reached at Čierna and Bratislava.

The Bratislava Declaration placed emphasis on "the indoctrination of the popular masses in the spirit of the ideas of socialism and proletarian internationalism" as well as on the "implacable struggle against bourgeois ideology and all antisocialist forces."[12] Nevertheless, these general statements failed to make clear the basic demand of the bureaucrat-ideologists: reimposition of censorship on the Czechoslovak public media, which at that time continued successfully to disseminate ideas of democratic socialism in the Soviet Union.

Indeed, in the spring of 1968 there were some signs of growing ferment in intellectual circles as a response to the trials of two Soviet writers, A. Ginzburg and Yu. Galanskov, and to the encouragement prompted by the democratization of society in Czechoslovakia. On April 30, 1968, the clandestine human rights movement began to publish the periodical *Khronika tekushchikh sobytii* [Chronicle of current events]. Subsequently, the greatest number of foreign items reprinted by the *Khronika* in the spring and summer of 1968 came from the Czechoslovak press and media. Since by this time Czechoslovak newspapers had disappeared from the book stalls in the Soviet Union, it was through the *Khronika* that Soviet intellectuals became acquainted with the speeches of Czechoslovak reformist leaders such as Dubček, Smrkovský, and others (which were often reported in the

Soviet press in a slanted way, or not at all), and with many germane documents (such as the Action Program of the Czechoslovak Communist Party, which was distorted by the official Soviet press, and the full text of the Two Thousand Words Manifesto).[13]

It can be surmised that for bureaucrats charged with maintaining ideological purity and supervision (who more than any other group in the Soviet leadership considered the internal politics of other Communist countries their own special province), the Bratislava truce did not resolve satisfactorily the aspect of the Czechoslovak issue that they considered the most dangerous: the threat of Czechoslovak reformism feeding back to Soviet intellectuals and dissidents. Indeed, the sympathy of small groups of intellectuals and students toward Dubček's reformism existed long before the invasion and the subsequent demonstration by several dissidents on August 25 in Red Square. There were already isolated, but nevertheless alarming, indicators during the spring and summer of 1968 that not only some intellectuals and students but also some courageous reformist-oriented CPSU members were beginning to consider the Prague Spring an example for the Soviet Union to follow. One was the circulation of handbills at the University of Gorky in April 1968 urging people "to follow the Czech example."[14] The following month Soviet writer Konstantin Simonov stated in an interview with the Czechoslovak journal *Reportér* that the success of the Prague "experiment . . . will mean a great contribution to world socialism."[15] Shortly before the negotiations at Čierna nad Tisou, as the possibility of military invasion gained increasing support in the Soviet Politburo, a group of members of the CPSU headed by General Grigorenko delivered a letter to the Czechoslovak embassy in Moscow. The letter was addressed to the Czechoslovak Party and to all the Czechoslovak people. It condemned the Soviet pressure on Czechoslovakia and expressed approval of Prague reformism. Similarly, the Soviet dissident writer A. T. Marchenko, also fearing invasion, expressed his support of the Prague Spring in an open letter to three Czechoslovak newspapers. During the Čierna negotiations on August 1, several intellectuals in Leningrad were arrested shortly after they began collecting signatures on their letter of protest against Soviet pressures on Czechoslovakia.[16] The point was made most persuasively by Academician Sakharov's manifesto, which urged the Soviet leadership to adopt some parts of the Czechoslovak reformist programs—e.g., to draft a similar law ending "irresponsible and irrational censorship." Sakharov also called for limits on the influence of the Central Committee bureaucrats who supervise ideological matters, as in Czechoslovakia during the Prague Spring. As an example of abuse, he mentioned the notorious Trapeznikov, "who enjoys too much influence."[17]

I do not mean to suggest here that the gradual development in the USSR of a Soviet version of the Prague Spring was real. My own experience during a trip to the USSR in June 1968 proved that the sympathy and encouragement on the part of quite a few intellectuals and students was accompanied by apathy and even hostility on the part of the general population. Only a courageous minority voiced its support of and sympathy toward Czechoslovakia. What is significant is that the developments mentioned above played into the hands of bureaucrat ideologists such as Trapeznikov. Having been personally attacked by writers such as Sakharov, they had good reason to fear that the infection of Dubčekism would spread to the whole of Eastern Europe and even to the USSR. To these bureaucrats and ideological watchdogs, men like Sakharov who advocated reformism in the USSR were simply the Soviet equivalent of Czechoslovak reformers.

These fears seem to have been reflected in the pages of *Sovetskaia Rossiia.* Its post-Bratislava editorial indicated tacit disapproval of the performance of the noninterventionists at Čierna and Bratislava, and of their acceptance of Dubček's reforms. While the editorials in *Pravda, Izvestiia, New Times,* and other periodicals stressed all the main features of the Bratislava Declaration, including both "general laws" and "specific national features and conditions" of socialist countries, *Sovetskaia Rossiia's* editorial (consistent with its policy line adopted at the time of the April Central Committee session and pursued during the Czechoslovak crisis) omitted reference to the portion of the Bratislava Declaration that alluded to "national peculiarities."[18] This omission was significant. It apparently implied disapproval of the parts of the declaration that referred to the relative independence of the domestic politics of socialist countries. On August 8, only two days after the Soviet Politburo had approved the Bratislava truce, *Sovetskaia Rossiia* unleashed another anti-Czechoslovak polemic, using (as in April) cryptic Soviet political language: "nationalist, revisionist and politically immature elements," and attempts at "liberalization and modernization" in socialist countries.[19]

The disapproval and pressure of the bureaucrats who supervise Soviet intellectuals and writers was reflected in comments published by the periodical *Literaturnaia gazeta.* This newspaper, published under the auspices of the Board of Soviet Writers Union and supervised by Markov and Gribachev, continued its complaint against Czechoslovakia even during the Čierna negotiations, when other Soviet periodicals had ceased their polemics.[20] Simultaneously, it was conducting a campaign against Soviet dissident writers. It was also the first Soviet periodical to revive the open campaign against the Prague reformists—beginning on August 14, well before the Soviet decision to intervene was taken. It rejected the interpretation advanced by the Czechoslovak press that Bratislava meant *de facto,* as well as *de jure,* recognition of Dubček's leadership.[21]

The bureaucrats responsible for ideological supervision perceived the Čierna-Bratislava truce and its implementation as an insufficient barrier against feedback to the Soviet Union and the East European countries from Prague reformism. They realized that controlling the Soviet dissident and intellectual communities would be much more difficult if Dubček and his supporters were to succeed in carrying their program to a successful conclusion at the Party Congress on September 9. They were apparently determined to support those Soviet decisionmakers who advocated intervention, and they would undoubtedly have put pressure on the more reluctant or wavering members of the Soviet Politburo and Central Committee to overturn the Bratislava agreement. (The truce was approved by the Soviet Politburo but not by the Central Committee, which, like the Czechoslovak Central Committee, was apparently not informed in great detail about the verbal assurances made at Čierna.)

This suggestion is supported by the fact that demands for the reimposition of censorship on and control of the Czechoslovak media (not specifically included in the Bratislava Declaration) were incorporated in the Moscow Protocol concluded after the postintervention negotiations between the Czechoslovak and Soviet leaders in Moscow on August 23–26. According to the Moscow Protocol, the Czechoslovak leaders were obliged to give top priority to measures for "controlling the information media so that they will serve the cause of socialism fully, . . . with a view to ending anti-socialist demonstrations on radio and television. . . . " The Czechoslovak leadership was required to "remedy the situation in the press, the radio, and the television by means of new laws and regulations," and through essential personnel changes in the leadership of the press and broadcasting.[22]

Needless to say, after the intervention, with controls reimposed on the Czechoslovak media, references to the Prague Spring gradually disappeared from Soviet underground periodicals. Whereas before the invasion Czechoslovak reformism was a subject of great interest and appeal among Soviet intellectuals and dissidents, afterwards the latter came to view it with an equal degree of skepticism. In the words of the exiled Soviet writer Zhores Medvedev, "Prior to August 1968 the abolition of censorship in Czechoslovakia and the general democratisation of society under Dubček had served as an attractive model for many intellectuals in the USSR, and had stimulated many speeches in favor of reform." The invasion, however, was devastating to this trend, and following it "all those reforms took on the appearance of a Utopian dream, a thing of the distant future, so that many liberal-minded people in the Soviet Union switched to a cautious wait-and-see position."[23]

This outcome was a payoff to the bureaucratic supervisors. Their fears (perhaps exaggerated) and demands probably contributed to the changing perceptions in the Politburo concerning the seriousness of the threat posed by Czechoslovak reformism to stability in the USSR.

The Pressure of the Ukrainian Party Bureaucracy

There is scattered evidence that the Party bureaucrats in the Ukraine (and probably also in Belorussia and the Baltic Republics), who were outspoken advocates of the intervention, were also dissatisfied with the results of the Čierna-Bratislava compromise. While most of the Soviet press ceased attacking Dubček's leadership, *Pravda Ukrainy* was apparently unwilling during the Čierna negotiations (as in May after the Kosygin-Dubček compromise) to cease its polemic against Czechoslovakia, maintaining that West Germany had tried to exploit the situation by interfering in Czechoslovak affairs.[24] In general, the Party bureaucracies in the Soviet West did not seem overjoyed about the outcome of the Čierna-Bratislava negotiations. On the contrary, some periodicals in the non-Russian republics of the Soviet West, such as *Sovetskaia Estoniia,* began to publish articles devoted to the question of ideological subversion and espionage in the western Soviet national republics.[25] This new campaign was similar to that conducted by *Sovetskaia Rossiia.* The implication might have been that the negotiations with Czechoslovak leaders did not solve the impending problem of the impact on the Soviet West of subversive western ideas (coming through Czechoslovakia).

The Čierna-Bratislava agreement did not curb the dissemination of Czechoslovak ideas of liberalism and federalization through the public media to the western national republics. Bureaucrats responsible for the Soviet West were much less sensitive to foreign policy implications than they were to the threatened "infection" of their own national republics. Like other Soviet bureaucrats, they were aware that the Czechoslovak leadership did not intend to forsake its obligations to the Warsaw Pact or to COMECON. But the wording of the Bratislava Declaration, which obliged the Czechoslovak leadership to follow a common foreign policy line, seemed insufficient to them.

As we have seen, such bureaucrats as Il'nitskii from the Ukraine, Lithuanian Party leader Snechkus, and Latvian Party leader Voss voiced concern about the liberal infection from Prague. Weighing the foreseeable consequences of nonintervention, the Party bureaucrats from the Soviet West probably considered the Bratislava Declaration a bad agreement.

The spokesman for the Soviet interventionist coalition, First Secretary of the Ukrainian Party Shelest, had good reason to be worried about the cost of a noninterventionist policy. As the well-researched study by Grey Hodnett and Peter J. Potichnyj, *The Ukraine and the Czechoslovak Crisis,* suggests, there were indeed important "linkages" between the situation in the Ukraine and that in the Prešov region in Czechoslovakia, with its Ukrainian population. In the summer of 1968, there were some indications that the Czechoslovak experiment with federalization had encouraged Ukrainian nationalist sentiments. The Ukrainian minority in Czechoslovakia decided to renew the activities of the post–World War II Ukrainian National Council, which had been abolished in the early 1950s. The congress of this organization, which based its program on the idea of the equality of Czechoslovak national minorities, was scheduled for August 23, a date that probably did not go unnoticed in the Soviet Ukraine.[26] Ukrainian intellectuals saw developments in Czechoslovakia as providing support for their own striving. The unresolved Czechoslovak crisis heightened Ukrainian bureaucratic anxieties over the rise of nationalism in their republic.

It is conceivable that after Bratislava, Shelest feared that his unsuccessful drive for intervention—demonstrated so persuasively by his attempts to break off negotiations at Čierna and by the rising domestic problems in the Ukraine (unrest among intellectuals, signs of the poorest grain harvest since the 1963 disaster)[27]—would cast a shadow on his policy of "Ukrainian autonomy," as well as on his prestige and position in the Politburo.[28] Perhaps in an effort to bolster his position in the Ukrainian Party apparatus as well as in the Soviet Politburo, Shelest and his supporters began to signal disapproval of the Bratislava truce and to remobilize support for military intervention.

The disapproval of the Čierna-Bratislava truce by the Ukrainian Party bureaucracy seemed to be again reflected in an important August editorial of the theoretical organ of the Ukrainian Communist Party, *Kommunist Ukrainy* which supported the tough stand that Shelest had taken at Čierna. It again attacked the concepts of "democratic socialism" and "liberalization of socialism" and its advocates. It recalled the "counterrevolutionary uprisings in Hungary and Poland in 1956" and pointed out that the United States, in trying to undermine the Warsaw Pact, once again counts on these "right-wing anti-socialist forces, revisionists and nationalists." Finally it called for "struggle against the counterrevolution." Like *Sovetskaia Rossiia, Kommunist Ukrainy* made no reference to those parts of the Bratislava Declaration that might have been interpreted as limited Soviet approval of a continuation of the Prague reforms—such as "specific national features and conditions." On the contrary, it stressed only those portions of the declaration that could be perceived as Soviet disapproval of Czechoslovak reformism—such as "unshakable fidelity to Marxism-Leninism" and "implacable struggle against bourgeois ideology and all antisocialist forces."[29]

Apparently, the Čierna-Bratislava compromise and its policy implications did not fully satisfy the leadership of the Ukrainian Party. It is interesting to note that *Kommunist Ukrainy,* unlike *Kommunist* (Moscow), *New Times,* and other periodicals, did *not* publish the test of the Bratislava Declaration in its August issue. Yet the text of the Warsaw Letter (produced at the Warsaw Conference, where Shelest was present and Suslov absent), along with the text of the Bratislava Declaration, was published in the

September issue of *Kommunist Ukrainy* with the approval of the July session of the CPSU Central Committee on the Warsaw Conference.[30] It seems plausible that the Ukrainian Party bureaucracy reaffirmed the priority in importance of the Warsaw Letter over the Bratislava Declaration, and of Shelest's performance at Warsaw over Suslov's at Čierna and Bratislava.

Implementation of the demands of the Warsaw Letter was the payoff for the Ukrainian Party bureaucracy. This was particularly true of demands regarding the Czechoslovak public media (the Ukrainian-language broadcasts of Radio Prešov, and such newspapers as *Nove Zhyttia* and *Duklia*), all of which carried favorable accounts of reformism and federalism and even an occasional critique of the situation in the Soviet Ukraine. These key demands had not been repeated in the Bratislava Declaration, but after the intervention they would be emphatically restated in the Moscow Protocol.

The August editorial in *Kommunist Ukrainy* reminded its readers that although imperialist tactics may differ, the objective is the same: "export of the counterrevolution," as happened during the "counterrevolutionary" revolts in Hungary and Poland in 1956. The policy implication of the editorial comments in *Kommunist Ukrainy* was clear: the major struggle at the present time should be conducted against the "counterrevolution" in Czechoslovakia, where developments threaten cohesion among the countries in Eastern Europe as well as in the Soviet West. Perhaps referring to the noninterventionist coalition, the editorial (probably reflecting Shelest's views) rejected "factionalism" and "factional struggles," pointing out (as Shelest had in his speech in July) that in the struggle against counterrevolution "there cannot be any room for passivity, neutralism and concessions." (Apparently this was a cryptic criticism of attempts to find a compromise with Dubček the noninterventionist.)

Shortly after the Bratislava Conference concluded, Shelest reportedly indicated to the Soviet Politburo his disapproval and uneasiness regarding the truce. He pushed to have the agreement revised. Apparently, he supported his arguments with reports about the alarming situation in the Ukraine and the deteriorating situation in Czechoslovakia.[31]

The Pressure of Interventionists in the KGB

Most of the intelligence assessments provided to Soviet decisionmakers come from the KGB.[32] This organization conducts intelligence and counterintelligence activities as well as operations directed against dissidents at home. It has even greater responsibilities and powers than its American counterpart, the CIA. KGB departments can influence Soviet decisionmaking by screening and interpreting intelligence information and delivering to the Politburo only reports its top officials believe are important.

The extent of KGB officials' role in Soviet management of the Czechoslovak crisis still remains unknown in the West. Fragmented evidence suggests, however, that the KGB officials responsible for operations in Eastern Europe must have been deeply concerned about the ability of their services to conduct their intelligence role, not only in Czechoslovakia but also elsewhere, if the reformist "infection" were to spread to neighboring countries, particularly East Germany and Poland. Prague reformism also presented a potential threat to the KGB officials responsible for Soviet domestic operations (as it did to the bureaucrats in charge of ideological supervision) by providing impetus to the growing number of dissidents and human rights activists in the Soviet Union. Both groups of KGB officials probably sought to nudge Soviet decisionmaking in the direction of intervention. On the other hand, it is possible that other KGB bureaucrats feared that the invasion would be detrimental not only to long-term Soviet interests in Czechoslovakia but also to joint Soviet-Czechoslovak intelligence operations abroad and thereby to the organizational interests of the KGB departments responsible for conducting intelligence operations in the West. (This actually happened between 1968 and 1969, when several high officials of the Czechoslovak intelligence service, Ladislav Bittman and Josef Frolík among others, defected because of the invasion. Their revelations were extremely damaging to both Czechoslovak and Soviet intelligence operations in the West.)

As we saw earlier, the KGB officials who supported the invasion very likely tried to "produce," through intelligence collection and covert action, proof of counterrevolution (the caches of secret weapons "discovered" in July are a case in point) to support arguments in favor of military intervention. In particular, KGB interventionists strove to create an impression of widespread opposition to Dubček's supporters among "healthy elements" in the Party. Although overt and covert KGB actions may have been of secondary importance alongside the political pressures and psychological warfare of the Warsaw Pact Command, they nevertheless influenced the final resolution of the crisis. As a former high official of the Czechoslovak intelligence service, L. Bittman, put it: "The active role of the Soviet intelligence service in the events of 1968 and 1969 in Czechoslovakia centered on the systematic implementation of political provocation, disinformation, and propaganda campaigns aimed at influencing Czechoslovak public opinion, terrorizing a selected group of liberals, and creating supportive arguments for the legitimization of the Soviet invasion."[33]

KGB officials and their agents in the Czechoslovak State Security were apparently active in producing and distributing leaflets, letters (such as that of the ninety-nine Prague workers), and anonymous pamphlets which expressed disagreement with Dubček's reformist policies and attacked him and his reformist supporters as "opportunists," "right-wingers," and even "traitors." These KGB collaborators were also involved (and this is not well known in the West) in certain actions which were thought at the time to have been organized by radical supporters of reform—for example, the campaign for the dissolution of the People's Militia—but which in reality were KGB-backed provocations organized by antireformists in the Czech State Security. According to information provided by Czechoslovak Minister of the Interior Pavel, at least fifty of the persons who agitated in support of the anti-People's Militia campaign in early August on the famous downtown Prague street of *Na Příkopěch* were Czech State Security agents.[34] Furthermore, KGB officials were undoubtedly behind attempts to discredit, terrorize, and intimidate prominent Czechoslovak supporters of reform, particularly the KGB's enemy number one, Czechoslovak Minister of the Interior Pavel.

This is not to say that the KGB alone was responsible for all the intelligence operations directed against the Prague reformers. The East German and Polish secret services were probably also very active during the crisis. Thus, other actions, such as the attempt to prove an "international Jewish conspiracy" (the famous Wiesenthal letter), may have been the work of General M. Moczar's Polish intelligence service.[35]

The Čierna-Bratislava *modus vivendi* (concluded without KGB representation, and perhaps over KGB objections) did not revoke the decision made during the Prague Spring—and vigorously implemented by Czechoslovak Minister of the Interior Pavel—to dismiss most of the KGB agents in Czechoslovakia (roughly 80–100 men). Obviously, these dismissals, as well as other measures taken by Pavel (such as his decision to dismantle security surveillance), had made Soviet security operations in Czechoslovakia much more difficult. (Under the earlier system, which was revoked by Pavel, KGB specialists were, for example, directly invited by the heads of various departments of the Ministry of the Interior for "task work" without the knowledge of the Czechoslovak leadership.) As a result of Pavel's policies and the subsequent polarization of the Czechoslovak State Security into two groups—reformists and young officials sympathetic to reform and those who were pro-Soviet—the KGB ceased to trust many of the Czech agents and began to have recourse instead to the intelligence-gathering service of the People's Militia.[36] On the other hand, Pavel's decision to dismantle the surveillance intelligence system left the Czechoslovak intelligence service without information on the plotting of the KGB and the Czechoslovak antireformist coalition against Dubček's leadership.[37] In July, when Soviet pressure mounted, Pavel reportedly established a "mobilization staff," which was ordered to keep track of the movement of troops in and around Czechoslovakia,[38] and of KGB agents, who at that time were streaming into Czechoslovakia in unprecedented numbers.

On the second day of the intervention (August 21), the high KGB official

Vinokurov (possibly a pseudonym) stated that the Warsaw Pact countries occupied Czechoslovakia mainly because of the growth of "counterrevolution" in Czechoslovakia and the inability of the Czechoslovak leadership to suppress it. This was manifest primarily in the "anti-Soviet demonstrations of the youth and in the additional actions aimed against the People's Militia." Then, however, he indicated clearly the KGB's main concern about Prague reformism: he charged that a number of Czech State Security members "had been arrested or dismissed and that their families had been persecuted." Almost all of the people mentioned by Vinokurov were those on whose behalf KGB General Kotov (chief Soviet KGB adviser in Czechoslovakia) had intervened unsuccessfully by demanding of Pavel that they be kept on.[39]

The KGB agents in the Czechoslovak State Security prepared for the military action against Czechoslovakia, knowing that they would be asked to participate. Directed since June 1968 by the head of the Czechoslovak State Security and a Soviet agent, V. Šalgovič, they worked actively with Soviet KGB officials. On the first day of the intervention they assisted in the arrest of Dubček and his reformist supporters in Prague.[40]

Some top KGB officials were apparently concerned about a reevaluation of the past operations, particularly those activities in Czechoslovakia that touched on the Jan Masaryk case and the political trials in the 1950s. The preliminary report on the political trials, prepared for the Czechoslovak Party Congress in September 1968, was well known among the KGB leadership and was considered to be politically explosive. The desire to prevent its publication and to restore the organizational mission of the KGB in Czechoslovakia, in view of the dismissal of most of its agents in that country (as indicated by a report of Czechoslovak Prime Minister Černík), contributed to the Soviet decision to intervene.[41]

The organizational interests and demands of the KGB officials responsible for supervising East European and domestic affairs were incorporated into the text of the Moscow Protocol, which was concluded after the intervention, in specific, concrete language. The protocol stated that the "activities of the Ministry of the Interior will also be examined fully" and that "appropriate measures will then be taken to strengthen the direction of this ministry."[42] The first steps of policy implementation after the intervention were the abrupt dismissal of Minister of the Interior Pavel and the gradual removal of Czechoslovak officers who had "lost the confidence of the KGB,"[43] thereby restoring the KGB mission and capabilities in Czechoslovakia. The invasion also removed a potential threat to the KGB mission in the USSR itself. Presumably after the invasion, the KGB domestic service received new guidelines allowing it to be less cautious in its operations; for example, it was allowed to make regular political arrests aimed at preventing the growth of the human rights movement and to coordinate actions against the dissidents. These changes were payoffs for the interventionists in the KGB, and played a role in inducing the Soviet leadership to intervene militarily in Czechoslovakia.

The Pressure of Interventionists in the Armed Forces

It appears that segments of the Soviet military elite were dissatisfied with the *modus vivendi* with Czechoslovakia and began to press the political leadership for a modification of the Čierna-Bratislava truce.

No Soviet Armed Forces representatives were at either meeting, since these focused mainly on Czechoslovak domestic politics. Hence, Warsaw Pact military and strategic questions were touched on only in general and ambiguous terms, such as "whether within the framework of the Warsaw Pact there could not be found additional possibilities for a common defense."[44]

As John Erickson has suggested, Soviet policy is conducted in bureaucratic compartments.[45] Because of varying bureaucratic responsibilities, the claims, interests, and policies of the various segments of military leadership may well differ from those of the political leadership. In addition, the Soviet military bureaucracy itself, as I have argued in Chapter 1, is not a unified bureaucratic elite, but a conglomeration of various groups with some differing organizational missions and capabilities—all seeking influence and often competing with each other. Apparently, these groups came to see quite different facets of the Czechoslovak issue and disagreed on ways of resolving it. Among the military elite, the officials responsible for the Warsaw Pact, under Commander-in-Chief Marshal Iakubovskii; the officials responsible for the newly restored (December 1967) Ground Forces Command, under Commander-in-Chief General Pavlovskii; and perhaps the generals of the old generation, with their backgrounds and responsibilities in the Soviet Ground Forces, were the groups that contained the most outspoken advocates of military intervention. They were dissatisfied with the absence of the Soviet Armed Forces from Czechoslovakia and considered Prague reformism a dangerous development. General Pavlovskii, who became commander-in-chief of the Soviet forces invading Czechoslovakia and, temporarily, the chief occupation authority in Czechoslovakia, may have perceived the military operation against Czechoslovakia as an opportunity to improve further the role, position, and prestige of his branch of the armed services, which during the Khrushchev era (because of strategic reforms) had been a "major source of disobedience, bureaucratic obstructionism, and general decline of military efficiency."[46] (The Ground Forces Command was abolished in September 1964.)

Debate on the Czechoslovak issue may have been viewed within the military elite as having some effect on long-standing defense budget demands or on competition between the various services, notably the Ground Forces and the Strategic Rocket Forces. In the Soviet armed forces, doctrinal demands often are made (and crisis situations used) to justify the autonomy and budgetary requests of the various services. In fact, some advocates of intervention among the Soviet military elite, such as Generals Shtemenko and Iakubovskii, belonged among those who, after Khrushchev's fall, argued that Soviet military doctrine does not exclude limited, nonnuclear warfare, thus reaffirming the importance of the Soviet Ground Forces.[47]

It should be recalled that another military bureaucratic group, the Main Political Administration of the Soviet armed forces (headed by General Epishev)—a peculiar Soviet military-ideological institution charged with political and ideological supervision of the Soviet armed forces—belonged among the bureaucratic groups advocating intervention, and that General Epishev reportedly advocated such an action in April 1968. Another military group which may have pushed for intervention was the Chief Intelligence Directorate (GRU), the Soviet military intelligence agency. Like the KGB, this smaller and less powerful agency also had organizational interests in Czechoslovakia which it perceived as being jeopardized by the Prague Spring. The dismissal of its men from the Czechoslovak Army apparently seriously affected the GRU's intelligence capabilities and mission.

Some other segments of the Soviet military establishment, however, were not happy with the momentum of the interventionist coalition. Even the armed forces newspaper *Krasnaia zvezda* kept a low profile on the Czechoslovak issue until the time of the emotional reaction to General Prchlík's press conference.[48] The generals responsible for the Strategic Rocket Forces, commanded by Marshal Krylov, may have been unenthusiastic about the prospect of Soviet intervention in Czechoslovakia, perhaps because they did not consider Prague reformism to be a real threat to their organizational interests. According to some reports, this view was shared by other Soviet generals of the younger generation, "modernists," also with backgrounds and bureaucratic responsibilities in the Strategic Rocket Forces. Whereas the Czechoslovak leadership, both before and during Dubček's tenure, had consistently refused to consent to the stationing of Soviet Ground Forces units on Czechoslovak soil, in 1966 Novotný was said to have already approved the stationing of strategic weapons and 8,000 specialists in Czechoslovakia.[49] There were no demands raised by reformists for removal of these troops. Some Soviet generals also feared the invasion would have detrimental effects on the Czechoslovak armed forces and on Soviet-Czechoslovak military ties.

Even at the top of the Warsaw Pact Command there were apparently misgivings about intervention. General Kazakov, the chief of staff of the Warsaw Pact forces (and commander of the Warsaw Pact forces during the June 1968 maneuvers in Czechoslovakia), was unexpectedly replaced only two days after the Bratislava Conference by the Ground Forces "lobbyist" and continuing admirer of Stalin,[50] General S. M. Shtemenko, who, during the Čierna and Bratislava negotiations, was included in the Soviet military team that conferred with the East German minister of defense. This personnel change may have been due in part to Shtemenko's experience with coordinating and planning delicate military operations; but it perhaps owed something as well to his predecessor Kazakov's skepticism of the wisdom of military intervention. In John Thomas's words, "As a former commander of the Southern Group of Forces in the 1950s involved in the suppression of the 1956 Hungarian revolt, Kazakov could in 1968 foresee the disruption that the use of force against an East European ally would cause. Then, too, having worked with the Czechs up to the time of his removal just before the invasion, Kazakov undoubtedly had qualms about military action against the only 'natural' ally of the Soviet Union in Eastern Europe."[51] Thomas further notes that "Kazakov was replaced by Shtemenko ostensibly because of 'illness,' but later he attended Western embassy receptions in Moscow and appeared in good health."[52] Kazakov's uneasiness about the intervention was apparently shared by some high-ranking officers. According to Soviet dissident General P. G. Grigorenko, several of them participated in the invasion and were most unhappy about these developments.[53]

On balance, however, it is reasonable to assume that powerful elites within the Soviet armed forces—the Warsaw Pact Command, the Ground Forces Command, the Main Political Administration, and the GRU—were dissatisfied with the Čierna-Bratislava *modus vivendi.* They probably considered certain provisions in the Bratislava Declaration, such as raising "the defense capabilities of every socialist state and the whole socialist commonwealth" and the strengthening of "military cooperation" in the Warsaw Treaty Organization,"[54] to be loosely and ambiguously worded.

According to Erickson, after the 1966 Vltava maneuvers the Soviet High Command had begun to lose confidence in the tactical performance of the Czechoslovak armed forces.[55] Perhaps in line with the emphasis on flexible response *(gibkoe reagirovanie)* as an addition to Soviet strategic doctrine, the generals responsible for the Warsaw Pact may have favored the forward deployment of Soviet Ground Forces on Czechoslovak territory.[56] Whatever the reasons, since 1966 they had evinced interest in stationing their troops in Czechoslovakia. These pressures became more intense during the early months of the Czechoslovak crisis because of the escape to the United States of Novotný's supporter General J. Šejna and the suicide of deputy Minister of National Defense, General V. Janko (who was said to be involved in the planning of a pro-Novotný coup to be backed by some Soviet generals) and because of the general weakening of the combat readiness of the Czechoslovak armed forces, a situation about which Czechoslovak Minister of National Defense Dzúr, who did not favor reform, complained to the commander-in-chief of the Warsaw Pact Forces, Iakubovskii.

Iakubovskii's revealing reply was that "a friend has understood another friend."[57] This lack of confidence in the Czechoslovak armed forces led to increased calls for the stationing of Soviet ground troops in Czechoslovakia. These reached their peak in July when a "memorandum," prepared on the initiative of a team of officers from the Klement Gottwald Military-Political Academy in Prague, and favoring multilateral decisionmaking in the Warsaw Pact, was published under the title "How Czechoslovak State Interests in the Military Sphere Are To Be Formulated." The glamour surrounding the affair of General Prchlík in July 1968 accelerated these pressures.

Thus, observing that the Czechoslovak issue was affecting its ability to perform its missions effectively, the Soviet generals responsible for the Warsaw Pact must have been extremely displeased with the decision of the political leadership to withdraw all Soviet units from Czechoslovakia on August 3, after several months of efforts to obtain Czechoslovak consent to the stationing of Warsaw Pact troops. (Marshall Iakubovskii had wanted to keep the Warsaw Pact troops deployed in Czechoslovakia until the congress of the Czechoslovak Communist Party in September.) Shortly before the negotiations in Čierna, Soviet Major General S. Zolotov (in charge of Soviet units of the Warsaw Pact in Slovakia), in a discussion with officials of the Slovak Party, said that "Czechoslovakia is threatened by a return to capitalism and Soviet soldiers are ready to prevent it."[58]

The preparation for intervention in Czechoslovakia must have posed significant logistic and technical problems. As Erickson has pointed out, "The key to the invasion of Czechoslovakia was logistics, rather than battle troops or anything else."[59] If the *modus vivendi* had continued, the Soviet leadership would have had to dismantle the military buildup at the Czechoslovak borders, thus depriving the Soviet Army of the logistic advantage of a "prearranged" war posture.

The importance of the so-called Rear Services exercise and the logistics of possible invasion seem to have escaped the notice of analysts of the Czechoslovak crisis. The Soviet generals responsible for the Warsaw Pact organization spent much time and effort preparing the military buildup. Not only were regular units involved in the several exercises conducted prior to the invasion, but by late July and early August thousands of reservists were called up and thousands of motor transport vehicles from throughout European Russia were mobilized from civilian resources in a large logistic rehearsal from the Baltic Sea to the Black Sea. Besides the supporting services, the Class II and Class III divisions stationed in the three westernmost districts of the USSR were put through preliminary maneuvers. It is possible that the Rear Service exercise during the midsummer, particularly the shortage of civilian trucks and manpower thus created, had some detrimental effects on the 1968 harvest in the Soviet Union and on manufacturing and production.[60] Commander-in-Chief of the armed forces Rear Services, Army General Mariakhin, stated in his evaluation of the summer military exercises:

It is no secret that the exercises made urgent the temporary requisition of thousands of units of powerful technical equipment and motor transportation from the national economy and the removal of thousands of reservists from kolkhoz and sovkhoz fields, as well as from industrial enterprises and state institutions, at a time when the heavy work of the harvest was at its highest peak throughout the country. . . . one also had to consider the circumstances—that this was a conditional prearranged war and that we were, naturally, unable to make full use of the country's communication arteries purely for the needs of our troops. This would entail disruption of the national economy and its transportation.[61]

Soviet generals had also probably learned a lesson from their own experience in Hungary in 1956—where the two armored divisions used in the first military intervention were not sufficient, and the second intervention required the deployment of ten divisions—and perhaps from the U.S. experience with gradual escalation in Vietnam. They knew that a military intervention ought to be an efficient, rapid, and overwhelming action. Such an action, however, required military deployment around the Czechoslovak borders. The Soviet military could (and apparently did) argue that, because of logistic problems, the Soviet leadership had only two options: either to dismantle the huge and costly military buildup, or to go in. The indefinite deployment of roughly 500,000 Soviet troops around the Czechoslovak borders, which, as we saw, continued after Bratislava, was impossible logistically, strategically, and psychologically. Such considerations apparently served as powerful arguments against those in the Soviet leadership who argued for a wait-and-see policy.

It is also conceivable, although there is no direct evidence, that some generals in the Soviet armed forces considered the results of the Čierna-Bratislava negotiations as an insult to the national pride of the Soviet Union and its military.[62] The dissatisfaction of segments of the Soviet military elite with the results of the Čierna-Bratislava negotiations was reflected in a post-Bratislava editorial in the military newspaper *Krasnaia zvezda,* which emphasized only those statements in the Bratislava Declaration that referred to "further strengthening of socialist countries," to dangers of "imperialist subversive activities," and to the "irreconcilable struggle against bourgeois ideology and all anti-socialist forces."[63]

The military exercises of the Warsaw Pact forces continued after Shtemenko's appointment, although there were signs that the troops that withdrew from Czechoslovakia were regrouping into a "prearranged" war posture at military bases in neighboring countries near the Czechoslovak borders.[64] In fact, probably because of pressure from the interventionists in the armed forces, the large-scale maneuvers of the Soviet Army did not actually come to a formal end. While on August 10, the logistic exercise *Nemen* formally ended, on the next day, August 11, new major air defense maneuvers (code-named Sky Shield) began, along with another exercise of "communication troops" in the Western Ukraine, Poland, and East Germany.[65] (Intriguingly, the *Nemen* exercise was evaluated in the Belorussian capital of Minsk only in the presence of Party and government leaders of the Belorussian Republic.) While the political leadership (at least the Politburo majority) was reportedly on holiday but apparently still closely following Czechoslovak developments, the interventionist group within the Soviet Army—led by Iakubovskii and Shtemenko of the Warsaw Pact, Epishev from the Main Political Administration of the Soviet armed forces, and Minister of Defense Grechko—began a remarkable series of meetings with East German and Polish military officials (and perhaps played brinksmanship by lobbying with the political leaders of their East European allies, Ulbricht and Gomułka), between August 14 and 17—when the final decision to invade was made.

On August 16, the maneuvers were extended for the first time during the crisis to Hungary, with participation of the Hungarian Army and the Southern Group of Forces. At that time the pressure of several segments of the Soviet armed forces in favor of military invasion was reflected on the pages of the armed forces newspaper *Krasnaia zvezda*. The deputy chief of General Epishev's Main Political Administration of the armed forces, General S. P. Vasiagin, recalled on August 15 that the Soviet armed forces had been ready to provide "fraternal assistance" to Czechoslovakia in May 1945: "You called us and we came." Vasiagin was signaling the willingness of the interventionists in the armed forces to provide "fraternal assistance" to Czechoslovakia. "Yes, this is what the Soviet soldier is like. At the first call he always comes to the aid of his brothers."[66] Obviously, the remarkable activities of the interventionists within the Soviet armed forces were not the only force that drove the Politburo to military action. Yet the bureaucrats responsible for the Warsaw Pact, the Ground Forces Command, and the Main Political Administration apparently pressured the Politburo for revision of the Bratislava truce.

The pressure of the interventionist group in the military elite was significant, as indicated by the inclusion of their demands in the postintervention Moscow Protocol. At the Moscow meeting, in contrast to the one at Bratislava, the armed forces were represented by the minister of defense, Marshall Grechko.[67] According to the Moscow Protocol, the invading Soviet armed forces were supposed to be withdrawn in "stages" (problems related to "the troops temporarily stationed in Czechoslovakia" were to be the subject of future negotiations). The protocol also suggested that the "problem of the security of Czechoslovakia's borders with the German Federal

Republic will be the subject of a special analysis."[68] These—and the granting of the organizational and personal demands presented to the Soviet political leadership when the Kremlin debate on the Czechoslovak issue reached its peak in mid-August—were the payoffs to the generals in charge of the Warsaw Pact and Soviet Ground Forces for their alliance with the interventionists.

The Pressure of the Interventionists in Eastern Europe

East German Pressure. The Čierna and Bratislava negotiations proved that Ulbricht's fears about the possibility of a dangerous compromise, which he expressed at the Warsaw Conference and which were reflected on the pages of the Party newspaper *Neues Deutschland* even during the negotiations at Čierna,[69] were justified. The Soviet Politburo again adopted a wait-and-see attitude toward Czechoslovakia. The Politburo's endorsement of the Bratislava agreement indicated that the majority of Soviet decisionmakers were, under certain circumstances, willing to live with Dubček's leadership and that the advocates of military intervention (such as Shelest and his allies) were in the minority. Ulbricht's behavior at the Bratislava Conference indicated that the truce had put him into a most awkward position. If the compromise had lasted, its consequences for Ulbricht would have been far-reaching. A peaceful resolution of the Czechoslovak crisis would undoubtedly have encouraged some sort of liberalization of the East German regime. In the long run it might also have contributed to a gradual rapprochement between West Germany and the socialist countries, thereby further isolating Ulbricht both from his East European allies and from the Soviet leadership—a development that Ulbricht had tried for years to prevent.

One of Ulbricht's East German critics, Professor Robert Havemann, an advocate of democratic socialism and a former member of the Socialist Unity Party (SED), was quoted in the Czechoslovak magazine *Svět v obrazech*, as having argued that "the solution of the German question in the sense of socialism and democracy would be unimaginably accelerated and made easier if the road now being taken by Czechoslovakia were also to be taken in our country."[70] Ulbricht, as much as his allies in the Soviet leadership, doubtless perceived the Bratislava agreement as an unsatisfactory one because it did not curb the main danger of the Prague Spring: the spreading of Czechoslovak reformism to East Germany through Czechoslovak German-language newspapers published for the German minority in Czechoslovakia (e.g., *Volkszeitung*), Prague Radio broadcasts in German, and East German tourism. The frustration of East German officials with Czechoslovakia even led to a demand that copies of *Volkszeitung* be removed from the stands of the Czechoslovak Cultural House in Berlin.[71]

Immediately after the Bratislava agreement was concluded, Ulbricht, irritated with the wait-and-see attitude of the majority of Soviet Politburo members, evidently began to work to overthrow the agreement by a round of political maneuvers. His actions proved that he was closer disciple of Machiavelli than of Marx. The East German press restrained its hostility until the very day of the intervention. But Ulbricht, fearing not only for the future of his regime but also for his own position, began to maneuver for a quick solution to the Czechoslovak crisis.

Several days after the Bratislava summit, most of the Soviet leaders went on holiday. Ulbricht did not follow their example; he stayed in East Berlin to launch a new political offensive. On August 9, only three days after the Soviet Politburo endorsed the Bratislava agreement, Ulbricht, in one of his most conciliatory speeches, proposed an exchange of high missions and a discussion of economic cooperation with West Germany. The East German *Volkskammer* (parliament) adopted his proposal to appoint a state secretary for future negotiations with West Germany. The most intriguing aspect of this proposal was that for the first time he backed away from his previous insistence on West German recognition of his country as a precondition. (Only a few weeks earlier, on June 21, Ulbricht had categorically rejected Brandt's offer of dialogue, naming a number of preconditions, including formal recognition.)

Ulbricht's moderation was probably more than an attempt to appease the Czechoslovak leaders. It may have been the result of pressure from "flexible elements inside the SED," as Philip Windsor suggests.[72] Perhaps Ulbricht's "new course" was a reflection of his assessment of the balance of power in the Kremlin. His overture to West Germany seemed to demonstrate to his critics in the Kremlin his "reasonableness" and flexibility (showing that he was willing to act in the "Bratislava spirit" and support the "peace-loving forces" in West Germany), and perhaps his ability to act independently—although one can safely assume that he had consulted the Soviet leadership in advance. After the intervention, Ponomarev would blame the "damage" caused by the intervention on, among other things, "the ambitions of Ulbricht."[73]

In reality, Ulbricht did not make a major concession on the German question. It is unlikely that he was really interested at that time (or ever) in a serious dialogue with West Germany. He offered to negotiate with West Germany in the field of economic cooperation, where he had the least to lose and the most to gain. Actually, Ulbricht might have hoped to gain leverage vis-a-vis Prague and a bargaining advantage in the forthcoming negotiations with Dubček—his next political move.

Ulbricht met with Dubček in Karlovy Vary on August 12, after refusing to travel to Prague. At that time it was thought that Ulbricht's visit was aimed at coming to terms with the Czechoslovak leadership. Postinterven-

tion evidence, however, indicates the contrary: the East German leader
probable purpose was to grapple directly with the danger threatening t
isolate his regime and to test Dubček's determination to pursue his ow
path. On the one hand, during the negotiations on August 12, while makin
reference to the Bratislava Declaration, Ulbricht was said to insist tha
Dubček guarantee the tenure of Czechoslovak antireformists at the upcom
ing Party congress. On the other hand, Ulbricht was reported to be rathe
uncertain, or at least to behave in an uncertain manner, during the negotia
tions—a rather clear indication that at that time the decision to intervene i:
Czechoslovakia had not yet been taken by the Soviet Politburo.[74] By the en
of his visit Ulbricht reportedly told Dubček: "Now I am satisfied. I see tha
you are on the right path and I can go for a vacation in the Crimea."[75]

There is some evidence, however, that upon his return from Czechoslo
vakia around August 13, apparently dissatisfied with the situation i
Czechoslovakia, Ulbricht, instead of going on a vacation, sent an importan
report to the Soviet Politburo stating that Dubček and his reformist sup
porters were unrepentant and unwilling to live up to the Bratislava agree
ment. His report allegedly provided evidence (for reasons of self-interest
but probably on the grounds of national security) of secret dealings betweer
Prague and Bonn and other Western capitals, and rumors that Czechoslo
vakia and Rumania intended to leave the Warsaw Pact, and that thei
"desire for neutrality would be the death knell of the 'socialist community
in Europe."[76]

Even during the short-lived post-Bratislava period in which Ulbricht tried
to demonstrate his "flexibility"—indeed, since late July—the East Germar
Volksarmee (regular units and mobilized reservists) had been preparing for
military action against the "enemy" in Czechoslovakia and were not al
lowed to leave the assembly area in the Thuringian Forest on the Czechoslo
vak borders.[77] Knowing that resolution of the crisis depended on the
balance of power between the interventionist coalition and the noninterven
tionist coalition, Ulbricht tried to influence the Kremlin to his advantage.

Ulbricht's post-Bratislava actions signaled to the coalition-ridden Soviet
leadership that the Bratislava agreement made the East German position
vulnerable and perhaps raised the danger of an "autonomous" East Ger
many. They had the choice of either "losing" East Germany (and perhaps
all of Eastern Europe) or restoring control by military force over Czechoslo
vakia. Ulbricht's pressure must have had at least marginal influence in trig
gering the Soviet decision to intervene in Czechoslovakia. In Melvin
Croan's words, it "must be counted as a significant contributory factor in
the Kremlin's fateful decision to intervene in Czechoslovakia."[78]

Polish Pressure. Like Ulbricht, Gomułka and his supporters in the Polish
leadership considered the Čierna-Bratislava *modus vivendi* a serious

mistake, as well as a sign of weakness and a serious blow to Soviet prestige. The Bratislava agreement seemed to exclude the possibility of a separate rapprochement between Czechoslovakia and West Germany, but it did not provide a way whereby the "cancer" of Czechoslovak reformism could be contained and kept from spreading to Poland. More important in the framework of Polish domestic politics, the Bratislava agreement made Gomułka's position more vulnerable. It encouraged his opponents in two competing coalitions: one led by Silesian leader E. Gierek, later Gomułka's successor, and the other led by General Moczar. As J. B. Weydenthal puts it, "The sudden appeasement of the Czechoslovak crisis was detrimental to Gomułka's authority. The apparent failure of his Czechoslovak policy, based on the anticipation of a tough Soviet attitude, created an imminent danger of a revival of factional tensions and internal controversies."[79]

This point was driven home by the heads of the competing coalitions in the Polish leadership. On August 15, Gierek implicitly criticized the performance of Gomułka's leadership, calling for greater intraparty democratization and rejuvenation of policymaking personnel.[80] At that time Gierek was generally considered to be a spokesman for the more flexible elements in the Polish leadership, and a man who could soon replace Gomułka. (This hope—probably shared by some Czechoslovak reformers—was expressed in the Czechoslovak magazine *Mezinárodní politika,* which hinted in May 1968 that Gierek's position on the March student demonstrations and on the purge in the Polish leadership was not so "hard" as that of other Polish politicians.[81] Later, Gomułka asserted that Czechoslovak leaders were extremely hostile to him and had even made an attack on him at the Bratislava Conference.) The other coalition leader, Moczar, described the outcome of the Čierna-Bratislava negotiations as a "decisive defeat of Gomułka's line."[82]

Thus, like Shelest and Ulbricht, Gomułka perceived the Bratislava agreement as a personal defeat and a blow to his policy that could, in turn, be detrimental to his bureaucratic position. Through a Party reshuffle in the Polish Politburo in July, Moczar and his supporters gained some ground, and it was expected that Gomułka's power would continue to decline seriously at the November congress of the Polish Party.[83] Hence, Gomułka and his supporters, perceiving a tentative Soviet compromise with Czechoslovakia in terms of domestic politics, tried to identify his fate, as had the troubled Czechoslovak leader Novotný in December 1967, with the "security" of the Soviet Union and the socialist camp. Gomułka signaled to the Soviet leadership that he favored a revision of the Čierna understanding because the Soviet leadership faced "serious consequences for the whole socialist camp." He gave "national security" reasons (much as Ulbricht had done) which were obviously self-serving.[84]

In short, the East European advocates of intervention, Ulbricht and

Gomułka, seem to have felt personally threatened by the Čierna-Bratislav moderation of Soviet policy toward Czechoslovakia. They evidently put a their hopes on their ability to convince the coalition-ridden Soviet leadei ship of the necessity to resolve the Czechoslovak crisis by military force The payoff for both men was a temporary improvement in and endorse ment of their positions. (For various reasons, however, both had to resig within three years.) Gomułka's position in particular depended entirely o bringing Czechoslovakia to order, even if this involved the use of force. In deed, in view of the ongoing factional struggle, the Soviet leadership ma have feared that Poland was in a situation similar to Czechoslovakia's prio to Novotný's fall in December 1967.

To be sure, East German and Polish pressure alone could not bring change in the Soviet decision. The Soviet Politburo was the final determine of Czechoslovakia's fate. Nevertheless, as in earlier stages of the crisis Gomułka's and Ulbricht's pressures served as factors *sui generis* in th Soviet bureaucratic tug-of-war by supporting the arguments of the Sovie interventionist coalition. Their disapproval of the Čierna-Bratislava truc was based on the grounds that the *élan* of Czechoslovak reformism hac threatened the cohesion of the Warsaw Pact. Even though their influenc was limited, pressure from the East German and Polish leaders was a signi ficant factor in changing the equilibrium in the Soviet Politburo and in forc ing the final decision.

Developments in Czechoslovakia from August 3 to August 20:
Pressure of the Antireformist Coalition

The Czechoslovak antireformist coalition perceived the Bratislava agree-ment as a defeat for its anti-Dubček policies. It appeared, at least for a while, that the antireformist coalition would have to defend its interests alone, without Soviet assistance. In the first post-Bratislava days, members of the antireformist coalition, confused by the Soviet decision, seem to have tried to save their positions by identifying themselves with the main goals of the Party congress, such as preparation of the new Party statutes. The spokesman of this coalition, Indra, who served as chairman of the commis-sion for the preparation of the new Party statutes, unexpectedly defended one of the important features of the new statutes at a press conference. He said that the minority "right . . . to keep its views, even after having been outvoted," is a "Leninist feature."[85] (It is not known whether Indra meant his own "minority," antireformist coalition, or Party reform *per se*.)

Yet it soon became an open secret in Prague that at the Party congress, most of Dubček's opponents would lose their positions. The Prague munici-pal Party organization prepared and circulated what was called a blacklist iving several dozen names of members of the Central Committee (full and lternate) who ought not to be recommended for Central Committee nembership at the Party congress. The situation was such that Dubček's upporters would very likely have carried the day at the congress. Among hose who probably would not be reelected at the Party congress were In- ra, Kolder, Švestka, Kapek, and some others—all of whom opposed the eformist movement and some of whom, during the negotiations at Čierna, ided with the Soviet leaders.[86] The date of their presumed defeat (Septem- er 9) was nearing. For Bilak, the Slovak secretary and an intimate friend of helest, the critical date was even closer because of the decision to hold the lovak congress first, on August 26.

Politics is full of irony. It was G. Husák, Dubček's successor in 1969 as irst Secretary of the Party, who in 1968 supported Dubček and the 'democratization" of Slovakia and managed to secure Dubček's consent to prepare Bilak's demotion (with Husák as Bilak's replacement) at the forth- coming Slovak Party Congress.[87] Bilak was put on the defensive by the ad- rance of the date of the Slovak congress from mid-October to August 26, as igreed upon by the Slovak Central Committee at a meeting on July 18. He was rapidly losing popularity in Slovakia in a struggle for power with Husák. Upon the arrival of the Czechoslovak delegation to the Bratislava Conference, the Slovaks welcomed Bilak, a former tailor, with calls of 'Něch šije Bilak" instead of "Něch žije Bilak"—a play on Slovak words, meaning "Long sew Bilak" instead of the usual "Long live Bilak."[88] Bilak felt threatened by the Slovak Party Congress and was reluctant even to pub- ish a list of candidates for the Central Committee of the Slovak Party. As late as August 16, he made a major effort to recover his position in a radio and television interview in which he defended the process of reformism in Slovakia.[89]

The only hope for the antireformist coalition at this stage was to continue the tactics it had used since early July of not providing support for, and even sabotaging, Dubček's efforts to stabilize the situation in Czechoslova- kia. Its goal was to convince the Soviet Politburo that there was an acute danger of political instability and "counterrevolution" in Czechoslova- kia—i.e., that the Presidium was disintegrating, that radicals were taking over, and thus that the Party congress would have to be prevented. This tac- tic became obvious at the Presidium sessions of the Czechoslovak Party on August 6 and 13, when Bilak and some of his supporters made critical remarks about Dubček's cult of personality, arguing that "he enjoys too much personal popularity and that he is not making use of this popularity to increase the authority of the body over which he presides."[90] The session of the Czechoslovak Presidium on August 13, during which Brezhnev made a first warning call to Dubček and Smrkovský, was characterized by nervous anticipation of the Fourteenth Congress and strong pressure from the antireformists to undermine Dubček's position. The Czechoslovak Presidium became deeply divided and almost disintegrated.[91]

On August 12, the Presidium had received an extensive report on the general political situation in Czechoslovakia in connection with the forthcoming Party congress—the so-called Kašpar report.[92] This report, which was not discussed at the August 13 Presidium meeting, had been prepared by the information bureau of the Central Committee, led by Jan Kašpar. Because of its political exploitation by antireformist coalitions, the report became one of the contributing factors in the decision to intervene.

Kašpar's report was an attempt to evaluate future political developments in Czechoslovakia after the Party Congress of September 1968. The report predicted that a stable Central Committee and a firm leadership could not necessarily be expected as an outcome of the congress. The report warned that continuity of the previous Party leadership would not be certain, because except for "a narrow part of the leading core of the Party, practically the entire Central Committee would be replaced." Although the report did not reach any definitive conclusions about the results of the Party Congress, it pointed to some of the uncertainties arising from it, warning that "the future of the central organs and their cadre composition appear very unclear." This would result in serious consequences for the Party and its policy in the post-congress period. Extremist forces imbued with "romantic political opinions" would probably seek to stir up hostility toward the USSR and discredit those who were committed to counteractions.[93]

Kašpar's report was used as a political weapon by the antireformists in their struggle with the reformists. In the light of information contained in the report, antireformists Indra and Kolder were instructed by the Presidium to evaluate it and prepare a list of specific measures for implementing the Čierna-Bratislava agreement for the next scheduled Presidium session, which was to be held on August 20, the very eve of the intervention. Although Kolder and Indra prepared such a list, they did not present it to the Presidium. Naturally, they were not interested in implementing an agreement that did not secure their personal positions. Instead, they presented an alarming memorandum, based on the tendentiously reworked conclusions of the Kašpar report and discussing the political situation as a reason for struggle against "extremist forces."[94] There is a strong likelihood that a copy of this position paper was delivered about the same time to Soviet Ambassador Chervonenko.[95]

The antireformists also seemed to be worried about the international support and recognition that Dubček's supporters were receiving from Yugoslav President Tito and Rumanian leader Ceauşescu, who were visiting Prague at that time. Another antireformist, Švestka, editor-in-chief of the Party newspaper *Rudé právo,* unexpectedly ordered the censoring of reports on Tito's visit to Prague.[96] Also, on August 14 Švestka demoted

ree of his reformist deputies at *Rudé právo,* and shortly before the inter-
ention (August 17 and 19) he published reports about the alarming situa-
on in Czechoslovakia, detailing discoveries of leaflets that demanded
hysical liquidation of the People's Militia, describing young rowdies
emonstrating in front of Party headquarters, and describing the threats
gainst the ninety-nine class-conscious Prague automobile workers whose
tter was printed in *Pravda* in July.[97] In a major article, Švestka criticized
spects of reformist policies and the activities of "antisocialist forces."[98]

The Czechoslovak antireformists had become controversial figures and
ere unlikely to be elected. Undoubtedly, their fears about their fate were
nared in some Soviet circles. Yurii Zhukov, in an anti-Czechoslovak article
ublished after Bratislava, warned that "the imperialists have begun to
veave a new net of intrigues" against Czechoslovakia. He described, for ex-
mple, the situation of Presidium member Švestka, who, while "defending
ne foundations of socialism," would probably be "deprived of his high of-
ice" at the Party congress.[99] Zhukov is both a leading Soviet commentator
nd a member of the Party's Central Auditing Commission. Because of his
onnections, he is, like a Soviet-style C. L. Sulzberger or James Reston, a
natural recipient of information leaks and tips about prepolicy discussions
f the highest Soviet decisionmaking body.[100] His article clearly indicated
trong concern in the Soviet leadership about the dark future of the Czecho-
lovak pro-Soviet fifth column.

Following the visit of Tito and the Presidium meeting of August 13,
everal members of the antireformist coalition—Indra, Bilak, Švestka, and
Kolder—changed their tactics and were "taking no more part in the Congress preparation,"[101] obviously to demonstrate to the Soviet leadership the
disintegration of the Czechoslovak Presidium, as well as to give their interventionist supporters convincing evidence that the Bratislava agreement ac-
ually encouraged the reformists' drive for power. They went for a holiday
at Orlík (a government spa near Prague) on August 18, "where they were to
be seen with their associates not behaving like holidaymakers, but like poli-
icians on the eve of a big campaign."[102]

In fact, apparently none of the antireformists was included in the Czechoslovak delegation that negotiated with Rumanian leader Ceausescu when he
visited Prague on August 16. However, the antireformist leader, Bilak, was
ncluded in the Czechoslovak team that met several days earlier, on August
9 and 10, with Tito.) The situation of the Czechoslovak leadership was
somewhat reminiscent of that of the Hungarian leadership in October 1956,
when E. Gerö, in the divided Hungarian Politburo, deliberately created a
situation that would render Nagy incapable of bringing about political
stability and would provide a rationale for the Soviet intervention.

The inexperienced Dubček and his supporters, concentrating on their
own intragovernmental games and maneuverings for the Party congress,

misinterpreted the signals of increasing pressure from advocates of militar
intervention at home and abroad. Like most Western observers, they er
roneously considered these signals, even after Čierna, to be elements o
psychological pressure similar to those used in May and July. They prob
ably believed that those within the Soviet leadership who feared the negativ
consequences of intervention would win the debate on Czechoslovakia.[10]
By the same token, the Czechoslovak antireformists had tried, behind th
scenes, to identify their fate with that of the Soviet interventionists. The
pressured the Soviet leadership by transmitting alarming signals and report
through Soviet Ambassador Chervonenko, the KGB, the public media, an
allies in the Soviet Union (e.g., Shelest) about the danger of a "right-wing"
counterrevolutionary coup d'état in Czechoslovakia. Through Soviet in
tervention, the reformists would be denied their victory at the Party con
gress. This would be the payoff to the Czechoslovak antireformist coalition

V

*In Washington, we sadly watched the destruction
of an attempt to give the Soviet structure what the Czechs
called a human face. No one was happy at our inability to
do anything constructive in regard to Czechoslovakia. But
despite the constant searchings which went on in the department, no one came up with any ideas that made sense in the
circumstances.*—Charles Bohlen

*I do not believe that such a lunatic decision was taken
unanimously.*—Ernst Fischer

An Anatomy of the Decision

The Role of Information in the Soviet Decisionmaking Process

We have seen that the participants in the Soviet decisionmaking
process try to influence its outcome by maneuvering. Like their Western
counterparts, they have to rely on information from diplomatic, intelligence, and various evaluative sources about political developments in other
countries. A continuous flow of reliable information is extremely important
to the formation of an accurate picture of developments in other states. Inaccurate or unreliable information, then, directly affects Soviet decisions
and their implementation.[1]

In Eastern Europe the formal Soviet information and communications
system has at least four main components: (1) the State Security (KGB),
whose representatives report directly to the foreign sections of the KGB; (2)
the Warsaw Pact and GRU military intelligence representatives, who report
directly to the Warsaw Pact Command and to the Chief Intelligence Directorate of the Soviet General Staff; (3) Party representatives, who report
directly to the Department of Liaison with Communist and Workers Parties
(DLCWP); and (4) the Ministry of Foreign Affairs representatives (ambas-

sadors and their staffs), who communicate directly with the Central Committee and, at present, with Secretary General Brezhnev's office—and not to the Foreign Ministry (except for reports essentially of legalistic or protocol significance).

The Czechoslovak crisis illustrates the importance of the information process in Soviet decisionmaking. There are signs that during the crisis the Soviet decisionmakers lacked accurate information about political realities in Czechoslovakia, particularly in regard to the ruling elite. Certain essential information sources of the Soviet surveillance system—e.g., the regular network of KGB and GRU *rezidenturas*—were curtailed. Among other things, 80–100 KGB agents were dismissed by Czechoslovak Minister of the Interior Pavel. Soviet officials were thus forced to seek alternative channels of information on critical Czechoslovak issues. Some of these alternatives provided a dubious and self-serving view, like that of the alarming reports from East Germany and Poland. The reports of East German leader Ulbricht and Polish leader Gomułka were especially significant. Ulbricht's report of his visit to Czechoslovakia and of his negotiations with Dubček, which must have reached the Soviet Politburo around August 13–14, is a case in point.

Another alternative source of information was the Czechoslovak antireformist coalition and its supporters. To create consensus for a given policy (particularly a risky one), Soviet decisionmakers must be able to demonstrate that it is vital to Soviet national security. Apparently, the arguments must be based, not on organizational or personal grounds, but on national security interests consistent with the shared images of Soviet decisionmakers (in the case of Czechoslovakia, "Western subversion," "danger of breaking up the Warsaw Pact," and so on).

As we have seen, the organizational interests of the KGB, particularly its East European and domestic services, were put in jeopardy during the Prague Spring. This fact probably influenced the "objectivity" of the intelligence collection of this agency, imposing constraints upon its choice of information to report. Thus, apparently, small and relatively insignificant features of Prague reformism (such as student rallies or the existence of various clubs) were not only reported but also, judging from the importance attached to them by the Soviet leaders during the negotiations, presented as proof of "counterrevolution" and "Western subversion." Some of the more sensational reports—those regarding the discoveries of "secret weapons," the leaflets threatening the People's Militia, etc.—were probably fabricated. As Soviet behavior during the first days of intervention revealed, Soviet decisionmakers may also have been provided with "facts" supporting the KGB stand and that of Ambassador Chervonenko—for example, that Dubček and his associates lacked support among the popula-

ion, and that his group was in the "minority" in the Presidium, had no
support in the Party organizations, either civil or military, and was unpopu-
ar except with the "revisionist sections" of the intelligentsia.[2] The controversial views expressed by individual Czechoslovak newspapermen were
presented as the basic posture adopted by Dubček's leadership.

The organizational interests of the GRU, as well as of the KGB, were affected by the developments in Czechoslovakia in 1968. Many Soviet sources
of information were lost through the dismissal of collaborators from the
Czechoslovak Army.[3] As a result, most GRU information on the strength,
morale, and defense capabilities of the Czechoslovak Army (particularly on
Czechoslovakia's Western borders) probably reflected the stand of the
GRU leadership.

The DLCWP segments of the Soviet–East European information system
were also affected by the Prague Spring. This department (run since April
1968 by Secretary Katushev) seems to have been less hostile to the Prague
Spring than was the KGB or the GRU. Yet even here, the dismissal of some
Czechoslovak officials from the department caused Soviet bureaucrats
responsible for the DLCWP to seek new suppliers of information.

Reports from the fourth information channel—the Soviet Embassy in
Prague—significantly influenced Soviet decisionmaking. The activities of
Ambassador Chervonenko and Minister-Counselor I. I. Udaltsov during
the crisis indicate that the notion prevailing among Soviet-watchers that
Soviet diplomats are merely "messenger boys of the Kremlin" may not be
entirely true. Obviously, the conduct, performance, and reporting of Soviet
envoys are extremely important. There are unexplained delays in Chervonenko's delivery of important Soviet messages during the crisis, a case in
point being the last warning letter of the Soviet Politburo (discussed at
length below), dispatched on August 17 but received by Dubček only on
August 19. More important, Chervonenko's ambassadorial handling of
Czechoslovak affairs and related information raised many questions.

Chervonenko launched his career in the Ukrainian Party apparatus. In
the early 1960s, he had the rather unfortunate position of Soviet ambassador to China when the Sino-Soviet dispute erupted.[4] During the Prague
Spring he probably feared that if things got out of hand he would be accused of losing another socialist country. Chervonenko did not anticipate
the fall of Czechoslovak President Novotný in the autumn of 1967. His
report about an explosive situation in the Czechoslovak leadership came to
Moscow after Novotný had already sought Brezhnev's assistance. Reportedly, Chervonenko was criticized for his tardiness by his superiors.[5] In late
1967 and early 1968, during the early stage of the crisis, Chervonenko stub-
bornly supported Novotný, whom he described to the Soviet eyewitness M.
Voslensky in March of 1968 (several days before Novotný's resignation) as

"our friend," in spite of his shortcomings.[6] Chervonenko had been unwilling to accept the reformists from the very beginning and, after Novotný's dismissal, established intimate relations with the nascent antireformist coalition. Afterwards, Chervonenko provided Soviet decisionmakers in general, and Brezhnev in particular, with information about the clearly antisocialist forces at work in Czechoslovakia and about the danger of counterrevolution there. According to the same eyewitness, as of March 1968 Chervonenko already viewed the situation in Czechoslovakia as being very complicated and getting steadily worse, so much so that, in his words, a "second Hungary" was possible.[7] Chervonenko's reports were similar to those of the KGB officials. According to both sources, Dubček did not have the situation in Czechoslovakia under control and enjoyed support only from a few pressure groups and extremists; he lacked support among the masses, especially among the workers. Chervonenko reported that the great majority of workers supported the USSR, and that a "handful of rightists" prevented them from expressing their opinion. In his judgment the first opportunity would give a victory to healthy forces in the Party.[8] Chervonenko's reports probably indicated that Dubček and his supporters would be defeated in the Czechoslovak Presidium in a confrontation such as the one that occurred on August 20—the very day of the intervention. The inaccuracy of Chervonenko's reports from Prague was acknowledged in April 1968 by Zagladin, who stated to M. Voslensky: "We know that the embassy does not send objective information."[9] Secretary Ponomarev reportedly also complained after the intervention about the "incompetence of Chervonenko."[10] In the view of exiled Soviet historian A. Nekrich, Chervonenko, as well as Minister-Counselor Udaltsov in Prague, had actually engaged during the Czechoslovak crisis in a systematic misinformation of the Soviet leadership.[11]

Because of Chervonenko and Udaltsov's close connection with Novotný and Novotný's supporters in Czechoslovakia, the reformists were hostile to Chervonenko, and Smrkovský complained about Chervonenko and Udaltsov's activities during his June 1968 discussion with Brezhnev. Smrkovský told Brezhnev that the two diplomats "do not inform you accurately" and indicated that the Czechoslovak reformists wished they would be recalled.[12]

Chervonenko and Udaltsov had been in steady contact with the Czechoslovak antireformists, who were anxious to inform the Soviet Politburo about the counterrevolutionary developments in Czechoslovakia. Smrkovský said that one such "informer," a deputy of the National Assembly, Madame Dohnalová, admitted after the invasion that "we took care to inform the Soviet comrades about everything that had been done in our country at that time [prior to the invasion]."[13]

After the invasion the Soviets would claim that thousands of loyal

Czechoslovak Communists had requested "fraternal assistance" from the Warsaw Pact, a great exaggeration, it would seem, when, in fact Chervonenko and Udaltsov succeeded in collecting only a dozen or less names of still unidentified Czechoslovak officials who would on the eve of invasion (August 20) legalize Soviet "fraternal assistance."[14]

To be sure, the information and reports of antireformist officials were important. For example, it is very likely that two antireformists—Indra and Kolder—sent a very important report (representing their "standpoint" on the political situation) to the Soviet Central Committee via Chervonenko about August 13–15.[15] Their "standpoint" was based on the conclusions of the Kašpar report regarding the political situation in Czechoslovakia, but was much more tendentious. The Indra-Kolder position on the situation in Czechoslovakia was presented at the crucial last Czechoslovak Presidium session, held on the eve of the intervention, August 20. It revealed a "trick" connected with the Congress and the praising of certain individuals and discrediting of others for the purpose of influencing the elections of delegates to the Fourteenth Congress.[16]

Since some of the ideas in Indra and Kolder's prepared memorandum were later repeated in the last letter of the Soviet Politburo to Dubček (August 17) and in *Pravda's* postintervention attack,[17] as well as in many Soviet analyses of the crisis, we can assume that it played an important role in the Soviet Politburo's evaluation of post-Bratislava developments in Czechoslovakia. It is possible that another urgent report from the Czechoslovak antireformist coalition came in the post-Bratislava period from the Slovak leader Bilak, who shortly after Bratislava probably concluded that his position as head of the Slovak Communist Party was in jeopardy. Bilak probably transmitted his own evaluation of the situation in Czechoslovakia, based on his perception of the outcome of the congress of the Slovak Communist Party on August 26, 1968, to his ally in the Soviet Politburo, Shelest. (The formulation of the first Tass communiqué on the intervention, which stated that assistance had been requested by Party and government leaders [or, in Dubček's words, "a self-appointed group of Czechoslovak representatives"],[18] suggested that communications between the antireformist coalition and the Soviet Politburo probably affected the final assessment of the balance of forces in Dubček's leadership and in particular the willingness of an antireformist coalition to dissociate itself openly from Dubček and create a new, pro-Soviet leadership.) The importance of the distorted information provided by the Czechoslovak antireformist coalition in Soviet decisionmaking was stressed after the invasion by Dubček himself. He concluded from his own experience that the Czechoslovak allies received and credited "information that was obviously nonobjective and twisted about solutions we intended to give internal problems of the Party and soci-

ety and about the actual correlation of forces . . . provided by all those
who . . . were about . . . to lose or had already lost . . . their confidence
and their personal positions."[19]

Dubček apparently got this impression during negotiations with the Soviet leadership after the intervention. According to him, the subjective, distorted, and exaggerated information transmitted to the Soviet leadership by
antireformist Czechoslovak politicians was aimed at an "evocation of
fears" about future developments in Czechoslovakia.[20] These information
sources as pointed out by another Czechoslovak leader, Mlynář, played an
important role in Soviet decisionmaking, for they supported the arguments
of the Soviet leaders in favor of military intervention.[21] This is probably
also true of the reports provided through such other sources as the KGB, the
Soviet Embassy, and East German and Polish channels.

It can be assumed that much of this information had been used to form
an estimate of the situation that would support the stand of the interventionist coalition in the long Soviet debate on how to resolve the Czechoslovak crisis. As we have noted, not all of the Soviet decisionmakers were convinced that the benefits of a military intervention would outweigh the costs,
and perhaps some of them doubted the reliability of the information provided by Chervonenko. Reportedly, in 1973 the Politburo established a
committee for the reexamination of policy options, which concluded that
the developments in Czechoslovakia were dangerous but did not "necessarily require military intervention."[22]

The alarming reports in the short-lived post-Bratislava period of truce—
especially the KGB's estimate of the outcome of the Czechoslovak Party
congress and the memorandum of Indra and Kolder—apparently reached
the Central Committee on August 13-15, and were transmitted to the Politburo as high-priority material. These reports were undoubtedly exploited in
the August debate by the interventionist coalition to convince their more
reluctant colleagues that the only option available to the Soviet Politburo
was military intervention.

The Risks of Intervention: Soviet Perceptions of the U.S. Response

The assessment of the risks involved in military intervention played an
important role in Soviet decisionmaking on the Czechoslovak crisis. The
main concern was to assess possible U.S. responses to such an action and
the repercussions on U.S.-Soviet relations. In the first months of Dubček's
tenure, the United States was silent, except for isolated statements such as
those of Eugene Rostow and Robert McCloskey on April 28 and May 2
regarding U.S. "sympathy" toward the developments in Czechoslovakia.
The Soviet leadership, therefore, had an unclear picture of how the United

States and NATO would respond to a Soviet military intervention and of the extent of damage to Soviet-U.S. relations.

Several times in the past, Soviet leaders had been unpleasantly surprised by U.S. responses, such as the U.S. intervention in Korea in 1950, Kennedy's blockade of Cuba in 1962, and the decision to bomb North Vietnam while Kosygin was visiting Hanoi in 1965. As Soviet Foreign Minister Gromyko once complained to U.S. Ambassador J. L. Beam: "You're so unpredictable. We can't count on American policy."[23] During the first months of Dubček's tenure the possible U.S. response to intervention was conjectural. Moreover, until the end of July, it was not clear whether the Czechoslovak Army would resist a Soviet invasion. If it had, the confrontation might have spilled over into West Germany and Austria. Czechoslovakia borders West Germany, and the possibility of a confrontation with NATO forces could not be excluded: if the Soviets followed the retreating Czechoslovak Army across the border in hot pursuit, then the Soviet leaders had a very dangerous situation to manage. Moreover, from a purely military-logistic point of view, U.S. forces in West Germany provided a deterrent factor in Soviet military calculations. Logistically, Czechoslovakia was equally accessible to both superpowers. Thus from a military point of view, the risk for the Soviet leadership seemed to be greater than it had been during the Hungarian crisis.

But during the Čierna-Bratislava negotiations and subsequently, the scenario changed. Shortly before the Čierna Conference, the dismissal of General Prchlík made it obvious that the Czechoslovak leadership had given up the option of armed resistance. The possibility of a confrontation with NATO stemming from a widening of the conflict could be avoided by skillful management of the military operation. Both Soviet and U.S. policymakers probably got indications at the time from Czechoslovak sources that the Czechoslovak Army would not fight.[24] This was one of several reasons for Washington's lack of concern about Soviet pressure upon Czechoslovakia. According to President Johnson's national security adviser, Walt Rostow, the different U.S. response to a perceived threat to Rumania on August 30, 1968, when President Johnson issued a delicate public warning to the Soviet Union, was influenced by the fact that U.S. policymakers were aware that Rumania might in fact resist Soviet intervention with military force.[25] U.S. decisionmakers, perhaps like their Soviet counterparts, were clearly worried about the unforeseeable consequences of a limited war in Europe, which, as Rostow pointed out, "could get out of hand."[26]

The attitude of Johnson's administration toward Czechoslovakia became much clearer to the Soviet leadership during the summer months of 1968, after the Soviet-U.S. diplomatic offensive had been launched. President Johnson was preoccupied with a desire for an early start to the SALT negotiations and for a summit with Soviet Premier Kosygin before the November presidential election;[27] perhaps he hoped that this policy would help the Democratic presidential candidate. Hence, U.S. behavior during the height of the Czechoslovak crisis, from June to August 1968, was perhaps even more cautious—as must have been noticed by the Soviet "Americanologists"—than U.S. behavior during the Hungarian crisis in October–November 1956.[28] The so-called hotline between the Kremlin and the White House (a means of communication that was active during the Arab-Israeli war of 1967) was not used, even on the day of intervention.

The Czechoslovak crisis erupted at a difficult time for the West, just as the Hungarian crisis had in 1956. While in 1956 two NATO countries— Great Britain and France—were engaged in the Suez adventure, in 1968 the United States, having just suffered through the Tet offensive, was deeply involved in Vietnam and was going through a period of antiwar disturbances at home.[29] Soviet awareness of the troubled period in America was clearly indicated in the speeches of Shelest and Brezhnev in July.

In fact, the behavior of the Johnson administration in the summer of 1968 demonstrated that the United States wanted to avoid the mistakes of the Dulles policies of the mid-1950s, when attempts to "roll-back" Soviet hegemony in Eastern Europe had been promised but not delivered on. The policy of "building bridges," or of "peaceful engagement," advocated by President Johnson in 1966, had never really been implemented. Like the "roll-back" policy, it remained only an empty phrase. There had been improvements in the commercial sphere, but no attempts had been made to bring about fundamental changes in Eastern Europe. Between June and August, it became clear to Soviet decisionmakers that the United States had given up its "bridge-building" policy in favor of a limited U.S.–Soviet détente. Interestingly, only when the Czechoslovak crisis was reaching its peak was significant progress made in improving U.S.–Soviet relations.

Even in the absence of the peculiar external and internal developments of 1968, it would have been difficult for the United States to present a psychologically credible deterrent to Soviet invasion. As Adam Ulam puts it, "Even without Vietnam and the appalling domestic situation, the U.S. government could and would have done nothing to stop the Soviet move. After all, it had done nothing about the Communist coup in Prague in 1948 or about the Soviet move into Hungary in 1956, when forceful diplomatic action *might* have made a difference. Yet, there can be no doubt that the deplorable situation of this country both at home and abroad furthered the Russians' belief that they could move with impunity."[30]

Another, perhaps minor reason behind the Johnson administration's unwillingness to do anything on Czechoslovakia's behalf—even when the threat of intervention became obvious in July and August—was (as Secretary of State Rusk frankly admitted) the perception of Czechoslovakia as a "troublemaker," which with its economic and military assistance was supporting so-called national liberation movements in underdeveloped countries, particularly Vietnam.[31] Czechoslovakia, because of its industrial capabilities, then ranked third among socialist countries in providing this kind of assistance, after the Soviet Union and China.

For these reasons, among others, the United States was unwilling and unprepared, in Rostow's words, "to make any kind of commitment,"[32] and displayed a rather cold attitude toward Dubček's leadership. The United States deliberately decided to pursue a policy of silence, giving every possible signal of noninvolvement. No move was made to grant Czechoslovakia most-favored-nation status in trade or to settle the question of Czechoslovak gold. Giving highest priority to détente, Johnson's administration made no statement warning the Soviet Union of the harmful effects of a military invasion on U.S.–Soviet relations. The only voices during the crisis that suggested a revision of U.S. policy vis-a-vis Czechoslovakia came from Congress, most notably that of Senator Claiborne Pell, the former U.S. consul in Bratislava. After his visit to Czechoslovakia and talks with Czechoslovak leaders, he recommended on July 11 at a press conference in Prague that the United States recognize Czechoslovak claims to low tariffs within the General Agreement on Tariffs and Trade (GATT), and that it appoint a "federal mediator" to deal with Czechoslovak financial claims in the United States and with U.S. claims for compensation for property nationalized in Czechoslovakia.[33]

In July officials in the U.S. State Department began to take seriously the danger of a Soviet intervention. A special intelligence committee on Czechoslovakia that had been set up in the State Department in the same month went on a twenty-four-hour watch. Ambassador Bohlen, who during the July crisis visited the Soviet Union as head of a delegation aboard the first Pan American World Airways flight to open direct air travel between Moscow and New York, was under orders to cancel the flight if Soviet troops moved into Czechoslovakia before he landed in Moscow.[34] After the Bratislava truce, however, high officials in the Johnson administration, like most policymakers in the West and the East appear to have believed that the Soviet-Czechoslovak *modus vivendi* would endure at least temporarily. Few of them believed that an intervention could take place at any time, and most of them thought it would not happen at all.[35]

Meanwhile, at about the time of the Čierna-Bratislava conferences, the Soviet Politburo received unmistakable signals that the United States would do nothing if Warsaw Pact forces were to intervene in Czechoslovakia. At the end of July Secretary of State Rusk denied publicly and in a conversation with Soviet Ambassador Dobrynin that the United States had any intention of being involved in the Czechoslovak situation. In Rusk's words, the Johnson administration "did not want to give any impression that the U.S. was behind the events in Czechoslovakia or that the U.S. tried to encourage the anti-Sovietism in this country,"[36] as maintained by some articles in the Soviet press. In addition, the U.S. command in Europe received strict orders in early July forbidding it to increase air or ground patrols on the Czechoslovak borders, or to undertake any activity that might be interpreted by the Soviets as supportive of Dubček's regime.[37]

There is some evidence that the Soviet assessment of U.S. attitudes and actions in the last phase of the crisis in July and August, among other factors, may have influenced the final decision. Shortly after the Bratislava Conference, on August 7, 1968, Radio Moscow denied reports that a U.S. warning had been transmitted to the Soviet leadership "not to bring troops into Czechoslovakia," because "the United States would be compelled by public pressure to defer the project of bilateral disarmament negotiations [SALT talks]." Radio Moscow emphasized that no U.S. official—including Ambassador Bohlen, who visited Moscow in July—had issued any such threat: "No one in Moscow noted such warning."[38]

It is likely that the overcautious U.S. attitude, far from deterring the Soviet Union from military action, had the opposite effect of giving a powerful argument to the interventionist coalition. The advocates of military intervention could finally demonstrate, during the last debate on Czechoslovakia, that a Soviet invasion would neither precipitate American involvement (whether direct or indirect) in Czechoslovakia nor do serious damage to U.S.–Soviet relations. As Kenneth Myers and Dimitri Simes point out, "An influential group within the Soviet leadership sought to persuade its colleagues that an invasion into Czechoslovakia contained extraordinary dangers. Ponomarev, Secretary of the CPSU Central Committee . . . argued that a Soviet military incursion into Czechoslovakia could seriously jeopardize Soviet relations with the United States and push the Americans into Chinese arms." In this light, Rusk's statements "served to convince the pro-invasion forces of the validity of their position, and thus to undermine the foes of invasion. In retrospect, the American interest would have been better served by the promotion of doubts and uncertainties as to possible American reactions to a Soviet move against Czechoslovakia."[39]

In addition, there were signs that during the crisis Soviet analysts were beginning to fear that Richard Nixon would be successful in his bid for the American presidency. These fears became obvious shortly after the Bratislava negotiations, when Nixon won the nomination at the Republican Convention. At the time, Soviet foreign policy experts viewed Nixon as the candidate who would cause more harm to Soviet interests, particularly in the field of arms control, than would his Democratic opponent, Hubert H. Humphrey. Soviet writers, identifying Nixon with a policy of U.S. military superiority, feared that he would try to recapture a more visible U.S. lead in the arms race. Thus, the Soviet Trade Union newspaper *Trud*, while defending the results of the Bratislava negotiations as being timely and necessary, described Nixon as a politician of "big business," who would favor a "position of strength," and "further expansion of the U.S. military budget."[40] Perhaps *Trud's* analysis, in cryptic Soviet political language, tried to establish a connection between the resolution of the Czechoslovak crisis and the result of the forthcoming U.S. election. The article seemed to imply that a Soviet intervention before the November election in America would weaken the chances of American advocates of SALT negotiations and enhance the electoral prospects of the anti-Communist candidate—who seemed less committed to arms control—Republican Richard Nixon.[41]

This is not to suggest that a different U.S. attitude toward Czechoslovakia or the USSR would have prevented the invasion. It is dubious whether anything that the United States might have done would have deterred the Soviet leadership from military intervention. Perhaps some sort of U.S. warning could have been exploited by the interventionists as proof of U.S. involvement in Czechoslovakia, and could therefore have increased the risks of Soviet retaliation. One can never be sure of policy effects. The balance of forces in the Soviet Politburo was precarious; it depended on many considerations—and not alone on perceptions of a possible U.S. response.

Still, the Johnson administration's policy of unconcern undoubtedly helped the interventionists in the debate and was a factor in encouraging the intervention. The Johnson administration could not have it both ways: an early start to SALT while Soviet troops were marching into Czechoslovakia—and all this two months prior to the presidential election. The linking of the two issues (SALT and Czechoslovakia), unfortunately, was understood by few. The Johnson administration not only continued, but speeded up, negotiations with the Soviet leadership—as if the Czechoslovak crisis were nonexistent—while making denials about U.S. involvement in Czechoslovakia.[42] U.S. policy toward Czechoslovakia, in Professor Griffith's words, was "short-sighted," because President Johnson "did not foresee that if the Soviets invaded Czechoslovakia, he would be compelled to acquiesce to a postponement of the ratification of the Non-Proliferation Treaty and the start of strategic weapons discussions with Russia."[43]

The Johnson administration could either have tacitly warned the Soviet leadership through diplomatic channels about the dangerous consequences of an intervention for both superpowers in the field of arms limitation, or have left the Soviet leadership guessing about a U.S. response. The latter would perhaps have been the better policy. The case is a classical one in the theoty of deterrence, where the decision depends to some degree on calculating the opponent's intentions. The outcome of the Soviet decisionmaking process was, of course, to be determined in part by events beyond U.S. policymakers' control, by the Soviet bureaucratic tug-of-war. Yet a situation of "genuine risk" with regard to U.S. intentions could have caused further uncertainties in the coalition-ridden Soviet Politburo. U.S. policymakers had nothing to lose; the right decision might have helped not only to deter the intervention, but also to ensure the early start of SALT negotiations—a matter in the interest of both superpowers.

The Rationale and Timing of the August Decision

So far, official Soviet sources have provided no satisfactory explanation of the reasons for the invasion. Most of the explanations have been *ex post facto* justifications. Soviet reasoning on this issue has changed several times, from an initial claim that the USSR responded to a call to "assist" a "group" of still unidentified Czechoslovak leaders to later claims that there was a need to put down an imminent "counterrevolution" or prevent the potential threat of Czechoslovak defection from the Warsaw Pact and counter the threat posed to that country by the "imperialist bloc" (primarily the West German "revanchists)". Numerous Western analysts have also tended to interpret the Soviet decision to intervene primarily in terms of Soviet national security and foreign policy considerations. Undoubtedly, broad international strategic and national security considerations—part of the shared images of Soviet national security decisionmakers—did influence the stands taken by the leadership on the Czechoslovak issue from the very beginning of the crisis. Soviet leaders attached great importance to Czechoslovakia because of its strategic geographic position as a buffer state between the Soviet Union and West Germany and because of its role as an important supplier of industrial equipment to the Communist countries and of military aid to Soviet clients in the Third World. They treated Czechoslovakia with special deference and stressed its importance on every possible occasion.[44]

Although Czechoslovak foreign policy during the Prague Spring was relatively less independent, and the risk of Czechoslovak withdrawal from the Warsaw Pact was very low, the perceived danger of a possible future defection was undoubtedly higher than it was in the case of Rumania. Prointerventionist arguments on the grounds of national security and foreign policy had been made throughout the April–August debate. All Soviet decisionmakers would have agreed that Czechoslovakia should not be allowed to become a "second Yugoslavia" or a "second Rumania." Brezhnev told the former Czechoslovak Ambassador Pavlovský at an earlier stage of the crisis that Czechoslovakia was not Rumania, or Yugoslavia and that they would not let Czechoslovakia go.[45]

Nevertheless, it is clear that Soviet and East European leaders did not believe that West German "revanchism" posed a real threat to Czechoslovakia. Although some of the arguments related to the West German threat were flaunted in Soviet and East European propaganda, treaties concluded in the early 1970s between the USSR and West Germany and between Czechoslovakia and West Germany showed that this factor served only as a temporary *ex post facto* justification rather than as a real motive for the invasion.

Moreover, it seems to have been clear to everyone in Moscow and Prague that the Dubček leadership would follow the terms of the Bratislava agreement strictly, at least in the realm of foreign policy, coordinating all important actions with the Soviet leadership. There was no indication that a fundamental change on the part of Czechoslovakia—withdrawal from the Warsaw Pact, a neutral course, or even Czechoslovak–West German rapprochement without Soviet approval—was envisioned. Soviet Central Committee officials did not doubt that Dubček would fulfill all obligations to the Warsaw Pact.[46] Thus, as late as August 17, the Soviet periodical *Za rubezhom* argued that the hopes of "Western politicians" that Czechoslovakia would leave the Warsaw Pact were "absurd."[47] In fact, during the short period of the Bratislava truce, the Czechoslovak government seemed somehow to be hardening its policy toward the West. On August 8, in the spirit of Bratislava, it protested officially against "the activities of the revanchists" in West Germany and their "anti-Czechoslovak speeches." These activities were said to be among the main obstacles in the normalization of relations between Czechoslovakia and West Germany. Similarly, on August 9, the Czechoslovak embassy in Washington protested a hostile anti-Czechoslovak campaign in the American press.[48] Even Soviet Ambassador Chervonenko had to admit, only several days prior to the intervention in discussions with the Czechoslovak minister of foreign affairs, Jiří Hájek, that there was no reason to reproach the Czechoslovak Ministry of Foreign Affairs or the minister, or to criticize the foreign policy pursued.[49]

More alarming in the Soviet leadership's perception were Czechoslovak relations and influence in Eastern Europe. East German and Polish leaders tried to convince the divided Soviet leadership that the northern flank of the Warsaw Pact was already to some degree "infected" by the cancer of Dubčekism in the summer of 1968. Indeed, Prague reformism provided impetus to polycentric and autonomous tendencies within Eastern Europe in general, while accelerating Rumanian defiance and drive for a more independent policy in particular. The Soviet leadership also worried about Czechoslovak influence in the southern tier of Eastern Europe. The Czechoslovak press published comments about instances of interwar cooperation among Czechoslovakia, Yugoslavia, and Rumania.[50] Perhaps Soviet leaders feared the potential development of a new "Communist Little Entente" in this area, which could undermine the Warsaw Pact.

Reports about the enthusiastic reception in Prague of Yugoslav President Tito and Rumanian Party leader Ceauşescu shortly after Bratislava apparently further irritated the Soviet leadership. The last warning letter from the Soviet Politburo to the Czechoslovak leadership on August 17 complained of "hints about the possibility of a reorientation of the alliance relationship of Czechoslovakia with the socialist countries"[51] (probably referring to hints in the Czechoslovak press, but not to the foreign policy of Dubček's leadership). But it seems inconceivable that the visits of Tito and Ceauşescu, which were planned in advance and had been postponed several times because of the prolonged Čierna-Bratislava negotiations, and which did not change the situation in any important way, were a major factor in the decision to intervene. These visits did not cause Czechoslovak foreign policy to shift in the direction of a "Communist Little Entente" subregional grouping. In fact, during his discussions with Czechoslovak leaders, Tito was critical of some features of Czechoslovak internal politics.[52]

More important, perhaps, in Soviet calculations were the unmistakable signs that the Bratislava agreement was perceived, not only in Czechoslovakia but in East European countries generally, as a sign of Soviet weakness and as a victory of the Czechoslovaks over the Soviets. The impact of Bratislava upon the East German and Polish leaderships has been mentioned. Its effects were also to be noted in other East European countries, such as Rumania (as hinted in Ceauşescu's speech before he flew to Czechoslovakia) and Albania where the reaction was more open.[53] The Soviet leaders naturally did not like to be taken as fools, and as their letter of August 17 indicated, they were concerned about the "one-sided meaning" of the Bratislava truce presented in the Czechoslovak media.[54]

In varying degrees, security considerations—the cohesion of the Warsaw Pact countries, the preservation of the *status quo,* and the political stability of Eastern Europe—contributed to the tipping of the scales in the Politburo during its August debate on the Czechoslovak issue. They do not entirely explain, however, the rationale or the timing of the Soviet decision very likely taken on August 17; neither can be reduced to any single motive. The fears of Soviet decisionmakers were not that Czechoslovakia would withdraw from the Warsaw Pact or COMECON, but that it would continue to *belong* to these organizations and that unrestricted and uncontrolled reformism would infect the other members and perhaps in the long run, the Soviet Union itself. Thus, the various segments of the interventionist coalition aimed primarily at reversing the moderate Čierna-Bratislava decision and preventing the Czechoslovak Party Congress from electing a homogeneous leadership and legitimizing the reformist program. The urgency that precipitated the invasion included unmistakable signs of a last-ditch effort to save the pro-Soviet elements in Czechoslovakia from total defeat. There is a strong likelihood that one of the factors that determined the *timing* of the intervention was the unexpected change of its *deadline*—i.e., the change in the date of the Congress of the Slovak Party from October to August 26.

At the Slovak Party Congress, significant changes in the Party leadership were supposed to take place. Shelest's ally Bilak would be replaced by Husák, at that time a supporter of reform. Urgent reports about the impending defeat of the antireformist coalition from Soviet Ambassador Chervonenko, the KGB, Ulbricht, and perhaps Bilak himself reached the Soviet Politburo around August 15. That these reports greatly influenced the perceptions of the Soviet leaders about the situation in Czechoslovakia is clearly indicated in the last warning letter from the Soviet Politburo of August 17. (Dubček received the letter on August 19 and read it to the Presidium members at the meeting on August 20, after the invasion had begun!)[55] The letter—the most telling evidence of the main concerns of the Soviet leadership before the invasion—was a tacit ultimatum, but it lacked two main elements of a classic ultimatum: a threat of penalty if the demands were not accepted and a time limit for compliance (it merely stated that "delays in this matter are extremely dangerous").[56] The letter was explicit regarding the points of main Soviet concern. It complained about unsatisfactory fulfillment of the "agreements" made at Čierna and Bratislava and about the "nationalistic" interpretation of these agreements. It also described "crude attacks . . . made on representatives of the Party and State who have evaluated objectively the results of the meetings at Čierna and Bratislava . . . they are threatened, public opinion is directed against them and they are labeled conservatives." The preparatory committee of the Social Democratic Party (which was mentioned only briefly in the letter) and Clubs K-231 and KAN (which at that time had almost ceased to exist) were not major considerations. The gravest danger was seen, not in a threat from the West or in Czechoslovak withdrawal from the Warsaw Pact, but in the campaign of "right-wing forces" against "the healthy forces" in Czechoslovakia. The letter hinted in places that the Soviet Politburo had received alarming reports on the outcome of the forthcoming congress of the Czechoslovak Communist Party on September 9. Reflecting the fears and reports of Czechoslovak antireformists, the letter complained that the Prague City Committee was playing the role of "a second CC [Central Committee]" and, with the backing of "forces" in the Czechoslovak Presidium, was attempting to influence the elections at the congress by "compiling 'blacklists' of Party officials who are not to be elected at the Fourteenth Party Congress to the new Central Committee." Thus, "in this way a situation has been created which allows the antisocialist forces to realize their plans—to deliver further blows to the Communist Party of Czechoslovakia."

A similar argument was advanced in the text with reference to "an appeal by a group of members of the Central Committee of the Czechoslovak Communist Party, the government, and National Assembly members [the antireformist coalition]" to governments and Communist parties of fraternal countries to render urgent assistance to the Czechoslovak people. This appeal depicted the danger of a reactionary coup which had been prepared by "right-wing forces" with the backing of "certain forces inside the Party, and Party bodies which actually met the right-wing forces half way" and which "organized a smear campaign designed to discredit individual functionaries, including some from the new leadership."[57] (This is an unmistakable reference to members of the antireformist coalition.)

Apparently, KGB intelligence estimates of the composition of the delegations to the Party congress and reports provided by the Czechoslovak antireformists Indra and Kolder supported Soviet interventionist arguments that the Fourteenth Extraordinary Party Congress, which was reluctantly and ambiguously approved at Čierna, would turn into a peaceful coup d'état, and bring about the defeat of the Czechoslovak fifth column. As *Pravda's* frankly worded editorial of August 22, 1968, put it, "The first and foremost matter causing serious concern and alarm is the situation in which the Czechoslovak Communist Party finds itself." *Pravda* stressed that

one could have hoped that the Czechoslovak Communist Party Central Committee Presidium would have used the preparation for the 14th Extraordinary Party Congress, scheduled for September 9, in order to end dismissal of cadres. This, however, did not happen. On the contrary, preparations for the Congress were used by the *rightwing forces* to step up their attacks against *healthy party forces,* to place their own people in district and provincial party organizations . . . . The press, under the control of the rightwingers, openly interfered in the election of delegates to party Conferences and to the Congress, and even published recommendations as to who should be elected to the future Czechoslovak Communist Party Central Committee and who should not. Hence, they clearly attempted to exercise inadmissible pressure on the delegates of the forthcoming Congress. Such was the state of affairs.[58]

The interventionist coalition apparently argued that recent developments in Czechoslovakia made necessary a new deadline for resolution of the crisis. Intervention, as one Soviet writer observed, was "an emergency measure, a forced measure dictated by the situation."[59] The decision whether to intervene had to be made before August 26, the date of the Slovak Party Congress. At this congress one of the most outspoken antireformists, Bilak, probably would not have been reelected, and the Soviets would have had to face a more homogeneous and reform-oriented leadership in the Slovak Party. The announcement of a visit to Prague by Secretary General of the United Nations U Thant to take place on August 23 may also have forced the Soviet leaders to reconsider the timing of the intervention. The timing was apparently not accidental. Perhaps deliberately, the Soviet leaders departed from the customary practice of invading on weekends or holidays, when many officials are unavailable. On August 20, when the intervention began, the Czechoslovak Presidium was supposed to meet for the last time before the Slovak Party Congress, and the Soviet

Politburo was certainly aware of this schedule, since the session of the Czechoslovak Presidium regularly took place on Tuesdays. It can be surmised that the interventionist coalition, using urgent reports from the KGB, Ambassador Chervonenko, Ulbricht, Gomułka, and the Czechoslovak antireformists, presented evidence that the antireformist coalition would make a successful bid for power at this meeting, and would outvote Dubček's supporters. Thus, the Soviet Army would only back up an internal coup d'état.

In their effort to win majority support in the Politburo, the interventionists presumably argued that the Soviet leadership could not wait any longer —certainly not until November, when the World Communist Conference and the U.S. election would take place. Brezhnev himself indicated that the timing of the intervention became an important factor in the Soviet decision. He was said to imply that there were those in the Politburo who argued in favor of delaying the Soviet decision: "From this point of view it would have been more favorable to wait until an open counterrevolution broke out in Czechoslovakia with all its consequences and only to interfere afterwards."[60]

The arguments of the interventionists against delay were apparently bolstered by Warsaw Pact and Ground Forces Command reports, which may have claimed, as General Mariakhin argued, that the Soviet armed forces could not continue in a "prewar" posture indefinitely. August 20 may have been presented by the interventionist coalition as the last appropriate deadline for curbing Czechoslovak reformism effectively and at least cost. As *Pravda* put it, "An atmosphere that was quite unacceptable for the socialist countries had been created. Under such circumstances it was necessary to act, and to *act purposefully and decisively without losing time*."[61] The interventionist coalition, one may surmise, estimated the costs of further delay as high as possible and was pressing to tip the scales in its favor.

The Decision to Intervene

The most important Soviet decisions in the post-Stalin era have been made by a ruling group of decisionmakers—in Soviet terminology, by the "collective leadership." Some of these decisions have appeared to Western observers as irrational, as taken by men who became victims of their own orthodoxy or, at best, of groupthink. On the other hand, some Soviet decisions have been interpreted as the rational actions of men who knew exactly what was best to do in the interest of their country.

It is difficult to label any decision "rational" or "irrational." All decisions are imperfect, those taken by individuals as well as those taken by groups. All have both rational and irrational elements. In the Kremlin, as in the White House, decisionmaking is not a science but an art, requiring judgment and reflecting compromise. It hinges on value- and preference-ordering. As numerous authors have pointed out, for a group to arrive at a preference-ordering is more difficult than for an individual. In Sidney Verba's words, "Different members will prefer different goals, and policy will often be formulated by bargaining among the members of a foreign policy coalition."[62] This is true of Soviet decisionmaking, where a collective body rules without a supreme authority such as a president and is composed of a heterogeneous group of men with divergent values, bureaucratic affiliations, constituencies, and responsibilities. Although from the perspective of each decisionmaker, his position represents a rational cost-benefit calculation, decisions made by the Soviet collective leadership seldom reflect united sets of national security interests. They appear to be taken in relation to a variety of inconsistent goals in internal and external policies, arising from participants with many differing personal and organizational interests.

In this respect, the hypotheses of bureaucratic politics can offer a tentative, if partial, explanation of how Soviet decisions are made. Under the conditions of collective leadership in the post-Stalin era, the major Soviet decisions have been made through discussions at Politburo sessions where senior decisionmakers often express, in Khrushchev's words, "different points of view."[63] The Politburo debate is aimed at reaching a consensus— in Soviet political terminology, a "unanimous point of view." Although most Soviet decisions are compromises, they are taken unanimously in order to preserve the unity and cohesion of the Politburo. According to Soviet leader Mikoian, "If a consensus were unobtainable, the Politburo would adjourn, sleep on the matter [while apparently intensifying the internal bargaining], and return for further discussion until unanimity was reached."[64] Occasionally, during a debate on a controversial issue like the Czechoslovak one, when the Politburo is sharply divided, a vote may be taken. As Khrushchev put it, "If on some question, unanimity cannot be reached, the problem is decided by a simple majority vote."[65] Brezhnev asserted in 1973 that collective leadership is still the major force in Soviet decisionmaking. He noted that the Politburo reached most of its decisions after long discussion, when consensus had been established.[66]

Soviet decisionmaking nevertheless remains a mysterious subject. Although we still do not know precisely how the Soviet decision to intervene in Czechoslovakia was made, we do have sufficient evidence to piece together a scenario that may have taken place in the Kremlin in mid-August 1968. The new debate on the Czechoslovak issue occurred in Moscow about August 15–17. On August 17, the Soviet press imposed a blackout on the activities of Soviet leaders. Prior to August 15, most of the Soviet decisionmakers had reportedly left Moscow (between August 7 and 9) for a holiday at a Black Sea resort.[67] Because the Czechoslovak issue remained unresolved, this was apparently a working holiday, during which Politburo members probably maintained steady contact with each other by telephone.

As we have seen, the Čierna-Bratislava negotiations did not solve all problems. It is reasonable to assume that the Soviet decisionmakers, who chose not to dismantle the military buildup at the Czechoslovak borders, had followed the developments in Czechoslovakia closely. The same pattern emerged as during the Čierna negotiations, when the Politburo members were also away from Moscow. Between August 9 and 15 only two full Politburo members—Kirilenko and Mazurov—were left in the capital in charge of Party and governmental affairs. (The Soviet press revealed that candidate members or secretaries Ponomarev, Katushev, F. D. Kulakov, and Grishin also remained in Moscow.) We still do not know precisely what happened during this period. The preceding analysis, however, suggests that the interventionist coalition (ideological supervisors, high Party officials from the Soviet West, the interventionists in the KGB and in the Soviet armed forces) and their East German, Polish, and Czechoslovak allies pressed again for a reversal of the moderate Soviet decision expressed in the Čierna-Bratislava understanding. There is no evidence of a demand for an extraordinary Central Committee session at that time. There is also no evidence, despite rumors, that such a session took place before the intervention.[68] (Such sessions had approved the results of the Dresden Conference and the performance of the Soviet negotiators at the Warsaw Conference in July.) Needless to say, discussion of such a sensitive issue as the military invasion of Czechoslovakia would be a risky undertaking in a forum of several hundred people. It is reasonable to assume that the Soviet decisionmakers were aware that the Čierna-Bratislava conferences would become a subject at the next session of the Central Committee and that the results would probably be examined by the committee. These considerations were doubtless in the minds of all the Soviet leaders. By August 14–15, they were perhaps acquainted with unmistakable signs of changes in the "bureaucratic mood,"—which may also have affected their calculations. Perhaps at the next Central Committee session the interventionist coalition would have received support from a majority of Central Committee members, especially since the Central Committee was not informed about the verbal agreements made at Čierna and Bratislava. The interventionists may have demanded in the post-Bratislava period that such a session be held to deal with the results of the negotiations with Czechoslovak leaders.

Inconclusive pieces of evidence available show that because of the pressure of the advocates of military intervention and their supporters at the Central Committee level, an "enlarged" session of the Soviet Politburo and the Secretariat, devoted entirely to the situation in Czechoslovakia, took place on August 16–17. At this session such advocates of intervention as Shelest[69] probably raised objections to the Bratislava truce. Perhaps they also presented the urgent reports of Chervonenko, Ulbricht, Gomułka, the KGB, and Czechoslovak antireformists Kolder, Indra, and Bilak as proof of counterrevolution, arguing that the deteriorating situation in Czechoslovakia threatened the political cohesion of Eastern Europe and stability in the Soviet West, and that the Politburo's only option was military intervention. The interventionists' arguments were presumably reinforced by logistic considerations and evidence that the Czechoslovak Army would not resist, and by indications that the United States would do nothing significant on behalf of Czechoslovakia. At this point it was not important whether Brezhnev had actually received from President Johnson on August 18 (as he told the Czechoslovak leadership) the answer to his inquiry, assuring him that the United States still honored the Yalta and Potsdam agreements[70] and, by implication, would not try to resist an invasion. By this date the Soviet Politburo already had enough signals from the U.S. government to know that it would not take action on behalf of Dubček's regime.

The seriousness of the Politburo debate was again, as in July, reflected by the publication on August 18, of an article in *Pravda* signed by I. Alexandrov. This semiofficial analysis described developments in Czechoslovakia in grave terms: intensification of subversive activities by antisocialist forces which are "undermining the foundations of the socialist system."[71] As in July, the interventionists were again trying to push the Politburo toward invasion.

The proceedings of the Politburo sessions may never be released. Nevertheless, even without hard evidence, one can, by examining the Soviet press, surmise the intensification of the Politburo debate that preceded the decision to intervene.[72] Brezhnev later admitted that the Politburo "thoroughly considered all aspects of the military intervention in Czechoslovakia" and implied that one view presented suggested that "this step would threaten the authority of the Soviet Union in the eyes of the people of the world . . . it would fan national passions and cause a loss of Soviet prestige in Czechoslovakia."[73]

Even during this debate, Suslov was said to express some reservations about military intervention, contending that "in spite of the undeniable upsurge of counterrevolutionary forces," it was still "possible to settle the Czechoslovak affair by political means."[74] According to various independent sources, several Soviet decisionmakers often mentioned—Suslov, Kosygin, and Ponomarev—questioned the wisdom of intervention, mainly on tactical grounds.[75]

The noninterventionists Suslov, Kosygin, and Ponomarev were said to be criticized in a report distributed to all Party organizations in the fall of 1968, apparently by the interventionists, for having "underestimated the danger of a counterrevolution in Prague."[76] An unsigned editorial in *Pravda* on August 22 criticized the "*soglashatel'skii podkhod* (compromising approach)" and "conscious belittling of the danger of counterrevolution" in Czechoslovakia.[77] It is conceivable that this criticism was directed not only against Czechoslovak reformists but also against the noninterventionists among Soviet decisionmakers. But there were similar signs of disapproval of intervention among some segments of the Soviet Party bureaucracies. A report of the Czechoslovak ambassador to the Soviet Union, V. Koucký, is said to have stated that at least 800 Soviet Party organizations (from a total of 60,000) were reluctant to approve the intervention. Some protests came from centrally located Party organizations with a high percentage of intellectuals (e.g., from Moscow and Leningrad, where the Prague Spring was considered an encouragement to Soviet reformism). Other protests came from similarly constituted Party organizations in the Soviet East (Siberia).[78]

Intriguingly, during this crucial session of the Soviet Politburo, a last desperate attempt was made to renegotiate a compromise with Dubček's leadership. As late as August 17, Hungarian leader Kádár met secretly with Dubček on the Czechoslovak-Hungarian borders, as they had in July. Kádár's still not fully explained mission, arranged at his own initiative, was a last effort, perhaps too late, to explore the possibility of political compromise.

Even Kádár must have been impressed by the emotional revival of the pre-World War II Czechoslovak-Rumanian-Yugoslav sentiment that followed Ceauşescu and Tito's visits to Prague. (The Little Entente was originally an alliance aimed primarily against Hungary.) Yet, during this last meeting, while the decision to invade was being made in Moscow, Kádár apparently tried to convince Dubček of the benefits of compromise with the Soviet leadership, and perhaps presented additional Soviet demands. Kádár was apparently reluctant to go along with military intervention—probably because of his assessment of its costs. After the intervention, he described his meeting with Dubček as one of his "efforts to find a simple, political solution to the Czechoslovak problem," and called the intervention "an unhappy necessity."[79] During their meeting, Kádár did not inform Dubček about the threat of intervention, apparently either because he did not know the outcome of the Soviet Politburo debate or because he was not authorized to pass along the information, if he did know. Dubček's impression after the meeting was that "Kádár had wanted to tell me something but he did not do so."[80] Probably believing that the noninterventionists could prevent an invasion, Dubček disregarded unmistakable signs of a new Soviet debate on Czechoslovakia and did not take Kádár's warnings seriously. He did not inform the Presidium about the details of his discussions with Kádár, or about the warning letter from the Soviet Politburo, which he received on August 19. (After the invasion had begun, Dubček read the letter to the Presidium.) Dubček may have not wanted to reveal the extent of Soviet pressure, fearing that it would create anti-Soviet feelings and be exploited by the antireformists. At any rate, he was again caught in a dilemma of various internal and external pressures. Concentrating on his own intra governmental game with the antireformist coalition, he badly misjudged the importance of these warnings, perhaps believing them to be still another form of Soviet pressure or a bluff.

In any case, Kádár's mission apparently came too late. The pressure of the interventionist coalition, which probably mounted on the night of August 17, was strong enough to influence some wavering senior Soviet decisionmakers to agree to the invasion. This seems to have been true of Brezhnev, who at this time probably changed his position again. Brezhnev's final stand on Czechoslovakia may have been influenced by his personal disappointment with Dubček. Unlike some of his colleagues in the Politburo, Brezhnev seems to have trusted Dubček, particularly at the beginning of the crisis, and may have believed Dubček cheated him during and after the negotiations at Čierna. As Brezhnev told Dubček during the post-invasion negotiations in Moscow on August 23–26, "I believed you and defended you against the others. . . . I said, 'our Sasha is a good Communist.' But you have disappointed us all terribly."[81] Thus, Brezhnev's disappointment with Dubček and his internal policies (particularly the appointments of high Czechoslovak officials, which Brezhnev complained were carried out without his prior understanding and approval)[82] reinforced Brezhnev's concern about the eroding effects of nonintervention on his own position. As we have seen, at Čierna and Bratislava Brezhnev had decided to join the noninterventionist coalition, but apparently not wholeheartedly. He was probably not entirely pleased with the outcome of the negotiations. At the crucial session of the Politburo on August 17, certain members of this body were said to have spoken critically of "hesitation and weakness" in dealing with the Czech question.[83]

That Brezhnev's performance at Čierna and Bratislava was overshadowed by that of Suslov, and that the truce received a cold reception from various important bureaucratic elites, did not enhance Brezhnev's position. His concern is evidenced by his telephoning Dubček on August 9 and 13 and by his personal letter to Dubček of August 16. It seems that in assessing the Czechoslovak issue Brezhnev also took into account the increasingly powerful influence of the interventionist coalition, which could weaken his position. As Brezhnev explained to Czechoslovak reformist B. Šimon in November 1968, during a private conversation in Moscow, "You thought that because you were in a position of power you could do as you pleased. This was your basic mistake. I also cannot do what I desire. I can actually realize perhaps only a third of what I would like to do. If I had not cast my vote in the Politburo in favor of military intervention—what do you suppose would have happened? Certainly you would not be sitting here. And *perhaps even I would not be sitting here either!*"[84] Fear, then, of not being on the winning side might help explain how Brezhnev and other undecided players made their final decision.

In the view of former Czechoslovak leader Mlynář, the advocates of military intervention in Moscow won the debate only during the last round of their offensive, which began about August 10. From this date until August 17 the pressure of the interventionist elements grew so strong that some of the wavering decisionmakers shifted to the side of the interventionists. Mlynář believes that Brezhnev, and even some of the skeptics of intervention, also joined the interventionist coalition at this time because of their fears of reprisals—e.g., forced resignation—should they not do so.[85] The evidence is insufficient to determine whether the final decision was reached by voting, as reported by some sources,[86] or by consensus without formal voting, and finally unanimously accepted despite the reluctance of some. We do not know exactly how the balance between the coalitions shifted between August 10 and August 17. We can only surmise that at that time the majority of Soviet decisionmakers accepted *l'ipotesi catastrofica* (the catastrophic hypothesis) about developments in Czechoslovakia. The Bratislava *modus vivendi,* which depended on a precarious balance of forces in the Soviet Politburo, was toppled by pressure from the interventionist coalition. Skeptics of military intervention were, for the first time during the long crisis, unable to resist the renewed pressure, because, as one of them put it, they "were unluckily in the minority."[87]

Implementation of the Decision

The implementation of Soviet foreign policy decisions is an intriguing and little-known part of the Soviet decisionmaking process. It is reasonable to assume that Politburo decisions are formulated in such a way as to give the Soviet foreign policy bureaucracies some room to maneuver. Moreover, instructions of the various Politburo members, and of the heads of national security agencies, to their men in the field can cause uncertainty even during the process of implementation and, under certain circumstances, contradictory and inconsistent actions.

This point is demonstrated by Soviet conduct during the first days after the decision to intervene in Czechoslovakia. As noted, this decision was probably taken on August 17[88] by the Soviet Politburo. That evening, three days before the actual invasion, the Soviet Army and KGB operatives apparently received an order to prepare final details of the action. On that day an airplane carrying special KGB units and the Czechoslovak STB collaborators reportedly landed at the Prague airport to prepare for the invasion.[89] That day, some Czechoslovak State Security members, led by Šalgovič, allegedly returned from the Soviet Union. At the same time the Soviet Warsaw Pact and Ground Forces Commands received an order to transform the contingency plans into an actual intervention. The operation was put under the overall command of Commander-in-Chief of the Ground Forces General Pavlovskii. It was evidently coordinated with the movement of units of the other Warsaw Pact countries under General Shtemenko, who stated, on August 20, that the Soviet troops were aware of "the entire complexity of the international situation" and of "their personal responsibility for the defense of the achievements of socialism."[90] On the eve of the invasion, once the troops were in position for deployment, command was transferred from the regular Warsaw Pact headquarters to the Soviet High Command.

The date of intervention was set for Tuesday evening, August 20—at a time when the Czechoslovak Presidium was in session. After the decision was made on August 17 the remaining time was probably devoted to final preparations: drafting and translating codes, final briefings, refueling vehicles, and painting the white stripes of invasion forces on tank turrets and hulls to differentiate them from their Czechoslovak counterparts. Western electronic surveillance of the buildup was impaired by the Warsaw Pact's use of electronic screens to cover the movement of troops and by the fact that the invading units kept radio traffic to a minimum. Nevertheless, some of the preparations of August 18–20, though still under the cover of summer maneuvers, did not pass unnoticed by U.S. and NATO long-range radar surveillance: heavy concentrations of flights over Poland, large-scale refuelings in Leningrad of military transports (which were lifting the Soviet airborne division into Prague on the night of August 20),[91] and the alert of the Soviet Strategic Rocket Forces.

Although military resistance was not expected, the Soviet General Staff was apparently ordered to take necessary precautions to avoid conflict with Czechoslovak Army units. Reportedly, during the summer the Warsaw Pact Command had lowered the Czechoslovak fuel and ammunition stocks by transferring those supplies to East Germany for more "exercises."[92] On August 19, the Warsaw Pact Command succeeded in securing the consent of the Czechoslovak Ministry of Defense for an unexpected military exercise of the Czechoslovak Army with the participation of Warsaw Pact observers. The exercises were to take place on August 21—the second day of intervention.[93] In reality, this was probably a maneuver to concentrate the Czechoslovak military forces in the western part of Czechoslovakia in order to minimize their opportunity to make contact with the invading troops, as well as to divert the attention of the Czechoslovak General Staff from the intervention.[94]

The Soviet Politburo, meanwhile, made some related decisions in foreign policy affairs. There is some evidence to indicate that the important decision to set a final deadline for the start of SALT negotiations was associated with the decision to intervene in Czechoslovakia. On August 19 President Johnson received Kosygin's short note agreeing to a summit meeting in Leningrad on September 30.[95] Kosygin's note suggested that a joint announcement be made on August 21; he apparently suspected that the president would cancel the visit. It is plausible that the decision to send such a note was taken to minimize the impact of the intervention on U.S.–Soviet relations, and indeed, Kosygin may personally have insisted on it. The wording of Soviet notes to the United States, Great Britain, and West Germany on the eve of the intervention clearly indicates the Soviet concern over the cost of its actions in the realm of international affairs. The Soviet note to the U.S. government stated: "We proceed from the fact that the current events should not harm Soviet-American relations, to the development of which the Soviet government *as before* attaches great importance."[96]

In a strictly military sense, implementation of the Soviet decision by the Warsaw Pact forces was a smooth and remarkably effective operation. The Soviet High Command showed considerable boldness and skill while ensuring that the invading troops (estimated number of "first-line forces," 250,000, "total strength," 500,000) did not spill over into West Germany and Austria. The commander of the invasion forces, General Pavlovskii, undoubtedly feared clashes with NATO forces and defections. Accordingly, five Soviet divisions were deployed directly south along the Karlovy Vary-Plzeň-Budějovice main highway and adjacent roads in a line about five kilometers back from West German territory and facing in both directions.[97] (The Czechoslovak special border brigades continued to operate without Soviet interference.) In thirty-six hours the Warsaw Pact armies had total control of Czechoslovak territory with no resistance.

Yet the intervention was not without defects. As I witnessed, for example, the invading forces were handicapped for several days by a lack of food, water, and fuel, sufficient supplies of which had not been brought in with the troops (suggesting their expectation that these would be provided by "healthy forces" in Czechoslovakia). Although there was no military resistance in Czechoslovakia, civilian resistance was strong enough to prevent the seizure of Czechoslovak supplies and fuel by the Warsaw Pact forces. These deficiencies in military planning reflected in some degree the acute political failure of the intervention.

In fact, the sharp gap between the military and the political aspects of the intervention again demonstrates that the decision to invade was made at short notice and based upon political misjudgments. It can be surmised that the decision of August 17 was founded (as *Pravda's* editorial of August 22 and initial Tass statements indicated) on the following faulty assumptions: (1) that Dubček and his supporters in the Czechoslovak Presidium were in the minority, were supported only by a few groups of "radicals," and could be outmaneuvered and outvoted; (2) that a new "revolutionary government of workers and peasants," like Kádár's in Hungary in 1956, would be established immediately by the antireformist coalition, supported by the Warsaw Pact forces; and (3) that there would be sufficient support for the majority of the Czechoslovak Presidium and Central Committee members and widespread support among the population for the Soviet action and for a new government. The original Soviet plan was to replace Dubček and his supporters with "healthy forces" and to create a new pro-Soviet government, led by the Czechoslovak antireformist Indra. This was clearly demonstrated during the first hours after intervention by the activities of the Soviet authorities in Czechoslovakia—Commander of Ground Forces General Pavlovskii, KGB officials, and Ambassador Chervonenko—who tried unsuccessfully for two days to create a pro-Soviet government. The original plan of the invasion called for a military intervention combined with an internal coup d'état. The antireformists were to create a confrontation, divide the Presidium, and form an anti-Dubček majority there. Then the Presidium was apparently expected to pass a resolution declaring counterrevolution imminent and to announce a postponement of the Party congress. Finally an appeal for assistance from the Soviet Army was to be broadcast by Czechoslovak radio.

August 20 was the Soviet D-day in Prague. On the afternoon of this day the Czechoslovak Presidium convened with two main issues on the agenda: Dubček's report on the preparation of the Party congress and discussion of the "standpoint" of Kolder and Indra regarding the position of the Czechoslovak Communist Party in the country.[98] The session began with a sharp confrontation over the procedure to be followed. Whereas Dubček and his reformist supporters wanted to discuss the documents prepared for the Party congress (the report and the draft of the resolution), the antireformists Kolder and Indra wanted to begin the Presidium session with a debate on their standpoint, which was based on the tendentious conclusions of the Kašpar report and which contained allusions to the internal threat to socialism in Czechoslovakia. Indra and Kolder had presumably anticipated that the Presidium's acceptance of their "standpoint" would provide a document that could be used to justify the intervention and also lead to Dubček's defeat and possible replacement. But the plan did not work for several reasons. First, the invasion seems to have been badly coordinated with the Soviet leadership. Some former officials of Dubček's regime believe there was uncertainty over the exact time of invasion because of the time differences involved: 1:00 A.M. Moscow time and 11:00 P.M. Central European time. The Czechoslovak antireformists expected the invasion to take place at 1:00 A.M. Central European time rather than at 11:00 P.M. when it actually occurred.[99] Second, Dubček vehemently rejected the change in procedure and insisted that the Presidium meeting begin with discussion of the Congress documents and only then proceed to the Indra-Kolder position paper. (It is conceivable that if the antireformists had forced the change in procedure, voting on the Indra-Kolder standpoint would have taken place, and two wavering leaders, Piller and Barbírek, might have voted with the antireformists.)[100] Finally, and perhaps most importantly, as an eyewitness of the meeting observed, the antireformists suffered from "terrible fears" and were hesitant during their attempts to carry out the planned coup. When news first came of the invasion and Kriegel talked about the 'betrayal of a people," the antireformist Bilak screamed repeatedly, "So lynch me then. Why don't you beat me?"[101] For all these reasons a resolution declaring a state emergency and calling for struggle against the 'counterrevolution" and for "fraternal assistance" was never voted upon. The discussion of the Indra-Kolder memorandum, which was heated and again demonstrated the sharp differences in the Presidium, took place only at the close of the Presidium session. The intervention was not legalized, directly or indirectly. On the contrary, when the first news of the invasion arrived, it was debated and condemned by a majority of the voting Presidium members (7:4) in a proclamation to all the people of Czechoslovakia. The antireformists Bilak, Kolder, Švestka, and Rigo (supported by the non-voting members Indra and Kapek) voted against that part of the Presidium proclamation that declared the invasion a breach of the fundamental relations among socialist states as well as of international law.

The next day, the antireformists, led by Kolder, Indra, and Bilak, appealed for cooperation with the Soviet authorities; but they were able to assemble in a meeting only fifty Central Committee members and candidates, a thin minority comprising about a third of the total number.[102] Neither they nor the Soviet authorities—General Pavlovskii, the KGB officials, and Ambassador Chervonenko—were able to organize sufficient support at the Central Committee level to constitute a new anti-Dubček Presidium and government.

Defeat of the antireformist coalition in the Czechoslovak leadership brought implementation of the Soviet decision into a state of confusion and contradiction. Soviet frustrations and indecisiveness, caused, among other things, by divisions among senior decisionmakers, were everywhere evident. The KGB officials and their STB collaborators, who arrested and kidnapped Dubček and his reformist supporters in the Czechoslovak Presidium (Smrkovský, Špaček, Kriegel, Černík, and Šimon) on August 21, informed them that in two hours they would stand in front of a "revolutionary tribunal" headed by Comrade Indra.[103] This decision was apparently reflected in *Pravda's* editorial on August 22, which described Dubček as "the head" of a "minority of the Presidium members" with "right-wing opportunist positions" (which in the Soviet vocabulary means something like "traitor"), who, "having paid lip service to their desire to protect socialism," were in fact, for a time, plotting "counterrevolution." The charges, which were very serious, were similar to those brought against Hungarian leader

Nagy on the eve of Soviet intervention in Hungary in November, 1956.[104]

The Soviet leadership had never negotiated with arrested Communist leaders who had been publicly labeled "right-wing opportunists." Yet it found itself doing so with the Czechoslovak reformists. Several hours after being kidnapped, Dubček and his supporters were taken first to the staff headquarters of the Warsaw Pact in Poland, then shortly afterward to the Transcarpathian Ukraine, where they were held as prisoners at the KGB prison. Only three days later, on August 23, they were brought to Moscow to negotiate with Soviet leaders.[105] The KGB agents seemed to have had contradictory orders about what to do with them. One day Dubček was treated as a traitor, several days later as a respected Czechoslovak leader.[106] The Soviet leadership was forced to allow the Czechoslovak reformists, whom it had abducted as "traitors" and had planned to try before a "revolutionary tribunal," to remain in power.

The contrast between the military near-perfection and the political blundering illustrates the hesitancy and perhaps still unresolved division in the Soviet leadership on this issue. The uncertainty of the Soviet leaders was also indicated (even during the first days of intervention) by some curious reports in the Soviet press, such as that in *Trud* depicting the actual reaction of the Czechoslovak populace to Soviet occupation.[107] Furthermore, at the first Tass report of intervention, signatures of Soviet leaders were conspicuously absent: until Podgorny's dismissal in 1977, all major announcements were customarily made over the signatures of a *troika*—Brezhnev, Podgorny, and Kosygin. No major address by a Soviet leader was given on this issue. The almost daily changes in Soviet policy toward Czechoslovakia, coupled with this lack of a high-level exposition on the subject, indicated that, even during implementation of the August 17 decision, some differences persisted within the Soviet leadership.

By August 23, a significant change occurred, bringing a new moderation. The leaders of both Czechoslovak coalitions were brought to Moscow for negotiations. The most important factor in the change was probably the situation in Czechoslovakia itself. Brezhnev recognized on the evening of August 22 that preintervention intelligence reports had been wrong.[108] The original decision had been based on distorted intelligence estimates.

The antireformist government was not instituted, and support in the Central Committee for the antireformists was minimal. Moreover, the reformist wing of the Czechoslovak Party succeeded in doing what the Soviet occupation forces had come to prevent—convening the Fourteenth Party Congress. Furthermore, loyal security forces in the Ministry of the Interior managed to arrest many pro-Soviet Czechoslovak agents. Undoubtedly, the Soviet leadership had deployed enough forces to impose its own government; but this action would have been too costly to the Soviet decision-makers responsible for foreign policy affairs. The first three days after the intervention brought some detrimental consequences that had been predicted by skeptics of the wisdom of military action.

President Johnson cancelled his planned visit to Leningrad, and the SALT talks had to be postponed.[109] The intervention was rejected and condemned not only by most governments in the West, but even by most of the Communist parties, whether ruling (Chinese,[110] Rumanian, Yugoslav, and Albanian) or nonruling (eighteen West European Communist parties). True, Brezhnev during the Moscow negotiations did not seem to be too impressed by the international opposition to the invasion. He told the Czechoslovak leaders that nothing that could happen would help Czechoslovakia: 'War will not break out; Comrades Tito and Ceausescu will give speeches, also Comrade Berlinguer. And what? You rely on the Communist movement in Western Europe [to help you], but it already lost its meaning fifty years ago!'[111] To be sure, the political failure of the intervention itself was a main factor in the Soviets' reconsideration of the original decision of August 17. But the first detrimental effects of the invasion in the international arena may have contributed to the Soviets' moderation and their willingness to bargain with Dubček and his supporters, despite Brezhnev's apparent remonstrations to the contrary.

The Politburo took another unprecedented step by deciding to compromise with a group of "right-wing" reformists against whom the Soviet troops had intervened—a paradoxical, almost incredible situation. The Soviet leadership reconciled itself to the continuance in office of reformists in the Czechoslovak leadership. The negotiations in Moscow, which were conducted under most unfavorable conditions for the Czechoslovak leadership, were nevertheless, like previous negotiations during the Czechoslovak crisis, a kind of hard bargaining session. Brezhnev's conduct throughout the negotiations was characterized by brutal attempts to extract concessions by threats and blackmail: "We have already got the better of other little nations, so why not yours too?"[112] According to Smrkovský, however, he seemed to be less interested in investigating who was "personally responsible for the situation we were in," because "one might discuss it forever,"[113] and more interested in negotiating a political compromise. The most delicate negotiations (particularly where there were serious disagreements) were again conducted between two bargaining teams of four, as in Čierna—the Soviets represented by Brezhnev, Suslov, Kosygin, and Podgorny, and the Czechoslovaks by Dubček, Smrkovský, Černík, and Svoboda.[114]

The outcome was the Moscow Protocol—an ambiguous agreement that was arrived at not only by hard bargaining between the teams of four and by internal bargaining within the delegations presenting drafts of the protocol, but also presumably through consultations with leaders of the four East European countries represented at the Dresden, Moscow, Warsaw, and Bratislava summits at earlier stages of the crisis: Ulbricht, Gomułka, Kádár, and Zhivkov.[115] The Soviet team included Minister of Defense

Grechko and Minister of Foreign Affairs Gromyko (who had not been part of previous delegations). The bureaucratic demands of interventionist in the armed forces and the KGB regarding the temporary stationing o troops in Czechoslovakia and the activities of the Czechoslovak Ministry o the Interior were included in the protocol. The demands of bureaucrat charged with ideological supervision regarding the Czechoslovak publi media were also specifically included. The Czechoslovaks had to consent to proclaiming the Fourteenth Party Congress "invalid." Yet the agreement concluded under such unfavorable circumstances, was still better than mos skeptics had expected.

Contrary to *Pravda's* August 22 editorial and the views of the interven tionists, the Moscow Protocol made no reference to Dubček's "right-wing opportunist" group and its policies or, because of Czechoslovak insistence to the threat of "counterrevolution" in Czechoslovakia or to officia appeals for "fraternal assistance." Neither was there a reference to the Warsaw Letter; only the Čierna-Bratislava negotiations were mentioned. Interestingly, at the September 1968 briefing of leading Soviet editors, Suslov reportedly proposed, in the spirit of the Moscow Protocol, a change in the phrase "open counterrevolution" (used by Soviet newspapers in the first days of the intervention) to "creeping counterrevolution."[116] The policy implication of this modification was obvious and consistent with Suslov's earlier argument that there was a danger of counterrevolution in Czechoslovakia, but that it was not imminent.

The protocol did not endorse the military invasion. The Czechoslovak reformists even succeeded in introducing a paragraph approving the contin-uation of Dubček's policies adopted at the January and May sessions of the Central Committee of the Czechoslovak Party and managed to have the word "temporarily" inserted in a paragraph referring to the presence of Soviet troops in Czechoslovak territory. (The original Soviet version had justified the invasion and stated that the Soviet troops would stay in Czechoslovakia.)[117]

Some of the Czechoslovak reformists, such as Smrkovský and Dubček, were reluctant to sign even this compromise version. The Czechoslovaks, represented by Smrkovský, Bilak, and Lenárt, were reminded of the political realities by Secretary Ponomarev: "If you do not sign now, you'll sign in a week. If not in a week, then in a fortnight. If not in a fortnight, in a month."[118] Finally, all the Czechoslovak leaders except "that Galician Jew" Kriegel signed the protocol.

The Soviet Politburo apparently made concessions at the insistence of the noninterventionists. Even these concessions were perhaps objected to by the interventionists, and certainly by Ulbricht, as indicated by the violent com-ments of the East German press.[119] Ulbricht and Gomułka were probably again dissatisfied with the compromise with the "revisionist" Dubček. The noninterventionists, who were defeated in the debate on August 17, nevertheless apparently insisted, during implementation of the decision, on using as little force as possible. The political mischief of the action, as well as the immediate foreign policy repercussions, gave them an opportunity to convince a majority in the Politburo about the benefits of a compromise with Dubček and his supporters. As Ponomarev told two Czechoslovak leaders in September 1968, "Although the presence of Soviet troops in Czechoslovakia was a *fait accompli* since the invasion," this does not mean one could not take a long look at the situation and "examine all possible political solutions not yet explored."[120] Ponomarev showed the Czechoslovak leaders his note to Brezhnev putting forward the program of "normalization" in Czechoslovakia, a proposal that was "moderate" and based on the decision to trust Dubček's team. Kosygin, during his private discussion with Mlynář in Moscow in August, also gave the impression of favoring a policy of compromise with the Czechoslovak reformists.[121]

The Moscow Protocol signaled the beginning of the end of the Czechoslovak experiment with reformism. Yet the Soviet leadership was forced to live, at least temporarily, with "right-wing opportunists" whom it had abducted as traitors. Implementation of the Soviet decision to intervene in Czechoslovakia was not successful, at least in the short run, and had to be modified into a compromise acceptable to all Soviet leaders. Some of the differences between the coalitions and the vacillation of the collective leadership which had surfaced during the preintervention debates persisted during the implementation stage. Soviet bureaucratic politics produced contradictory policies, even after the decision to intervene was made.

As a result of these contradictions, Dubček and many of his reformist supporters remained in power. Although several of them—Kriegel, Císař, Šik, and Pavel—were forced to resign, the Soviet leadership consented, at least temporarily, to the reformists' demands for demoting such antireformists as Kolder, Švestka, Rigo, and Kapek. Despite the military intervention, many features of the reformist program remained in effect. The Moscow compromise, which was concluded under unfavorable conditions when Czechoslovakia was already an occupied country, was translated into action slowly, becoming a policy dictate only after April 1969, when Dubček and his supporters were forced to resign. All remnants of Czechoslovak reformism were eradicated in the subsequent period between 1969 and 1971—the topic of another study.

VI

The Soviet invasion of Czechoslovakia in 1968 was the last straw. Any idea of internationalism ended for us . . . . If the term "Eurocommunism" had been invented in 1968, Dubček would have been a Eurocommunist. —Santiago Carrillo, 1977

Conclusions

The Value of the Bureaucratic-Politics Paradigm

It is beyond the scope of this study to provide a general analysis of Soviet decisionmaking in foreign policy. The bureaucratic-politics paradigm offers one means of approaching the subject. Some of the conclusions that follow are necessarily tentative, for, despite the unusual availability of some data, the present study has depended heavily on a personal interpretation of cryptic and incompletely known communications among Soviet decisionmakers. Furthermore, because of the lack of complete information and authoritative "inside" dates, it is impossible to structure certain unknown variables into the analytical framework or to capture all the complexities of the Soviet decisionmaking process. It should be borne in mind that the Czechoslovak crisis was an extraordinary event, one that challenged that process. This account can in no sense be regarded as the final word on the Czechoslovak crisis.

Nevertheless, application of the bureaucratic-politics paradigm—modified and tailored to Soviet circumstances—substantially illuminates certain aspects of the decisionmaking process leading to the intervention which have not previously received sufficient attention: the differing perceptions and interests held by central decisionmakers and the maneuvers they employed in an effort to arrive at a decision beneficial to them, to their internal constituencies, and to their external allies in Eastern Europe. In spite of the

154

limitations brought about by the peculiar rules of the Soviet decisionmaking game, the bureaucratic-politics paradigm provides a useful conceptual tool for the analysis of Soviet decisionmaking as a process of consensus building in the Politburo and the Central Committee bureaucracies and for the detection of signals of serious debate in these organizations (by deciphering the cryptic language of Soviet politics). It elucidates the importance of the players' perceived payoffs, the coalition politics and organizational maneuvering, and the silent bargaining among top bureaucrats. The coalitions that emerge in this process are heterogeneous, temporary conglomerates of bureaucratic elements with differing interests. Because these interests, or payoffs, are not necessarily consistent and may vary from issue to issue, coalition politics can lead to a shifting of the players' stands.

Moreover, the paradigm helps to explain the importance of a *deadline* in the Soviet decisionmaking game, which in the case of Czechoslovakia was the "action-forcing" Party congress scheduled for September 9, 1968. It also illustrates the bureaucratic constraints within which the game is played and how it can be conditioned by East European politics and pressures. It suggests that in building consensus for a new policy, its advocates need the active cooperation, or at least the approval and acquiescence, of a majority within the ruling elite. Consensus building requires internal maneuvering and bargaining, as noted during the procedures of two Central Committee sessions of the CPSU during the Czechoslovak crisis. In both cases it was apparently necessary for the interventionists to persuade wavering and uncommitted players and to reach out to a broader forum of supporters.

Seemingly, in Soviet politics, various changes in the rules of the game, such as adjustment of the decisionmaking circle to include or exclude players, can shape the outcome of a particular decision. Thus, during the Czechoslovak crisis, changes in personnel provided opportunities for seeking new decisions.

Finally, the paradigm is helpful in understanding the important role of communication and information in Soviet decisionmaking. It seems to suggest that even in the Soviet environment information collected by agencies abroad may be filtered or distorted, or messages may be manipulated, in an attempt to influence the outcome of an important debate. Cryptic signals based on misinformation may be sent to other nations in the absence of firm decisions.

Overall the study demonstrates that Soviet attempts to negotiate with Dubček's regime during the various stages of the crisis were *not* a ruse designed to create a false sense of security while plans for an intervention were being perfected. Although elements of deception were undoubtedly involved, the Soviet leadership decided to intervene only after a long period of hesitation and vacillation. Neither was the decision based on uniform perceptions of national security, such as fear about dramatic changes in

Czechoslovak foreign policy or about the threat from the West. Such possibilities were not taken seriously by Soviet officials. It was clear to them
particularly after Bratislava, that the Dubček government would not deviat
in its foreign policy orientation, and that talk of a NATO or West German
"threat" to Czechoslovakia had been exaggerated. This is not to say tha
the argument of the "threat from the West" was not *employed* in the debat
preceding the invasion in order to create bureaucratic and public support

The final decision was shaped by many factors: the various interests o
senior decisionmakers, perceived domestic political consequences and
foreign policy linkages, East European politics, instability and pressures
clear signals of the Czechoslovak military's nonresistance and of over
cautious U.S. noninvolvement, manipulated information, logistic con
siderations, and finally the bureaucratic tug-of-war resulting in shaky com
promises and tradeoffs between various elements in the Politburo. In brief
the final decision was essentially the outcome of a contest among variou
bureaucracies with differing foreign, domestic, and organizational policy
interests.

In view of the ambiguous nature of the Čierna and Bratislava agreements
and the signs of division within the Soviet Politburo, the decision to invade
Czechoslovakia seventeen days after the negotiations should not have been
so difficult to predict. The ambiguity of the outcome of the negotiations
was indicated by the Soviet decision to withdraw Warsaw Pact troops from
Czechoslovak territory but not from the Czechoslovak borders. Thus, intervention was still being considered as one of the options open to the Politburo. In fact, the negotiations—while seemingly successful—intensified the
ongoing bureaucratic struggle within the Soviet leadership. Elements of the
interventionist coalition—such as the Party leaderships in the Soviet
Union's western non-Russian republics, the departments of the Central
Committee of the CPSU concerned with ideological supervision and indoctrination, interventionists in the armed forces and in the KGB—communicated to the Politburo their dissatisfaction with and disapproval of the
Čierna-Bratislava agreement, with its sudden moderation of Soviet policy.
Pressures from East German leader Ulbricht and Polish leader Gomułka
were also on the increase. Both men advised the Soviet leadership that the
"soft" nature of the Čierna-Bratislava compromise might have unfavorable
consequences for their countries. Czechoslovak antireformists, fearing their
defeat at the forthcoming Party congress, signaled to the Soviet leadership
that the congress would result in a "right-wing" takeover and should be
prevented.

These pressures and signals, and the information provided on the critical
Czechoslovak situation, were extremely important. With the personnel
changes made under Dubček's leadership, Soviet leaders lost control over
some channels of information; they seem many times not to have had ade-

quate or accurate information. Thus, they were forced to seek data from alternative East German, Polish, and Czechoslovak antireformist sources. In addition, intelligence estimates provided by KGB officials in Czechoslovakia and by Ambassador Chervonenko were distorted by parochial and personal interests. Finally, KGB-sponsored provocations and disinformation operations provided evidence of the "counterrevolution" in Czechoslovakia and support for the interventionist stand in the Politburo. The resulting faulty intelligence reports, on which the final decision was based, led in part to the initial political fiasco of the invasion.

In the final debate, the interventionists probably grounded their arguments on the USSR's need to be in a position of control because of the unpredictability of developments in Czechoslovakia after the upcoming Party congress. They probably also pointed to the need to mitigate the impact of the congress on the USSR, primarily in the Ukraine, and on Soviet dissidents and reformists, as well as on Eastern Europe (where it might have aggravated the unstable conditions in the Polish and East German leaderships and the autonomous tendencies in Rumania). The military intervention could not be delayed any longer; if Czechoslovak reformism was validated at the congress, dealing with it would be much more difficult. This argument was apparently reinforced by logistic considerations of the Soviet armed forces, particularly as expressed by the general supervising the Rear Forces. General Mariakhin seems to have argued that a military buildup around Czechoslovakia could not be maintained indefinitely.

In assessing in advance the costs of the invasion it was not difficult for the advocates of intervention to argue after the Čierna-Bratislava negotiations that the Czechoslovak invasion would be a low-risk operation. The unwillingness of Dubček's leadership to fight and the clear signals of U.S. noninvolvement strengthened their case and appreciably increased the probability of success.

Increasingly, Soviet decisionmakers came to share ideas, propagated by certain bureaucracies, which disposed them toward intervention. The view that the Soviet Union should prevent the "spread of anti-Communism" and "the unnecessary shedding of the blood of Czechoslovak Communists," together with the image of Czechoslovakia as a "second Yugoslavia," apparently struck a chord among uncommitted senior decisionmakers.

Feelings of betrayal by Dubček and the sense that the Čierna-Bratislava agreement and its Czechoslovak interpretation and implementation were an insult to the pride of the Soviet Union were probably not absent in the calculations. The one-sided characterization given in Czechoslovakia, in the countries of Eastern Europe (particularly Rumania and Albania), and in the West—of the Čierna-Bratislava agreement as a "Czechoslovak triumph" and a "Soviet defeat"—may have touched Soviet decisionmakers in a sensitive spot, moving them in the direction of intervention. Change in the bureaucratic mood in the Central Committee and a substantial shift in perceptions of the negative payoffs of the policy of nonintervention may also have affected the calculations of the hesitant decisionmakers. In the post-Bratislava period, Secretary General Brezhnev, in particular, apparently decided to join the interventionist coalition in the face of signals and pressures from several powerful Soviet bureaucracies which threatened to undermine his position of *primus inter pares* in the Politburo. This might explain how some of the other players joined the coalition that argued in favor of intervention in mid-August, and the consequent reluctant decision to use military force.

One of the salient conclusions of the study is that Soviet perceptions of the risks involved in using military force had a major influence on decisionmaking. Although some analysts believe that Dubček's preparations in the early stages of the crisis (mobilization of the Czechoslovak armed forces and civilians) might have triggered an earlier invasion, I think it more likely that a firm posture accompanied by credible demonstrations of the Czechoslovak will to resist, consistently pursued—as in the case of Yugoslavia in 1948–49, Poland in 1956, Albania in 1961, and Rumania in the mid 1960s—could have considerably increased the political risks of invasion and even altered the debate in the Kremlin. The Soviet Politburo would then have had to choose between limited war against a "socialist ally," with the danger of a possible spillover into West Germany and Austria and confrontation with NATO forces, and nonintervention, with the problem of East European and domestic containment. Not to be overlooked in the USSR's calculations of risks involved in the use of military force is its perception of the possible U.S. response. The case of Czechoslovakia, as well as others (the Korean War of 1950, the Hungarian uprising of 1956, the Cuban missile crisis of 1962, and the 1975 civil war in Angola, for example), suggests that U.S. policymakers should be aware that their sometimes unconscious signals are factors in policy debates in the USSR. The U.S. hands-off policy and its well-advertised noninvolvement, accompanied by the belief on the part of President Johnson's advisers that there would be no invasion, apparently helped the interventionist school of thought to prevail in the Soviet debate on the Czechoslovak issue. Had the signals about Czechoslovak nonresistance and the U.S. hands-off policy been lacking, and had the reformists appeared to be in firm control, the invasion might not have come to pass.

On balance, the findings of this study support the earlier conclusions of other writers who argue that the rational-policy approach alone is inadequate to explain Soviet foreign policy decisionmaking. True, the Soviet system, with its different Leninist political culture and rules of the game, limits the diffusion of power in the bureaucracies, thereby generating a circumscribed style of bureaucratic politics which affects Soviet foreign policy.

Despite these limits, however, Soviet decisions are also influenced by the exigencies of bureaucratic affiliation and by the ability of some players to outmaneuver rivals, and not solely by the merits of the situation or the arguments put forward by individual decisionmakers. Although conflict and debates over policy issues have been more difficult to detect in the post-Khrushchev era, they do, nevertheless, exist, and the Czechoslovak case provides a telling example of this. That the skeptics of intervention lost on this particular policy issue but yet did not also lose their jobs in the aftermath suggests that policy cleavages in Brezhnev's leadership may not necessarily be viewed as dysfunctional; they may rather be viewed as unavoidable occurrences in the consensus-oriented decisionmaking processes.

The prediction of Soviet actions is a venturesome exercise, and this study does not make the Soviet decisionmaking process much less mysterious. Neither does it intend to foster the impression that greater focus on bureaucratic politics during the crisis could necessarily have enabled analysts to foresee the Soviet invasion. First of all, the Soviet Politburo's decision to invade was made at the last minute and then reluctantly. Perhaps only the presence of an agent inside the Politburo could have made possible an exact prediction. Second, it might be argued that by using the very data that I have had at my disposal, and by applying the bureaucratic-politics paradigm to the Soviet debate, analysts could have concluded that some other outcome than military intervention was possible. I think it likelier, however, that consideration of the bureaucratic politics involved in Soviet decisionmaking would have led the analysts, if not to anticipate the invasion, at least not to discount it as a possible outcome of the debate. To say the least, more sensitivity to the bureaucratic-politics factor might have improved the analysts' chances of detecting the signals of serious controversy in the Politburo. As with the Japanese attack on Pearl Harbor in 1941, the German attack on the USSR in the same year, and the Yom Kippur War of 1973, the Czechoslovak case illustrates flaws in intelligence gathering, as well as a tendency not to read, or in any event to misread, the available signals.

As it happened, the brave but indecisive Alexander Dubček, at times naïve and in foreign affairs inexperienced, chose to believe that his reform Communist ideology and his good intentions and personality could "convince" the Soviet Politburo to abstain from the use of military force in Czechoslovakia. It seems that he was aware of the differences in opinion among Soviet leaders as to the means of resolving the Czechoslovak crisis.[1] Nevertheless, he did not try to exploit these differences to Czechoslovak advantage. His failure to take seriously the Soviet option of military intervention and the subsequent need for a Czechoslovak defense strategy was clearly signaled by the dismissal of General Prchlík. This move, designed to diffuse the crisis, and Dubček's inability to control his internal enemies, actually strengthened the cause of the interventionists in Moscow.[2] Dubček did not understand that the Soviet Politburo was much more likely to intervene if the advocates of such action could demonstrate that the USSR would encounter little or no military resistance from Czechoslovakia. He and most of the other reformist leaders and their advisers failed to anticipate the invasion as one of the options of the Soviet Politburo. His advisers had not seriously researched Soviet politics, nor did they take seriously the signs of debate and the changing "bureaucratic mood" in the Politburo. Thus, for their part, they failed to understand the significance of the internal dynamics of the Soviet Politburo and the signals among its members. This deficiency proved fatal.

It is my hope that the present study will facilitate comparative analyses leading to a better understanding, and thus to more accurate explanations, of Soviet behavior. The continuing search for a paradigm designed to provide insights into the complexities of Soviet bureaucracies is of great value in elucidating Soviet national security and foreign policymaking.[3] It can perhaps be helpful in predicting Soviet behavior and in averting disasters like the one experienced by the Czechoslovak leadership in 1968. The need for this capability will be particularly acute during the 1980's, as suggested by the Soviet invasion of Afghanistan.

Reassessing the Costs of Intervention

Substantial benefits, primarily the stabilization of Eastern Europe, accrued to the USSR as a consequence of the intervention in Czechoslovakia. Yet the costs have been much greater, it would seem, than a superficial judgment might suggest.

The invasion affected adversely the Soviet posture in world politics. The immediate consequences for Soviet relations with the West were rather unpleasant. The invasion was a temporary setback for the Non-Proliferation Treaty, providing arguments for opponents of the treaty in the U.S. Senate and delaying its approval in several other countries, including West Germany and Japan. More important, it prevented an early beginning of SALT negotiations between the superpowers. President Johnson refused to go to Leningrad in September 1968 to launch strategic arms limitation talks with Soviet Premier Kosygin, and President Nixon hesitated for some time before signaling the start of SALT. Hence, the talks were delayed until the late fall of 1969 (and then entered into at a lower level than the chiefs of governments), more than a year after they might have begun. It may well be true, as former Secretary of State Rusk suggested to me, that the momentum in limiting strategic weapons was lost.[4] The delay, in effect, abetted both superpowers in the enormously expensive program of testing and developing MIRV technology. (Almost simultaneously with cancellation of the Kosygin-Johnson summit, the tests for perfecting MIRVs began).

Moreover, the invasion of Czechoslovakia had unfavorable effects upon Soviet policies vis-à-vis Western Europe and Japan. By creating an impression of Soviet unpredictability, it enhanced, at least temporarily, the authority of NATO and its disposition in Europe and the Mediterranean. Czechoslovakia produced, in 1968, an element of cohesion and reinvigoration in the NATO alliance. It also contributed to a temporary reversal or delay of the trend in several West European countries, as well as in the United States (under the advocacy of Senator Mike Mansfield) and Canada, toward a reduction of forces in Western Europe. The intervention also, at least temporarily, mobilized sentiment against the proposed European Security Conference (ESC) and jeopardized the Soviet leadership's hope that the ESC might be convened in Helsinki in the first half of 1970. Equally, it was a temporary blow to Soviet *Westpolitik* in general, and rapprochement with West Germany in particular. Efforts toward cooperation with the West German Social Democrats, led by Willy Brandt, had to be put off for at least another year.

Although the invasion called into question *Westpolitik* and its significance for East-West relations, the overall effect was not so traumatic as originally feared. But it slightly altered the military balance in Europe, adding some four or five Soviet divisions to Warsaw Pact forces and encouraging some Western countries to increase their military budgets. It also drove some increasingly independent West European countries back closer to the United States. De Gaulle's vision of a grouping of European states led by France, which would provide a counterbalance to both superpowers, was put in jeopardy.

Similarly, in Japan, the intervention had adverse consequences for the opponents of extending the U.S.–Japanese Security Pact, which was to expire in 1970. The invasion also had negative effects on Soviet relations with most developing countries in the Third World, which (with the exception of a few Arab countries) unanimously condemned it. Even Egypt, at that time the recipient of Soviet military and economic aid, was ambivalent in its attitude.

Overall, the Soviet intervention did not significantly alter the general pattern of East-West relationships. The Soviet leadership succeeded in keeping the total political costs of the intervention relatively low, certainly lower than expected. This happened partly because of Czechoslovakia's failure to actively resist Soviet forces and partly because of the Soviet use of maximum force and minimum violence in implementing the decision to invade.

The West correctly interpreted the intervention as a purely defensive move, aimed at preserving political stability in the Soviet Union and Eastern Europe. The intervention did not reverse détente, but only contributed to an alteration of its character. Instead of change through rapprochement, détente became rapprochement without change—at least during the terms of President Nixon and President Gerald Ford, from 1969 to 1976. Eventually, East-West negotiations resumed as if the intervention had never taken place. The Soviet posture of deterrence was strengthened and its policy of *Westpolitik* made more credible. In 1971 the Soviet leadership successfully concluded a Soviet–West German treaty, in 1972 the SALT I Agreement. Finally, in 1975, it scored with the convening of the European Security Conference.

The invasion had its most profound effect, not on East-West relations, but on the Communist movement as a whole. It caused, as the Soviet liberal-minded Marxist historian Roy Medvedev pointed out, "an extremely serious crisis in the international communist movement."[5] The postinvasion climate brought about an increasing willingness on the part of many Communist parties to challenge Soviet authority. The immediate casualties included the long-awaited Third World Communist Conference, which had been scheduled for November 25, 1968. Even though the conference was finally convened in June 1969, the Czechoslovak issue remained a serious obstacle to consolidation of Soviet supremacy in the international Communist movement.[5]

In Eastern Europe the intervention led to a temporary worsening of Soviet relations with Rumania and Yugoslavia, while providing one of the reasons for the formal withdrawal of Albania from the Warsaw Pact. After the invasion, the Rumanian and Yugoslav governments developed concepts of total national defense whereby newly created Patriotic Guards in Rumania and a perfected "territorial defense force" in Yugoslavia would fight alongside regular army units in a defense in depth, repelling any invaders.

On balance, the invasion demonstrated to the ruling parties the narrow limits of autonomy set by the Soviet leadership. Stability in Eastern Europe was actually increased by the Soviet invasion, since it served as a warning against repetition of the Prague Spring. But this will probably not be a lasting stability. The invasion did not signal an end to liberalist trends in Eastern Europe. Thus, the Kádár regime in Hungary has managed to maintain some of its domestic flexibility.

In some Communist parties in Western Europe and in Japan, the invasion has encouraged a trend toward "socialism with a human face" that embodies even greater departures from the Soviet model than the architects of the Prague Spring had contemplated. For several important parties (Italian, Spanish, and French), the invasion, which Ernst Fischer christened a manifestation of *Panzerkommunismus,* served both as a warning about the Soviet version of "proletarian internationalism" and as an inspiration, if not a model, for the road toward pluralistic socialism. As the Spanish Communist leader Santiago Carrillo pointed out, "The Soviet invasion of Czechoslovakia in 1968 was the last straw." With it, "any idea of internationalism ended for us."[6] Indeed, the Czechoslovak experiment seems to be continuing in several Communist parties of Europe. In the words of Carrillo, "If the term 'Eurocommunism' had been invented in 1968, Dubček would have been a Eurocommunist."[7] As the leader of the Italian Communist Party, Enrico Berlinguer, implied in 1976, membership in NATO may offer West European Communist parties the security necessary to develop a brand of Communism that the USSR and its East European allies strangled in Czechoslovakia.[8]

The invasion contributed to a deepening of the split with the PRC, as the Chinese leadership exploited the crisis to condemn the Soviet Union. Chinese leaders appear to have believed, correctly or incorrectly, that the intervention was the manifestation of a new Brezhnev doctrine of "limited sovereignty" seeking to justify Soviet intervention in any socialist country, including China. The intervention convinced the Chinese of the imperialist intentions of the USSR and served as a catalyst in Chinese domestic and foreign policies. The Soviet-Chinese border incidents of 1969 confirmed these convictions. The Chinese leadership reacted to the intervention by curbing the Cultural Revolution, reinforcing the Sino-Soviet borders, and establishing better relations with the United States as a counterbalance to the perceived Soviet threat.

Finally, and perhaps most importantly, the intervention was costly to future Soviet relations with Czechoslovakia—the only country in Eastern Europe other than Bulgaria without a long-standing anti-Russian tradition. As Charter 77 demonstrates, as late as 1977 Czechoslovakia still showed very few signs of accepting "normalization."[9] As seen in retrospect, then, the intervention was probably only a temporary solution.

There are grounds for believing that some Soviet decisionmakers were aware of the high costs of the invasion to the USSR, not only in terms of its relationship with Czechoslovakia but also as regards its interests in the international Communist movement. Former West German Chancellor Willy Brandt "had gained the impression that the Soviet leaders were not altogether happy about the intervention in Czechoslovakia." According to him, ". . . the Soviet Politburo's drastic step was resisted to the last. The voting was probably six to five. It later seemed that Brezhnev, who may well have cast the deciding vote, was unhappy about the decision of August 1968."[10] It is also interesting to note that Brezhnev's predecessor, N. S. Khrushchev, strongly disapproved of the Soviet invasion of Czechoslovakia. As Roy Medvedev reported, Khrushchev confided to his intimates that "somehow it could have been done differently" and that the invasion was a "big mistake."[11]

Evidence suggests that doubts in the Soviet leadership about military intervention as the only solution to the crisis may well have persisted into the 1970s. When Shelest was dismissed from the Politburo in 1973 because of "nationalist errors" and his objections to Nixon's trip to the USSR, he was also charged with having presented an inaccurate account of developments in Czechoslovakia in 1968. During this same period (1972–73) some former Czechoslovak leaders were said to have been contacted by Soviet officials in alleged efforts to reexamine the Czechoslovak crisis.[12] These doubts notwithstanding, it is unlikely that Soviet reappraisals will lead to an official revision of the resolution of the Czechoslovak crisis, or that former Czechoslovak reformist leaders will experience a political resurrection after the succession of Brezhnev (a hope reportedly cherished by Dubček himself).[13]

One can only speculate as to what the Soviet leaders might have learned from the Czechoslovak crisis and its resolution and as to how they might respond to similar challenges in the future. Although the Soviet leadership has strongly indicated that it would continue to resist trends toward "liberal reformism" in Eastern Europe, it does not follow that future Soviet responses to such challenges as the Czechoslovak crisis will necessarily be military ones. The Soviet determination not to permit adaptation of reformist, pluralistic Communism is one lesson of the Czechoslovak crisis. Another is that Soviet responses to such developments are neither automatic nor foreclosed. Faced in Eastern Europe with a situation similar to that in Czechoslovakia in 1968, the Soviet leadership might again respond heavy-handedly after weighing the pros and cons of military intervention. The final Soviet response would be determined by many factors, among the most salient of which might be the ability or inability of future reformers to draw appropriate lessons from the mistakes of Alexander Dubček and his supporters in the Czechoslovak leadership of 1968.

Notes

Preface

To keep the notes manageable, I have adopted the practice of giving most foreign-language titles in their English translation and the complete title only when first citing a work, using an abbreviated but clear form in subsequent citations. (More extensive notes to the material here are available in my doctoral thesis, "Soviet Foreign Policy Decisionmaking and Bureaucratic Politics: Czechoslovak Crisis, 1968." School of Advanced International Studies, Johns Hopkins University, 1975.)

1. For the most sophisticated discussion of such a conceptual framework for the study of Soviet foreign policy decisionmaking, see Vernon V. Aspaturian's "Internal Politics and Foreign Policy in the Soviet System," in *Approaches to Comparative and International Politics*, ed. R. Barry Farrell (Evanston, Ill.: Northwestern University Press, 1966), pp. 491–551; and Alexander Dallin, "Soviet Foreign Policy and Domestic Politics: A Framework for Analysis," *Journal of International Affairs*, no. 23 (1969), pp. 250–65. For the most innovative approach to the study of Soviet foreign policymaking see Jan F. Triska and David D. Finley, *Soviet Foreign Policy* (New York: Macmillan, 1968).

The literature on studies of Soviet foreign policy decisionmaking is rather small in scope and somewhat fragmentary. Perhaps the best case study employing the conflict model approach to Soviet foreign policy decisionmaking is Herbert S. Dinerstein, *The Making of a Missile Crisis, October 1962* (Baltimore: Johns Hopkins University Press, 1976). For other interesting case studies of this sort see Jon D. Glassman, "Soviet Foreign Policy Decision-making," in *Columbia Essays in International Affairs: The Dean's Papers,* vol. 3 (New York: Columbia University Press, 1967), pp. 373–402; Uri Ra'anan, *The USSR Arms the Third World: Case Studies in Soviet Foreign Policy* (Cambridge, Mass.: MIT Press, 1969); Robert M. Slusser, *The Berlin Crisis of 1961* (Baltimore: Johns Hopkins University Press, 1973); and Thomas W. Wolfe, "Soviet Interests in SALT," in *SALT: Implications for Arms Control in the 1970s,* ed. William Kinter and Robert Pfaltzgraff (Pittsburgh: Pittsburgh University Press, 1973).

For studies utilizing the conflict school approach in Soviet decisionmaking, mainly in domestic affairs, but also relating to Soviet foreign policy, see Robert Conquest, *Power and Policy in the USSR* (New York: St. Martin's Press, 1961); Carl Linden, *Khrushchev and the Soviet Leadership, 1957–1964* (Baltimore: Johns Hopkins University Press, 1966); and Michel Tatu, *Power in the Kremlin: From Khrushchev to Kosygin* (New York: Viking, 1969).

For studies focusing mainly on Soviet decisionmaking in domestic affairs see Roger Pethybridge, *A Key to Soviet Politics: The Crisis of the Anti-Party Group* (New York: Praeger, 1962); and Sidney Ploss, *Conflict and Decision-Making in the Soviet Union: A Case Study of Agricultural Policy, 1953–1963* (Princeton: Princeton University Press, 1965).

For studies weighing the importance of subgroups and groups in the Soviet political process, see Roman Kolkowicz, *The Soviet Military and the Communist Party* (Princeton: Princeton University Press, 1967); and H. Gordon Skilling and Franklyn Griffiths, eds., *Interest Groups in Soviet Politics* (Princeton: Princeton University Press, 1971).

For a much more extensive critical overview of studies on Soviet decisionmaking see Arnold L. Horelick, A. Ross Johnson, and John D. Steinbruner, *The Study of Soviet Foreign Policy: A Review of Decision-Theory-Related Approaches* (Santa Monica, Calif.: The Rand Corporation, 1973), R–1334.

Chapter 1

1. General James H. Polk, "Reflections on the Czechoslovakian Invasion, 1968," *Strategic Review* 5 (1977): 33. A clear exception was V. Zorza of the *Washington Post*.
2. Memorandum quoted in Charles E. Bohlen, *Witness to History, 1929–1969* (New York: Norton, 1973), pp. 530–31.
3. See the House Select Committee on Intelligence Report (also known as the Pike Committee Report), printed in the *Village Voice*, February 16, 1976, p. 77.
4. Graham T. Allison, *Essence of Decision: Explaining the Cuban Missile Crisis* (Boston: Little, Brown, 1971).
5. Hans Morgenthau, "Inquisition in Czechoslovakia," *New York Review of Books,* December 4, 1969, pp. 20–21.
6. Herman Kahn, "How to Think about the Russians," *Fortune* 78, no. 6 (November 1968); p. 127.
7. The document usually referred to as the locus of the Brezhnev doctrine is an article by S. Kovalev, "Sovereignty and Internationalist Obligations of Socialist Countries," published in *Pravda* on September 26, 1968. For a discussion of the Brezhnev doctrine, see Boris Meissner, *The Brezhnev Doctrine,* East Europe Monograph 2 (Kansas City: Park College Governmental Research Bureau, 1970).
8. On the question of divergent viewpoints within the Soviet Politburo toward Czechoslovakia, see Fritz Ermarth, *Internationalism, Security, and Legitimacy: The Challenge to Soviet Interests in East Europe, 1964–1968* (Santa Monica, Calif.: The Rand Corporation, March 1969), RM–5909–PR, pp. 84–117; Philip Windsor and Adam Roberts, *Czechoslovakia, 1968* (New York: Columbia University Press, 1969), pp. 62–79; Anatole Shub, *The New Russian Tragedy* (New York: Norton, 1969), pp. 95–110; David W. Paul, "Soviet Foreign Policy and the Invasion of Czechoslovakia," *International Studies Quarterly* 15, no. 2 (June 1971); 159–202.
9. For a discussion of the bureaucratic-politics model, see Graham T. Allison and Morton H. Halperin, "Bureaucratic Politics: A Paradigm and Some Policy Implications," in *Theory and Policy in International Relations,* ed. Richard Ullman and Raymond Tanter (Princeton: Princeton University Press, 1972), pp. 40–79; Allison, *Essence of Decision;* Morton H. Halperin et al., *Bureaucratic Politics and Foreign Policy* (Washington, D.C.: Brookings Institution, 1974). For a critique of the bureaucratic-politics approach, see Stephen D. Krasner, "Are Bureaucracies Important? (or Allison Wonderland)," *Foreign Policy,* no. 7 (Summer 1972), pp. 159–79.
10. On the shared images of national security interests held by American leaders, see Halperin, *Bureaucratic Politics and Foreign Policy,* pp. 11–12.
11. On the problems of Soviet foreign policy decisionmaking, see Vernon V. Aspaturian, "Soviet Foreign Policy," in *Foreign Policy in World Politics,* ed. Roy C. Macridis (Englewood Cliffs, N.J.: Prentice-Hall, 1962), and Triska and Finley, *Soviet Foreign Policy.*
12. For an examination of institutions involved in Soviet foreign policy decisionmaking, see Vladimir Petrov, "Soviet Foreign Policy-Making," *ORBIS* 17, no. 3 (Fall 1973): 819–50.
13. For a discussion, see Roman Kolkowicz, "The Military," in *Interest Groups in Soviet Politics,* ed. H. Gordon Skilling and Franklyn Griffiths (Princeton: Princeton University Press, 1971), pp. 160–64. For further discussion of the military elite and various subgroups in the Soviet decisionmaking process, see Kolkowicz, "Strategic Elites and Politics of Superpower," *Journal of International Affairs* 26, no. 1 (1972); 40–59; M. Mackintosh, "The Soviet Military Influence on Foreign Policy," *Problems of Communism* 22 (September–October 1973): 1–12. Also see the discussion of William E. Odom, "The Party Connection," ibid., pp. 12–26.
14. Andrew W. Marshall, "Bureaucratic Behavior and the Strategic Arms Competition," Southern California Arms Control and Foreign Policy Seminar, Research Paper 5, Santa Monica, Calif., October 1971; and Marshall, *Problems of Estimating Military Power* (Santa Monica, Calif.: The Rand Corporation, August 1966), P–3417. Heather Campbell's study of the debate over the Soviet Air Force's building new airships concludes that it was affected mainly by organizational competition. See Campbell, *Controversy in Soviet R&D: The Airship Case Study* (Santa Monica, Calif.: The Rand Corporation, October 1972), R–1001–PR. For a

more skeptical treatment of organizational effects on Soviet military decisionmaking, see Matthew P. Gallagher and Karl F. Spielmann, *Soviet Decision-Making for Defense: A Critique of U.S. Perspectives on the Arms Race* (New York: Praeger, 1972).

15. Frederick C. Barghoorn, "The Security Police," in Skilling and Griffiths, *Interest Groups in Soviet Politics,* pp. 93–129. Also see Rowland Evans and Robert Novak, "The KGB Resistance to Soviet Détente," *Washington Post,* January 10, 1974; Michel Tatu, *Power in the Kremlin: From Khrushchev to Kosygin* (New York: Viking, 1969), p. 390.

16. Dimitri Simes and Gordon Rocca, "Soviet Decision Making and National Security Affairs," Georgetown University Center for Strategic and International Studies, Memorandum 20–KM–11–1, Washington, D.C., November 1973, pp. 25–26; Petrov, "Soviet Foreign Policy-Making," p. 826.

17. Robert Jervis, *Perception and Misperception in International Politics* (Princeton: Princeton University Press, 1976).

18. On this point, see Alexander Dallin, "Soviet Foreign Policy and Domestic Politics: A Framework for Analysis," *Journal of International Affairs* 23, no. 2 (1969): 259.

19. Milton Lodge, *The Soviet Elite: Attitudes since Stalin* (Columbus, Ohio: Merrill, 1969); Skilling and Griffiths, *Interest Groups in Soviet Politics;* Philip D. Steward, "Soviet Interest Groups and the Policy Process," *World Politics* 22 (October 1969): 29–50; Joel Schwartz and William Keech, "Group Influence and the Policy Process in the Soviet Union," *American Political Science Review* 62 (September 1968): 840–51; David E. Langsam and David W. Paul, "Soviet Politics and the Group Approach: A Conceptual Note," *Slavic Review* 31 (March 1972): 136–41.

20. For example, in the Soviet decisionmaking process on SALT 1, only broad institutional groups like those relating to foreign affairs, the scientific intelligentsia, the military, and segments of the R&D and industrial establishments exercised any leverage. See Thomas W. Wolfe, "Soviet Interests in SALT," in *SALT: Implications for Arms Control in the 1970s,* ed. William R. Kintner and Robert L. Pfaltzgraff (Pittsburgh: Pittsburgh University Press, 1973), pp. 28–38.

21. *Pravda,* May 16, 1953. This notion of collective leadership was expressed several weeks after Stalin's death; it was reprinted in the 1970s in *Kommunist* ("The Effective Forces of Leninist Principles of Party Leadership," *Kommunist,* no. 16 [1974], 3–15). The rationale of collectivity was presented by P. A. Rodionov in his book *Kollektivnost: Vysshii printsip partiinogo rukovodstva* [Collectivity: the highest principle of party leadership] (Moscow: Izdatel'stvo Politicheskoi Literatury, 1967).

22. See Roy A. Medvedev and Zhores A. Medvedev, *Khrushchev: The Years in Power* (New York: Columbia University Press, 1976), p. 175; and Jerome M. Gilison, "The New Factors of Stability in the Soviet Collective Leadership," *World Politics* 19 (July 1967): 580. For a more skeptical view of the stability and durability of collective leaderships, see Leonard Schapiro, "Collective Lack of Leadership," *Survey* 70–71 (Winter/Spring 1969): 193–200; and Robert G. Wesson, "The USSR: Oligarchy or Dictatorship?" *Slavic Review,* June 1972, pp. 314–22. See also Myron Rush, *Political Succession in the USSR* (New York: Columbia University Press, 1965), p. 204.

23. Mohamed Heikal, *The Road to Ramadan* (New York: Ballantine, 1975), p. 94.

24. See Tatu, *Power in the Kremlin,* p. 272. A new study by Herbert S. Dinerstein indicates that the predecision dialogue, which was reflected in the Soviet press, existed even among this restricted group. See Dinerstein, *The Making of a Missile Crisis,* pp. 184–229.

25. Thomas W. Wolfe, *The SALT Experience: Its Impact on U.S. and Soviet Strategic Policy and Decisionmaking* (Santa Monica, Calif.: The Rand Corporation, September 1974), R–1686–PR.

26. For a discussion of the Czechoslovak revolution of 1968 in relation to Czech and Slovak traditions, see Josef Korbel, *Twentieth-Century Czechoslovakia* (New York: Columbia University Press, 1977).

27. Lack of space precludes a detailed analysis. For an in-depth treatment of the origins of the Prague Spring, see H. Gordon Skilling, *Czechoslovakia's Interrupted Revolution* (Princeton: Princeton University Press, 1976); Galia Golan, *The Czechoslovak Reform Movement: Communism in Crisis, 1962–1968* (Cambridge: Cambridge University Press, 1971); Golan, *Reform Rule in Czechoslovakia: The Dubček Era, 1968–1969* (Cambridge: Cambridge

University Press, 1973); Pavel Tigrid, *Kvadratura Kruhu* (Paris: Svědectví, 1970); and Vladimír V. Kusín, *The Czechoslovak Reform Movement, 1968* (London: International Research Documents, 1973).

28. The foreign policy part was hastily added to the Action Program at the last minute (interview with Antonín Šnejdárek, former Director of the Institute of International Politics and Economics [UMPE] during the Dubček era, Paris, June 6, 1974).

29. Thus, the unexplained movements of Warsaw Pact troops in March, May, and July were unusually well publicized.

30. *New York Times,* April 30, 1968; *Financial Times,* April 30, 1968.

31. Deputy Minister of Light Industry P. I. Maksimov was reported to have said at a working session of CMEA in February, "I cannot imagine Soviet soldiers ever having to shoot at Czech soldiers" (interview with Mrs. Larisa Silnický, a former interpreter for the Czechoslovak government, Tel Aviv, September 24, 1973; see also her "Recollections of Bratislava," *Radio Liberty Dispatch* RL–195/74, July 2, 1974), p. 2.

32. Brezhnev revealed this to the Czechoslovak leaders during the postinvasion negotiations in Moscow on August 26, 1968. See the account of one of those present, Zdeněk Mlynář: *Nachtfrost: Erfahrungen auf dem Weg vom realen zum menschlichen Sozialismus* (Cologne: Europäische Verlagsanstalt, 1978), pp. 205–6. Mlynář was a secretary of the Central Committee of the Czechoslovak Party. He now lives in exile in Vienna.

33. Polk, "Reflections on the Czechoslovakian Invasion," pp. 31–32.

34. The differing perceptions of Soviet officials regarding the Czechoslovak crisis can be deciphered by content analysis of their speeches and public statements. In general, some officials consistently attacked the "nationalist" and "right-wing revisionist" elements, "various demagogues and renegades," and "degenerates," and their "models of democratic socialism" and policies of "limitless decentralism." They called for "revolutionary vigilance" in the USSR, and some of them began to hint at offers of "fraternal assistance" to the "healthy forces" in Czechoslovakia in their struggle "against imperialist intrigues."

Meanwhile, other officials consistently refrained from cryptic assaults on the Czechoslovak leadership, pledging respect for "each other's views," the "right of autonomy" and "noninterference in the internal affairs" of other Communist parties. Some of them occasionally expressed publicly their "confidence in the Czechoslovak Party." During the crisis this group, instead of attacking the "right-wing revisionists," consistently assaulted the "left revisionism" or "left adventurist perversion of Marxism" in the Chinese leadership as the main danger to the USSR. (The former group of officials, on the other hand, probably because of their preoccupation with the Czechoslovak issue—or because they saw the influence of Czechoslovakia as being the main source of danger to the USSR—did not express any concern regarding the policies of the Chinese leadership.)

Hereafter, in keeping with the purpose of this book, the public speeches and pronouncements of Soviet leaders will be referred to without going into lengthy analyses. For a comprehensive and detailed analysis of the differences in perceptions and policies of Soviet leaders on the Czechoslovak issue, see my previous work "Soviet Decisionmaking and the 1968 Czechoslovak Crisis," *Studies in Comparative Communism* 8, No. 1 & 2 (Spring–Summer 1975): 147–73; and my doctoral dissertation, "Soviet Foreign Policy Decisionmaking and Bureaucratic Politics: Czechoslovak Crisis, 1968." The speeches of Soviet leaders should be interpreted cautiously, but as we shall see in later chapters, the actions and pronouncements of several of these leaders during the negotiations with Dubček's leadership will confirm my interpretations of their divergent views on the Czechoslovak issue.

35. For Shelest's views related to the Czechoslovak crisis, see his speeches in *Pravda Ukrainy,* February 17 and July 5, 1968, and his article "Faithful Attachment of the CPSU" in *Voprosy istorii KPSS,* no. 7 (June 28, 1968), pp. 7–20 (also reprinted in *Kommunist Ukrainy,* no. 7 [July 1968], pp. 3–17). See also an analysis by Grey Hodnett and Peter J. Potichnyj, *The Ukraine and the Czechoslovak Crisis* (Canberra: Australian National University, 1970). For Masherov's views, see *Sovetskaia Belorussiia,* May 11, 1968. As shown below, in chapter 2, Shelest's and Maserov's views were shared by other high officials from such Soviet non-Russian republics as Latvia and Lithuania.

36. For Pelshe's views, see *Neues Deutschland,* May 4, 1968, and *Tribuna* (Prague),

March 26, 1969. Trapeznikov's militant view on the Czechoslovak issue is developed in his book *At the Turning Points of History* (Moscow: Progress Publishers, 1972), pp. 73–78. For Demichev's view see *Pravda,* June 20, 1968 and *Kommunist,* no. 10 (July 1978), pp. 14–35. For Grishin's, see *Pravda,* April 23, 1968. For Gribachev's, see *Komsomolskaia pravda,* July 25, 1968.

37. For the KGB position on Czechoslovak reformism see the memoirs of two former high officials of the Czechoslovak intelligence service: Ladislav Bittman, *The Deception Game: Czechoslovak Intelligence in Soviet Political Warfare* (Syracuse, N.Y.: Syracuse University Research Corporation, 1972), pp. 167–215; and Josef Frolik, *The Frolik Defection* (London: Leo Cooper, 1975), pp. 130–78.

38. For Suslov's views, see *Pravda,* February 29 and May 6, 1968. For the importance of the conference, see "On the Eve of the Consultative Meeting in Budapest," *World Marxist Review* (published under the auspices of the International Department) 11, no. 2 (1968), pp. 3–6. For Zagladin's views, see *Pravda,* April 29, 1968, and Radio Moscow, March 21, 1968.

39. *Izvestiia,* July 11–14, 1968; and *Europa-Archiv* 23 (1968): 361–88.

40. Dimitri K. Simes, "The Soviet Invasion of Czechoslovakia and the Limits of Kremlinology," *Studies in Comparative Communism* 8, nos. 1–2 (Spring/Summer 1975): 178. See also hints in "The Political Course of Mao Tse-tung on the International Scene," *Kommunist,* no. 8 (May 1968), pp. 95–108.

41. For Kosygin's views, see his speeches in *Sovetskaia Belorussiia,* February 15, 1968; *Pravda,* April 3, 1968; and *Izvestiia,* July 2, 1968. See also Dubček's address referring to Kosygin's performance at the Dresden Conference of five Warsaw Pact countries, *Rok šedesátý osmý: V usneseních a dokumentech ÚV KSČ* (Prague: Svoboda, 1969), pp. 86–87. For Kosygin's views on SALT see Lyndon B. Johnson, *The Vantage Point* (New York: Holt, Rinehart & Winston, 1971), pp. 484–485; John Newhouse, *Cold Dawn: The Story of SALT* (New York: Holt, Rinehart & Winston, 1973), pp. 89–94; an interview with Dr. Walt W. Rostow, National Security Adviser to President Johnson, Austin, Texas, July 26, 1974; and an interview with Secretary of State Dean Rusk, Athens, Georgia, July 31, 1974.

42. Simes, "The Soviet Invasion of Czechoslovakia," p. 178. See also A. Grigorysants and V. Rogov, "Leninist Ideas Are Invincible: The Policy of Anticommunism Meets with Failure—Richard Nixon Again," *Trud,* August 13, 1968.

43. Stephen F. Cohen, *Bukharin and the Bolshevik Revolution: A Political Biography 1888–1938* (New York: Knopf, 1974), p. 214.

44. Cohen, *Bukharin and the Bolshevik Revolution;* Robert C. Tucker, *Stalin as Revolutionary* (New York: Norton, 1973).

45. Max Jakobson, *The Diplomacy of the Winter War: An Account of the Russo-Finnish War, 1939–1940* (Cambridge, Mass.: Harvard University Press, 1961), pp. 144–49.

46. See Seweryn Bialer's narrative in Wolfgang Leonhard, *The Kremlin since Stalin* (New York: Praeger, 1962), pp. 103, 106–7.

47. Bohlen's impression after discussing the issue was that Zhukov urged "military action in Poland, but was overruled." Bohlen, *Witness to History,* p. 409.

48. Khrushchev admitted that some Soviet leaders wondered if "the Hungarian comrades were going to interpret correctly the fact of our coming to their aid." See M. Molnar, *Budapest, 1956* (London: George Allen Unwin, 1971), p. 289. See also Bohlen, *Witness to History,* p. 417.

49. Leonhard, *The Kremlin since Stalin,* p. 241.

50. See Robert C. Tucker, "The Anti-Party Group," *Problems of Communism* 12, no. 4 (July–August 1963): 43.

51. Leonhard, *The Kremlin since Stalin,* p. 241.

52. For an analysis, see Zbigniew Brzezinski and Samuel P. Huntington, *Political Power: USA/USSR* (New York: Viking, 1965), pp. 250–52; and Medvedev and Medvedev, *Khrushchev,* pp. 75–80.

53. See Tatu, *Power in the Kremlin,* p. 427; and Medvedev and Medvedev, *Khrushchev,* pp. 171–79.

54. On the theory of coalition politics, see William H. Riker, *The Theory of Political Coalitions* (New Haven: Yale University Press, 1962). For an important modification of

Riker's theory see Robert Axelrod, *Conflict of Interest: A Theory of Divergent Goals with Applications to Politics* (Chicago: Markham, 1970), pp. 165–85.

55. See such hints as "an extension of the rights of republican and local power" in Shelest's speech, Radio Kiev, July 6, 1968. Shelest was reported at the time to be taking an indulgent line toward Ukrainization in the cultural realm and to be promoting the Ukraine's regional economic interest. See an official criticism of the views expressed in Shelest's book *O Ukraine, Our Soviet Land* in the article "On the Serious Shortcomings and Mistakes of One Book," *Kommunist Ukrainy*, no. 4 (1973), pp. 77–82. The Ukrainian Party leadership was also reported to have pursued a policy in the late 1960s aimed at appeasement of extremist Ukrainian nationalism, including publication of vulgar anti-Semitic books, despite the stand of the central leadership in Moscow. See Boris Smolar, *Soviet Jewry Today and Tomorrow* (New York: Macmillan, 1971), pp. 29–31.

56. Trapeznikov, *At the Turning Points of History*, pp. 77–78.

57. See Andrei D. Sakharov, *Progress, Coexistence, and Intellectual Freedom* (New York: Norton, 1968), p. 57. *Literaturnaia gazeta*—a newspaper under the influence of ideological watchdogs like Markov—mounted a campaign during the Czechoslovak crisis against Soviet writers such as Solzhenitsyn *(Literaturnaia gazeta,* June 26, 1968). Another Soviet newspaper that adopted a strong anti-Czechoslovak line, *Sovetskaia Rossiia,* had also intensified its attacks on the liberal Soviet periodical of Tvardovsky *Novyi mir,* during the crisis. For example, see *Sovetskaia Rossiia,* May 8 and June 15, 1968.

58. Reported by *Politicheskii dnevnik* (Political Diary), no. 43 (April 1968), p. 38.

59. See Academician S. G. Strumilin's critique of Liberman and his "followers" in "Profit," *Komsomol'skaia pravda,* February 16, 1968. After the intervention, the Soviet press sharply criticized not only Šik's views *(Izvestiia,* September 20, 1968) but also Liberman's *(Voprosy ekonomiki* 21, no. 9 [September 1968]: 11–24). See also I. M. Mrackhovskaia, *From Revisionism to Betrayal* (Moscow: Progress, 1972), for a criticism of Ota Šik's economic views.

60. See M. Tatu, *Le Monde,* May 5–6, 1968. See also S. Budín, "Why All the Secrecy?" *Reportér,* May 15–21, 1968.

61. See Iakubovskii's statement in *Pravda,* May 14, 1968, and an analysis in the *Daily Telegraph,* May 3, 1968.

62. *Literární listy,* May 30, 1968. Zhadov stated this to a unit of Czech soldiers.

63. See Claire Sterling, *The Masaryk Case* (New York: Harper & Row, 1969).

64. Deutsche Presse-Agentur, April 4, 1968.

65. Radio Prague, May 3, 1968.

66. "Polsko, Warsava" [Poland, Warsaw], *Student* 4, no. 14 (April 3, 1968). See also Nicholas Bethell, *Gomułka: His Poland, His Communism* (New York: Holt, Rinehart and Winston, 1969), p. 262.

67. *The Reminiscences of Władisław Gomułka,* Radio Liberty Research Paper No. 50, Radio Liberty Committee (New York, 1974), p. 15. It should be noted that the authenticity of portions of Gomułka's memoirs is considered doubtful by some experts. (The original memoirs were said to have been smuggled out of Poland and published in Polish in Israel in *Nowiny-Kurier,* June 1, 1973.)

68. Erwin Weit, *At the Red Summit: Interpreter behind the Iron Curtain* (New York: Macmillan, 1973), p. 205.

69. *Večerní Praha,* April 22, 1968.

70. See A. Dubček's letter to the Federal Assembly of Czechoslovakia and the Slovak National Council of October 28, 1974 (henceforth referred to as Dubček's letter), *Listy* (Rome) 5, no. 3 (April 1975): 14.

71. See Pavel Tigrid, "Czechoslovakia: A Post-Mortem II," *Survey,* Winter–Spring 1970, p. 114. Here I am also indebted to P. Windsor, *Czechoslovakia 1968,* pp. 30–31.

72. See Dubček's letter, *Listy,* p. 14.

73. For reports about a secret SED document, see *Literární listy,* May 30, 1968; and F. Fejtö, "Moscow and Its Allies," *Problems of Communism* 17, no. 6 (November–December 1968: 36. For an attack on Smrkovský, see a speech by the East German ideologist Kurt Hager, *Neues Deutschland,* March 27, 1968.

74. See excerpts from the diary of a Soviet eyewitness, Professor M. Voslensky, a former arms control expert of the Central Committee of the CPSU now living in Munich: "This Will

Only Help the Americans," *Der Spiegel,* no. 34 (August 21, 1978), p. 126 (henceforth referred to as Voslensky's diary).

75. *Pravda,* February 29, 1968; "Communiqué of the Plenary Session of the CPSU Central Committee," *Pravda,* April 11, 1968.

76. See hints in Brezhnev's address, *Pravda,* March 30, 1968.

77. See Simes, "The Soviet Invasion of Czechoslovakia," pp. 177—78.

78. See John Erickson, "Towards a 'New' Soviet High Command: 'Rejuvenation' Reviewed," *Royal United Service Institution Journal* 144, no. 655 (September 1969): 43.

79. For Kádár's support, see a report in *Rudé právo,* April 19, 1968, and Czechoslovak minister of foreign affairs Jiří Hájek's comment on his visit to Budapest, Radio Prague, May 24, 1968.

80. See Zdeněk Mlynář's narrative, *Nachtfrost,* p. 199. Kádár made this remark to Dubček and Mlynář during the negotiations in Bratislava. Also see a report of an interview with Kádár in C. L. Sulzberger, *An Age of Mediocrity: Memoirs and Diaries, 1963—1972* (New York: Macmillan, 1973), p. 477.

81. See *Rudé právo,* May 7 and 8, 1968.

82. See Golan, *The Czechoslovak Reform Movement,* p. 48.

83. Reported by Czechoslovak leader Smrkovský at a public meeting (at which I was present) in Prague, March 20, 1968 and in his posthumous testimony as an interview (henceforth cited as an interview with Smrkovský), *Listy* [Rome] 5, no. 2 [March 1975]: 6).

84. Radio Prague, May 21, 1968. In February Brezhnev made positive reference to Dubček's January visit to Moscow and proclaimed the right of each Communist party to act "completely independently" (Radio Leningrad, February 16, 1968).

85. *Pravda,* March 30, 1968. According to Vasil Bilak, during the May negotiations Brezhnev said that Czechoslovakia would never be allowed to leave the socialist camp, even if the USSR had to pay the price of a third world war. He also suggested that the Soviet Army could share the burden of defending the Czechoslovak western border (interview with Bilak, *Rudé právo,* September 3, 1969).

86. An interview with Smrkovský, *Listy,* pp. 11—12; and Radoslav Selucký, "The Dubček Era Revisited," *Problems of Communism* 24 (January—February 1975): 40.

87. Interview with J. Zedník, deputy chairman of the National Assembly, *Lidová demokracie,* June 17, 1968. Emphasis added.

88. Ibid.

89. Pavel Tigrid, *Why Dubcek Fell* (London: MacDonald, 1971), p. 68. Most of Tigrid's information came from the officials of Dubček's leadership. This information, according to Tigrid, was gathered by Czechoslovak counterintelligence monitoring a conference of Soviet generals.

90. Weit, *At the Red Summit,* pp. 202—3.

91. Intriguingly, in April 1977, in a turnabout, Rusakov replaced Katushev in this job.

92. *Politicheskii dnevnik* (Political Diary), no. 43 (April 1968), p. 38. To my knowledge, only twelve of the seventy-two known issues of *Politicheskii dnevnik* (which was suppressed in the early 1970s) are available outside the USSR. *Politicheskii dnevnik* is believed to be a kind of *samizdat* produced for the first time in 1964 by a group of liberal Marxists, some of whom probably held positions in the Soviet bureaucracies, and edited by Roy Medvedev. For a discussion, see A. Astrachan, "Introduction—Documents: Soviet Union, *Political Diary,*" *Survey* 18, no. 3 (84) (Summer 1972): 210. For items in *Political Diary* concerning Czechoslovakia I consulted the *Arkhiv samizdata (Samizdat Archive)* compiled by the Department of Research of Radio Liberty and deposited in the library at the Center for International Studies at MIT.

93. See *Pravda,* April 10, 17, 1968.

94. *Politicheskii dnevnik,* no. 43 (April 1968), pp. 21—34.

95. *Pravda,* April 23, 1968. Emphasis added. A sarcastic Czech reporter made the comment that a careful reading of Grishin's speech "could induce someone to ask whether Comrade Grishin did not mean us after all" (E. Rosián, *Práca* [Bratislava], April 25, 1968). See also a commentary in *Mladá fronta,* April 25, 1968.

96. "Communiqué of the Plenary Session of the CPSU Central Committee," *Pravda,* April 11, 1968.

97. Kosygin's moderate behavior was reported on Prague television, May 22, 1968, and in

Zemědělské noviny, May 22, 1968, and an interview with a former deputy prime minister of the Czechoslovak government, Ota Šik, St. Gallen, June 5, 1974. Šik met with Kosygin at that time.
98. Tigrid, *Kvadratura kruhu,* p. 43.
99. *Borba* (Belgrade), May 11, 1968; also Radio Prague, May 12, 1968; *Rudé právo,* May 10, 1968; and *Práce,* May 13, 1968.
100. See hints in "The Recommendation of Herr Brandt" (signed "N. R."), *Neues Deutschland,* June 12, 1968.
101. The editors of *Sovetskaia Rossiia* were privately critical of developments in Czechoslovakia as early as 1967, as reported by Radoslav Selucký, who visited the USSR at that time (Selucký, *Východ je východ* [Cologne: Index, 1972], p. 77; Selucký to Valenta, October 23, 1974). During the Prague Spring, Selucký was an adviser to the Central Committee of the Czechoslovak Communist Party and to the Economic Council of the Czechoslovak government.
102. See, e.g., V. Gur, " 'Ethical Socialism' in the Service of Imperialist Reaction," *Kommunist Ukrainy,* no. 2 (February 1968), pp. 68–76; Editorial, ibid., no. 4 (April 1968), pp. 4–12; "The Great Ideas of Marx and Lenin Lighten the Path to Communism," ibid., no. 5 (May 1968), pp. 2–10; *Pravda Ukrainy,* May 24, June 4, 1968; *Radianska Ukraina,* June 6, 1968; *Literaturnaia gazeta,* April 3, May 8, 1968; *Sovetskaia Rossiia,* April 4, May 9, 1968.
103. M. Shiriamov, "Whose Interests Did President Masaryk Defend?" *Sovetskaia Rossiia,* May 14, 1968.
104. *Svobodné slovo,* July 3, 1968 as cited in Ermarth, *Internationalism, Security, and Legitimacy,* p. 78. However, a deputy editor-in-chief of *Sovetskaia Rossiia,* in an interview, reportedly stated that an article was published "because in Czechoslovakia there are people who want to revive the Masaryk type of democracy" (Radio Prague, May 14, 1968).
105. Here, particularly, see D. Volsky's positive comments on the developments in Czechoslovakia in *New Times,* no. 19 (May 14, 1968) and no. 25 (June 26, 1968), and a favorable report on Smrkovský, "People in the News," *New Times,* no. 20 (May 22, 1968). See also *Izvestiia,* March 11, May 6, 1968.
106. See *World Marxist Review* 11; "Action Program of the Communist Party of Czechoslovakia," *ibid.,* no. 5 (May 1968): 43–47; interview with Dubček, no. 6 (June 1968):5–8.
107. See the first article, published in April, "The Roots of the Current Events in China" (editorial), *Kommunist,* no. 6 (April 1968), pp. 102–13. The only indirect assault on Czechoslovak "revisionism" during the entire crisis was a reprint of Secretary Demichev's speech, in *Kommunist,* no. 10 (July 1968), pp. 14–35.
108. Yu. Zhilin, "The Main Trend," *Mirovaia ekonomika i mezhdunarodnye otnosheniia,* no. 4 (1968), p. 7.
109. See reports in *Pravda,* March 14, 27, April 3, 12, 17, and June 8, 1968.
110. *Pravda,* May 7, 1968.
111. *Pravda,* March 28, 1968.
112. For the most hysterical attacks of the East German and Polish press, see *Neues Deutschland,* March 27, May 12, 24, and June 12, 1968; *Berliner Zeitung,* May 9, 11, 15, 1968; *Trybuna Ludu,* May 9, 24, 1968; *Żolnierz Wolności,* May 4, 1968; and *Życie Warszawy,* May 4, 1968. For a more detailed analysis, see Robinson's "Czechoslovakia and Its Allies."
113. Favorable articles were published in the following Hungarian newspapers: *Magyar Nemzet,* June 23, 25, 1968 (FBIS, June 26, 27); *Magyar Hirlap,* May 31, 1968 (FBIS, May 29); and even (until July) the Party newspaper *Népszabadság,* May 9, 19, June 1, 1968 (FBIS, May 16, 21, June 4).
114. For a more detailed analysis, see Skilling, "Conflicting Tendencies in the Party," *Czechoslovakia's Interrupted Revolution,* pp. 493–525. See also the memoirs of the former Czechoslovak leader Zdeněk Mlynář, *Nachtfrost,* pp. 97–184.
115. Skilling, *Czechoslovakia's Interrupted Revolution,* pp. 518–21; Vladimír Horský, *Prag 1968: Systemveränderung und Systemverteidigung* (Stuttgart: Ernst Klett, 1975), pp. 60–71; and an interview with A. Indra, *Svoboda,* October 1, 1969.
116. A poll taken in May 1968 revealed that 87 percent of the secretaries of district and regional committees of the Party and 85 percent of Party members backed the reformist program. See *Rok šedesátý osmý: V usneseních a dokumentech,* p. 170.

117. Interview with Šik, St. Gallen, June 5, 1974.
118. For Kolder's views, see his articles in *Rudé právo,* May 29, 1968 (also reported by *Pravda,* May 30, 1968), and June 21, 1968. For Indra's views, see his alarmist speech, *Radio Prague,* May 9, 1968, and also a report by Dalimil in *Literární listy,* July 4, 1968. For Švestka's views, see *Rudé právo,* May 16, June 23, and July 14, 1968. For Bilak's views, *Pravda* (Bratislava), May 23, 1968, and *Rudé právo,* June 5, 1968.
119. See Eugene Steiner, *The Slovak Dilemma* (Cambridge: Cambridge University Press, 1973), p. 179. For reports on Bilak's contacts with the East German ambassador to Czechoslovakia, Florin, see Tad Szulc, *Czechoslovakia since World War II* (New York: Viking, 1971), p. 337.
120. An interview with Smrkovský, *Listy,* p. 8.

Chapter 2

1. "Two Thousand Words to Workers, Farmers, Scientists, Artists, and Everyone," *Literární listy,* June 27, 1968. The manifesto was signed by more than sixty Czech citizens.
2. An interview with Smrkovský, *Listy,* p. 10.
3. Kolder was on the list of candidates for delegates to the congress, but he was not elected at the regional conference in Frýdek Místek, having failed to get a 50 percent majority in the secret ballot (Radio Prague, July 7, 1968; *Práce,* July 7, 1968).
4. Zdeněk Hejzlar, former director of Prague Radio, as quoted in Horský, *Prag 1968,* p. 68. See also Zdeněk Mlynář, *Nachtfrost* (Cologne: Europäische Verlangsanstalt, 1978), p. 183.
5. Radio Moscow, May 4, 1968; *Public Papers of the Presidents of the United States: Lyndon Johnson* (Washington, D.C.: Government Printing Office, 1968), pp. 715–16.
6. R. Reston, "Cultural Exchange Talks Set by Soviets," *Washington Post,* May 29, 1968.
7. Newhouse, *Cold Dawn,* p. 103.
8. Interview with Rusk, Athens, Ga., July 31, 1974.
9. Newhouse, *Cold Dawn,* p. 104.
10. For more information on the June 1968 talks between Brandt and Abrasimov in Berlin, see "Berlin Secrets," *Politika,* June 23, 1968; and *Der Spiegel* 22, no. 26 (June 1968): 22.
11. "U.S. Offers Hints of Chinese Rapprochement," Radio Moscow, June 4, 1968.
12. "The Political Course of Mao Tse-tung on the International Scene" (editorial), *Kommunist,* no. 8 (May 31, 1968), pp. 97. The possibility of an American–Chinese rapprochement became the subject of numerous analyses in Soviet periodicals at that time.
13. Gromyko's speech was printed in *Pravda,* June 28, 1968.
14. See Johnson, *The Vantage Point,* p. 485.
15. *Izvestiia,* July 2, 1968.
16. *Pravda,* June 28, 1968. Here I am indebted to Newhouse, *Cold Dawn,* pp. 104–5.
17. See *Pravda Ukrainy,* July 5, 1968; Radio Kiev, July 6, 1968; and Shelest's similar article, "Faithful Attachment of the CPSU," *Voprosy istorii KPSS,* no. 7 (July 1968), pp. 7–20.
18. *Pravda Ukrainy,* July 6, 1968. Emphasis added.
19. *Pravda,* July 4, 1968.
20. Ibid.
21. *Pravda,* July 9, 1968.
22. *Pravda,* July 4, 1968.
23. Interview with Lt. Col. F. Kudrna, press secretary of the National Defense Ministry, Radio Prague, July 11, 1968. Also see Thomas W. Wolfe, *Soviet Power and Europe: 1945–1970* (Baltimore: Johns Hopkins University Press, 1970), p. 371. See also Eugen Löbl and Leopold Grünwald, *Die intellektuelle Revolution; Hintergründe and Auswirkungen des Prager Frühlings* (Düsseldorf: Econ, 1969), pp. 122–23.
24. Radio Belgrade, July 9, 1968; *Frankfurter Allgemeine Zeitung,* July 11, 1968.
25. *Izvestiia,* July 11–14, 1968.
26. "Der Deutsch-Sowjetische Meinungsaustausch zur Frage des Gewaltverzichts," *Europa-Archiv* 23 (1968): 361–88; G. Duckwitz, "Gewaltverzicht und Interventionsrecht," *Aussenpolitik* 19, no. 9 (September 1968): 519–36.
27. I. Alexandrov, "The Attack against the Socialist Foundation of Czechoslovakia," *Pravda,* July 11, 1968.

28. See "The 'Pure Democrats' Are Pushing for Power," *Literaturnaia gazeta,* July 10, 1968. *Sovetskaia Rossiia* also concluded that "Czechoslovakia has become the main object of the subversive activities" and that "the notorious 2000-Word Manifesto is an example of this" ("The Diversionists Are Looking for a Crack," *Sovetskaia Rossiia,* July 12, 1968).

29. Dubček's speech to the Central Committee, September 26, 1969; William Shawcross, *Dubček* (London: Weidenfeld & Nichilson, 1970), p. 286. See also Weit, *At the Red Summit,* p. 200.

30. *Le Monde,* July 20, 1968. According to Kolder, the objectors (besides himself) were Bilak, Švestka, and Rigo. See Kolder, *Fakta nelze zamlčet: Svědectví lidí a dokumentů* (Prague: Knihovna Rudého Práva, 1971), p. 105. Kolder expressed his disagreement with the decision of the Czechoslovak Presidium in a memorandum published later in *Tribuna,* September 10, 1969. See also V. Bilak, *Rudé právo,* September 3, 1969.

31. Gomułka's interpreter, Erwin Weit, who was present at the Warsaw Summit, stated that the meeting had been arranged "at very short notice." Weit was informed on the night of July 13. See Weit, *At the Red Summit,* p. 194.

32. See "Communiqué of the Warsaw Conference of the Five Socialist Countries," *Rok šedesátý osmý,* p. 235.

33. Interestingly, the East German delegation did not include Ulbricht's successor, Honecker, even though Gomułka's interpreter at the Warsaw Conference, Weit, was verbally informed that Honecker would participate (Weit, *At the Red Summit,* p. 196).

34. When reporters called it to his attention, Kosygin glossed it over with a jovial wave: "The standards of life in Sweden are very high. But for that matter, they are very high in Czechoslovakia" (Alan Levy, *Rowboat to Prague* [New York: Grossman, 1972], p. 260).

35. *Pravda,* July 15, 1968.

36. Ibid. Emphasis added.

37. See Dubček's address in *Rudé právo,* July 19, 1968.

38. Weit, *At the Red Summit,* p. 202. At about this time, Ulbricht's group sent an internal Party document to regional Party secretaries which expressed a readiness to take "all appropriate actions to strengthen the position of socialism in Czechoslovakia" *(Frankfurter Allgemeine Zeitung,* August 27, 1968).

39. Ibid., p. 202. While discussing ways in which the "healthy" forces could be assisted, Ulbricht reportedly suggested that the Warsaw Pact countries try to "stir up the Slovaks" and push things in that direction (ibid., p. 216).

40. Zhivkov's attitude seems to have been reflected by an anti-Czechoslovak campaign launched by the Bulgarian press in July. See, for example, *Rabotnichesko delo,* July 12, 15, 1968.

41. Weit, *At the Red Summit,* pp. 199-200. A hard-line view was also reflected in the Polish press. See *Trybuna Ludu,* July 14, 1968.

42. An interview with Czechoslovak general Václav Prchlík, Radio Prague, July 15, 1968. For the stiffening of Kádár's attitude, see his speech during a visit to Moscow in early July (*Pravda,* July 4, 1968).

43. Weit, *At the Red Summit,* p. 201. This stand seems to have been supported by the attitude of the Hungarian press after the conference, which was calmer and much less abusive than that of the East German and Polish press. See, for example, *Népszabadság,* July 17, 1968; and *Magyar Hirlap,* July 19, 1968 (FBIS, July 22, 1968).

44. Weit, *At the Red Summit,* p. 201.

45. Ibid., p. 203.

46. *Neues Deutschland,* July 13, 1968.

47. Interview with Zbigniew Brzezinski, New York, January 27, 1974.

48. Weit, *At the Red Summit,* p. 211.

49. Ibid., p. 209.

50. Ibid., p. 207.

51. Ibid., p. 210.

52. Ibid.

53. Ibid., pp. 210-11.

54. Ibid., p. 213.

55. *Politicheskii dnevnik,* no. 46 (July 1968), p. 19.
56. For the text of the Warsaw Letter, see *Pravda,* July 18, 1968.
57. Weit, *At the Red Summit,* p. 202.
58. Ibid. The East German position was also reflected in the press. See *Neues Deutschland,* July 6, 13, 1968.
59. Ibid., p. 215.
60. Ibid.
61. See Isaac Deutscher, "Moscow: The Quiet Men, Constellations of Lobbies," *Nation,* no. 14 (April 5, 1965), pp. 352–57.
62. See Aspaturian, "Soviet Foreign Policy," in Macridis, *Foreign Policy in World Politics,* p. 197.
63. As quoted in Leonhard, *The Kremlin since Stalin,* p. 103.
64. See M. Page, *The Day Khrushchev Fell* (New York: Hawthorn, 1965), p. 64.
65. For a list of speakers and discussants, see *Pravda,* July 19, 1968; Radio Moscow, July 17, 1968.
66. Richard Löwenthal, "The Sparrow in the Cage," *Problems of Communism* 18 (November–December 1968): 16–17.
67. Snechkus, "The April Session and Some of Our Tasks," *Kommunist,* no. 6 (June 1968), pp. 3–7. As early as April, *Kommunist,* the journal of the Lithuanian Central Committee, launched a sporadic campaign against revisionism. See "Marxism and Progress of Mankind" (editorial), *Kommunist,* no. 4 (April 1968), p. 3. After the invasion, Snechkus publicly complained about those who wanted to "modernize socialism," and sharply rejected attempts for the "liberalization of socialism" (Snechkus, *Kommunist,* no. 10 [October 1968], pp. 9–10).
68. A. E. Voss, "Some Questions of Ideological Work of the Party Organizations," first published in the Central Committee magazine *Politicheskoe samoobrazovanie,* no. 9 (1968), pp. 22–30. A month later, the article was reprinted in the theoretical magazine of the Latvian Communist Party, *Kommunist Sovetskoi Latvii* 24, no. 10 (October 1968 [signed for publication, September 30, 1968]): 7–15.

On July 30, the Latvian *Kommunist Sovetskoi Latvii* published an editorial that probably reflected the views of the Latvian bureaucracy in general and of Voss in particular. It described Czechoslovakia as "the object of furious attacks by the internal reaction and external imperialist forces" and strongly advocated the policy stated in the Warsaw Letter. See "In the Interest of Every Soviet Man," *Kommunist Sovetskoi Latvii* 23, no. 8 (August 1968): 9–10.
69. Hodnett and Potichnyj, *The Ukraine and the Czechoslovak Crisis,* p. 86.
70. See Il'nitskii's article in *Pravda Ukrainy,* July 29, 1968; and his "Our Banner Internationalism," *Kommunist Ukrainy,* no. 1 (1969), pp. 85–93. Also see Hodnett and Pitchnyj, *The Ukraine and the Czechoslovak Crisis,* pp. 144–45.
71. Hodnett and Potichnyj, *The Ukraine and the Czechoslovak Crisis,* p. 96.
72. In Leningrad, as in Moscow, the ideas of the Prague Spring were being echoed in intellectual circles, which later expressed resentment over the intervention. I witnessed this development while visiting Leningrad and Moscow in May and June 1968. According to several Soviet intellectuals whom I met at this time (and who must remain anonymous), Tolstikov had the reputation in Leningrad of being tough with intellectuals and was reportedly concerned about this trend.
73. See *Pravda,* April 1, 1968. See also an analysis of Keldysh's speech in *Politicheskii dnevnik,* no. 43 (April 1968), p. 3.
74. Sakharov, *Progress, Coexistence, and Intellectual Freedom,* p. 67.
75. Gribachev's article was an imaginary conversation, in which a Soviet youth posed a rather unusual question: "One often hears that Marxism is outdated in the contemporary world and cannot be a leading ideology for the building of the future. What do you think of this?" (N. Gribachev, *Komsomol'skaia pravda,* July 25, 1968).
76. Frederick C. Barghoorn, "Trends in the Top Political Leadership in the USSR," in *Political Leadership in Eastern Europe and the Soviet Union,* ed. R. Barry Farrell (Chicago: Aldine, 1970), p. 72.
77. *Pravda,* July 18, 1968.
78. *Pravda,* July 19, 1968. The Soviet Army newspaper *Krasnaia zvezda* and the Bulgarian

newspaper *Otechestven front* went even further, reporting additional discovery sites in Czechoslovakia. See *Krasnaia zvezda,* July 21, 1968; and *Otechestven front,* July 20, 1968.
79. See V. Ragulin and I. Chushkov, "The Adventurist Plans of the Pentagon and CIA," *Pravda,* July 19, 1968.
80. Interview with Rusk, Athens, Ga., July 31, 1974.
81. For details, see an interview with Smrkovský, *Listy,* no. 2, March 1975, p. 15; "Unsubstantiated Reports," *Zemědělské noviny,* July 23, 1968; J. Řezábek, "Let Us Pay Attention," *Mladá fronta,* July 23, 1968; and Tigrid, *Why Dubcek Fell,* p. 61.
82. "About Relations with Czechoslovakia," *Politicheskii dnevnik,* no. 46 (July 1968), p. 23.
83. *Pravda,* July 20, 1968. Another senior Soviet decisionmaker, Politburo member and Chairman of the RSFSR Council of Ministers G. I. Voronov, at the time of the session made no direct reference to Czechoslovakia, as Podgorny and his deputy Iasnov had *(Sovetskaia Rossiia,* July 20, 1968). He did, however, express support for the Warsaw Letter, pointing out: "The people of the RSFSR approve the decree of the plenary meeting of the CPSU Central Committee, the meeting in Warsaw, and the letter to the Central Committee of the Communist Party of Czechoslovakia adopted at that meeting" *(Sovetskaia Rossiia,* July 20, 1968).
84. Radio Moscow, July 19, 1968; Radio Kiev, July 19, 1968; *Pravda, Sovetskaia Rossiia, Trud, Krasnaia zvezda,* July 20, 1968.
85. Agence France Presse (AFP) (Paris), July 21, 1968.
86. *Krasnaia zvezda,* July 21, 1968.
87. Král denied that he had spoken or acted on governmental instruction (interview with Karel Král, New York, October 27, 1971).
88. Christian Schmidt-Haüer and Adolf Müller, *Viva Dubček: Reform und Okkupation in der ČSSR* (Cologne: Kiepenheuer & Witsch, 1968), p. 71.
89. *New York Times,* July 20, 1968.
90. Fritz Beer, *Die Zukunft funktioniert noch nicht: Ein Porträt der Tschechoslowakei, 1948–1968* (Frankfurt: S. Fischer, 1969), p. 323. Also reported by Ludvík Veselý, *Dubček* (Munich: Kindler, 1970), pp. 326–27.
91. As reported by Dušan Havlíček, an eyewitness and the former head of the press department of the Central Committee of the Czechoslovak Party, in an interview in Geneva, June 8, 1974.
92. *Pravda,* July 5, 1968. Emphasis added.
93. "Strengthen the Position of Socialism and Peace" (editorial), *Pravda,* July 19, 1968. A similar comment appeared in *Izvestiia* on the same day. The editorial in *Izvestiia* criticized Czechoslovakia but also stated: "There is no doubt that Czechoslovakia has adequate forces that can uphold socialist order and defeat anti-socialist elements" ("Strengthening Socialism Is Our Common Task," *Izvestiia,* July 19, 1968). These comments were similar to *Pravda's* important comment during the Hungarian crisis in 1956, on October 28, when the majority of Soviet decisionmakers still seemed to prefer nonintervention in Hungary: "The Hungarian working people, who fought heroically for the establishment of a socialist state in 1918 and who established their own people's rule after the defeat of Hitler's legion, dealt a crushing blow to the schemes of imperialist reaction. They are determined to defend their people's regime and to continue on the path of building socialism" ("Collapse of the Anti-Popular Adventure in Hungary" [editorial], *Pravda,* October 28, 1956).
94. Radio Prague, July 18, 1968.
95. Radio Moscow, July 14, 15, 1968; Paris AFP, July 17, 1968.
96. Interview with Franz Marek, Vienna, May 27, 1974. After the intervention, Marek was expelled from the Politburo of the Austrian Party for his stand on the Czechoslovak issue.
97. Michel Salomon, *Prague Notebook: The Strangled Revolution* (Boston: Little, Brown, 1971), p. 136. Salomon, who based his notebook on interviews with many Communist officials in Eastern and Western Europe, was a correspondent with *L'Express.*
98. "Irresistible Trend toward Unity" (editorial), *Kommunist,* no. 9 (June 1968), pp. 4–5. Emphasis added.
99. "Communiqué of the Working Group Set up to Draft Materials for the Conference of Communist and Workers' Parties," *World Marxist Review* 11, no. 7 (July 1968): 1.
100. See the text of the French transcript of the conversation, *L'Humanité,* May 18, 1970.

101. Interview with Havlíček, Geneva, June 8, 1974.
102. Italian Party leader Longo, as reported on Radio Prague, July 21, 1968.
103. *Pravda,* July 20, 1968.
104. Radio Belgrade, July 23, 1968.
105. See *Politika,* July 24, 1968.
106. The full text was published only in *Politicheskii dnevnik,* no. 46 (July 1968), "The reply of the CSCP/CC Presidium to the Warsaw Letter of the Five Communist Parties."
107. "The Viewpoint of the Presidium of the Czechoslovak Communist Party Central Committee," *Pravda,* July 22, 1968.
108. This plan was reported by an East German source, as quoted by D. Binder, "July Plan to Oust Dubček Reported," *New York Times,* August 9, 1968.

Chapter 3

1. The portions in the first part of this chapter dealing with the conference at Čierna nad Tisou are based mainly on Pavel Tigrid's account of the negotiations in *Why Dubcek Fell,* which in turn draws extensively on the minutes of the meeting. Other important sources of information were an interview of Czechoslovak Presidium member Josef Smrkovský, who participated in the conference *(Listy* [Rome], 5, no. 2 [March 1975]), and my consultations with other former officials of the Czechoslovak Communist Party. The second part of this chapter, dealing with the Bratislava Conference, draws primarily on the narrative of Zdeněk Mlynář, one of the participants in the conference and former secretary of the Central Committee of the Czechoslovak Communist Party, in his memoirs *Nachtfrost,* pp. 193–200, and on my interviews with Mlynář and with other former officials of the Czechoslovak Communist Party who were present at Bratislava.
2. Richard Löwenthal, "The Sparrow in the Cage," *Problems of Communism* 18 (November–December 1968): 18.
3. A Soviet commentator said: "I am certain that there is no need to explain to anyone the importance of the problems discussed there, an indication of which is the very composition of the delegations to the talks, attended on the Soviet side by the leading representatives of the 'PSU and the Soviet state" (D. Morozov, on Radio Moscow, July 30, 1968).
4. Radio Belgrade, July 30, 1968.
5. General James H. Polk, "Reflections on the Czechoslovakian Invasion, 1968," *Strategic Review* 5 (1977): 31.
6. For details, see "Withdrawal of the Lion," *Der Spiegel* 22 (July 29, 1968): 19–20.
7. Radio Prague, July 26, 1968.
8. See General Mariakhin's statement in V. Goltsev, "Master of Military Affairs," *Izvestiia,* July 30, 1968; and also an article by army general I. G. Pavlovskii, commander-in-chief of the Ground Forces, "Tactical Training and the Moral and Psychological Education of Troops," *Krasnaia zvezda,* July 26, 1968.
9. I was able to track down only a single report of the East German source about this meeting: Radio East Berlin, July 30, 1968.
10. Interview with Zdeněk Mlynář, Vienna, October 6, 1978.
11. See "Whom Is General Václav Prchlík Obliging?" *Krasnaia zvezda,* July 23, 1968; and *On Events in Czechoslovakia,* (Moscow, 1968), 7.
12. Jiri Pelikan, *Ein Frühling, der nie zu Ende geht:* pp. 260–61.
13. Radio Prague, July 26, 1968.
14. David Vital, *The Survival of Small States* (London: Oxford University Press, 1971), p. 29.
15. See Josef Maxa, *A Year Is Eight Months* (Garden City, N.Y.: Doubleday, 1970), p. 145.
16. Alexej Kusák, "Illusions of Czech Politics" in *Sborník, Systémové změny* (Cologne: Index, 1972), p. 147.
17. Zdeněk Mlynář, *Československý pokus o reformu, 1968: Analýza jeho teorie a praxe* (Cologne: Index-Listy, 1975), p. 238.
18. An interview with Smrkovský, *Listy,* p. 13.
19. The letter was read on Moscow Radio the day negotiations started (July 29, 1968), and was reprinted a day later in *Pravda.* Also see *Rudé právo,* July 31, 1968.

20. Reported by a Czechoslovak participant to Radoslav Selucký, "The Dubček Era Revisited," *Problems of Communism* 24 (January–February 1975): 41.

21. Morozov's comment on Moscow Radio, July 30, 1968.

22. See Roger Garaudy, *Die ganze Wahrheit: Oder, für einen Kommunism ohne Dogma* (Reinbek bei Hamburg: Rowolt Taschenbuch, 1970), p. 123.

23. "The Defense of Socialism: A Supreme International Duty" (editorial), *Pravda,* August 22, 1968.

24. An interview with Smrkovský, *Listy,* p. 13; Pavel Tigrid, "Czechoslovakia: A Post-Mortem," *Survey,* no. 73 (Autumn 1969), p. 161–62.

25. A proposal for an immediate convening of the Party congress was presented to the Czechoslovak Presidium on July 17, two days prior to the session of the Central Committee, but it was rejected. See Kolder, *Fakta nelze zamlčet,* 106.

26. See an interview with Smrkovský, *Listy,* p. 14.

27. See Schmidt-Haüer and Müller, *Viva Dubček,* p. 90; and Alexej Kusák and Franz Peter Künzel, *Der Sozialismus mit menschlichen Gesicht* (Munich: Südwest, 1969), p. 201.

28. An interview with Smrkovský, *Listy,* p. 13.

29. Mlynář, *Nachtfrost,* p. 194.

30. Maxa, *A Year Is Eight Months,* p. 146.

31. Radio Moscow, July 31, 1968.

32. M. Tatu, "New Light on Invasion: A Scenario That Was Months in the Making," *Le Monde,* August 20, 1969.

33. Colin Chapman, *August 21st: The Rape of Czechoslovakia* (Philadelphia: Lippincott, 1968), p. 30. Chapman, a foreign news editor of the *Sunday Times,* based his account on the information provided by the newspaper's special correspondent in Czechoslovakia.

34. Tigrid, *Why Dubcek Fell,* p. 87.

35. Windsor and Roberts, *Czechoslovakia, 1968,* p. 73.

36. Maxa, *A Year Is Eight Months,* p. 147.

37. An interview, with Smrkovský, *Listy,* p. 13.

38. Mlynář, *Nachtfrost,* p. 194.

39. Salomon, *Prague Notebook,* p. 151.

40. Tigrid, "Czechoslovakia: A Post-Mortem," p. 162.

41. Tigrid, *Why Dubcek Fell,* pp. 86–87.

42. "A Quarter of a Century of an Unpleasant Episode," *Svědectví* 12, no. 46 (1973): 268; interview with one of the members of the Czechoslovak Social Democratic Preparatory Committee, Přemysl Janýr, Vienna, May 25, 1974.

43. Radio Prague, July 29, 1968.

44. Dubček's speech of September 26, 1969, as reported in *Svědectví,* no. 38 (1970), pp. 275–76.

45. Tigrid, *Why Dubcek Fell,* p. 87.

46. Radio Prague, August 1, 1968.

47. Dubček's verbal assurances to Brezhnev were reported by Tad Szulc of the *New York Times,* who was told about them by a high Czechoslovak official. See Szulc, *Czechoslovakia since World War II,* p. 364. Dubček later admitted that "we also discussed the internal question of cadres" (Dubček's speech of September 26, 1969, as reported in *Svědectví,* no. 38 [1970], pp. 275–76).

48. An interview with Smrkovský, *Listy,* p. 14.

49. Ibid.

50. Dubček implied that he preferred to keep quiet about his private talk with Brezhnev for the Soviets' own interest (Dubček's speech, *Svědectví,* p. 276). See also Mlynář, *Nachtfrost,* p. 194.

51. According to Bilak, Brezhnev told the Czechoslovak negotiators: "Comrades, let us not sign any agreement. We believe in your Communist word, and we expect that you will act and proceed as Communists. If you cheat on us again, we shall consider it a crime and a betrayal and act accordingly. We would not sit with you again at the same table" (Bilak, *Pravda zůstala pravdou,* p. 169).

52. Radio Belgrade, August 1, 1968.

53. Reported by D. Lompar, special Yugoslav correspondent in Prague, Radio Belgrade, July 31, 1968.

54. Joint Communiqué on the Meeting of the Politburo of the CPSU Central Committee and the Presidium of the CPC Central Committee, *Pravda,* August 2, 1968.

55. "Conference of the Six Communist and Workers' Parties in Bratislava," *Czechoslovak Digest* (Prague), no. 32 (August 8, 1968), pp. 11–12.

56. Chapman, *August 21st: The Rape of Czechoslovakia,* pp. 34–35. According to Levy, Gomułka said: "I don't know why this meeting has been called, since everything has been already agreed upon" (Levy, *Rowboat to Prague,* p. 197).

57. Interview with Larisa Silnický, Tel Aviv, September 24, 1973; also her "Recollections of Bratislava," Radio Liberty Dispatch, RL 195–74, pp. 3–4.

58. Ibid.

59. See the Bratislava Declaration, published in *Pravda,* August 4, 1968. Italics in subsequent quotations from this declaration indicate emphasis added.

60. Tigrid, *Why Dubcek Fell,* p. 90.

61. Mlynář, *Nachtfrost,* p. 199.

62. Ibid., pp. 196–97.

63. See, for example, the Soviet statement announcing the invasion of August 20, in *Pravda,* August 22, 1968; the joint Soviet-Czechoslovak communiqué, *Pravda,* October 29, 1969; and the Soviet-Czechoslovak Treaty of May 6, 1970, *Pravda,* May 7, 1970.

64. Mlynář, *Nachtfrost,* pp. 196–97.

65. Ibid., pp. 197–98.

66. Maxa, *A Year Is Eight Months,* p. 152.

67. Interview with L. Silnický, Tel Aviv, September 24, 1973; and her "Recollections of Bratislava," pp. 4–5.

68. Smrkovský and Černik reportedly said, "We managed to convince them" (Pavel Kohout, *From the Diary of a Counterrevolutionary* [New York: McGraw-Hill, 1969], p. 270).

69. Václav Král, *Československo a Sovětský svaz, 1917–1971* (Prague: Práce, 1971), p. 77.

70. Tigrid, *Why Dubcek Fell,* p. 90.

71. Löwenthal, "The Sparrow in the Cage," p. 19.

72. The troops that withdrew from Czechoslovakia were reportedly relocated near the Czechoslovak-Polish borders (Radio Paris, August 9, 1968; Polk, "Reflections on the Czechoslovakian Invasion 1968," p. 32).

Chapter 4

1. "Strength in Unity" (editorial), *Pravda,* August 5, 1968. The phrase "wisdom, calm, thoughtfulness and patience characterize the conference in Bratislava" was repeated in Moscow Radio commentaries (Radio Moscow, August 5, 8, 1968).

2. Ibid.

3. *Izvestiia* (editorial), August 6, 1968; ibid., August 9, 1968; *Trud* (editorial), August 6, 1968; *New Times,* no. 32 (August 14, 1968); "Proletarian Internationalism: Banner of the International Communist Movement" (editorial), *Kommunist,* no. 12 (August 1968), pp. 24–30; and V. Vladimirov, "Socialist Countries and Political Strategy of Imperialism," *Mirovaia ekonomika i mezhdunarodnye otnosheniia,* no. 8 (July 1968), pp. 3–15. The last is the publication of the Institute of World Economy and International Relations (IMEMO).

4. CPSU Communiqué, "On the Results of the Talks between the Politburo of the CPSU Central Committee and the Presidium of the Central Committee of the Communist Party of Czechoslovakia in the Town of Čierna nad Tisou, and the Bratislava Conference of Representatives of Communist and Workers' Parties of Socialist Countries," *Pravda,* August 7, 1968.

5. Radio Budapest, August 5, 1968.

6. Hungarian satisfaction with the outcome of the Čierna and Bratislava conferences was reflected by other Hungarian officials and by the Hungarian Press. See a speech of Secretary of the Hungarian Party Z. Komócsin, Radio Budapest, August 9, 1968; and *Népszabadság,* August 6, 1968 (*FBIS,* August 8, 1968).

7. Radio Budapest, August 5, 1968; emphasis added. This part of Kádár's interview also appeared in *Pravda,* August 6, 1968.

8. From an interview with an official of a West European Communist Party.

9. Roy A. Medvedev, *On Socialist Democracy* (New York: Alfred A. Knopf, 1975), pp. 51–52 and 347, n. 5.

10. Y. Zhukov, "About the Discredited Prophets," *Pravda,* August 6, 1968.

11. See the text of the introduction and full-page coverage, with four articles, on this sub ject: "Whom Are the Diversionists of the Air Waves Serving?" *Sovetskaia Rossiia,* August 2 1968.

12. See the Bratislava Declaration in *Pravda,* August 4, 1968.

13. Peter Reddaway, *Uncensored Russia: Protest and Dissent in the Soviet Union* (New York: American Heritage Press, 1972), pp. 95–96, 365–67. In researching the *Chronicle o, Current Events* for material pertaining to Czechoslovakia I was fortunate in being able to con sult the *Arkhiv samizdata* (Samizdat Archive), compiled by the Department of Research o Radio Liberty and deposited in the library of the Center for International Studies at MIT. The references to the *Chronicle* used here are from the translation of eleven of its issues by Peter Reddaway in *Uncensored Russia.*

14. Reddaway, *Uncensored Russia,* p. 389.

15. *Reportér* 3 (May 8–15, 1968): 17.

16. Reddaway, *Uncensored Russia,* pp. 96–111, 381.

17. Sakharov, *Progress, Coexistence, and Intellectual Freedom,* p. 88. Trapeznikov must have noticed that the new Dubček leadership had satisfied one of the first demands of Czecho- slovak academic circles: it fired his counterpart in Prague, J. Obzina, head of the department supervising the science and higher educational institutions.

18. "For Friendship, Solidarity, and Unity of Action!" (editorial), *Sovetskaia Rossiia,* August 6, 1968.

19. G. Kibets and A. Stepanov, "Dictatorship of the Proletariat: Its Content and Forms," *Sovetskaia Rossiia,* August 8, 1968.

20. "So It Is Quite Specific: Anticommunism" (editorial), *Literaturnaia gazeta* July 31, 1968.

21. "The Political Milk of *Literární listy*" (editorial), *Literaturnaia gazeta* August 14, 1968. (This was in reply to an article by J. Válka, "From Warsaw to Bratislava," *Literární listy* 1, no. 24 [August 8, 1968].)

22. "The Moscow Protocol" in Tigrid, *Why Dubček Fell,* Appendix A, p. 211.

23. Zhores A. Medvedev, *Ten Years After Ivan Denisovich* (New York: Alfred Knopf, 1973), p. 108.

24. See, e.g., L. Katsoshvili, "Lies in the Air: The Real Aims of the Masters of Deutsche Welle," *Pravda Ukrainy,* August 1, 1968.

25. See *Sovetskaia Estoniia,* August 4–7, 1968.

26. See hints in an article by Z. Štastná, "Na Východní Výspě" [On the eastern outpost], *Reportér* 4 (March 13, 1969): 9–12.

27. On the grain output of the Ukraine in 1968, see *Pravda Ukrainy,* November 23, 1968.

28. There had already been signs of an aggravation of the situation in the Ukraine in 1968. The situation was strongly criticized by Ukrainian Marxist dissenter Ivan Dziuba *(Interna- tionalism or Russification?* [London: Weiderfeld and Nicolson, 1968]) and nationalist dissenter Vyacheslav Chornovil *(The Chornovil Papers* [New York: McGraw-Hill, 1968]).

29. "Fidelity to Marxism-Leninism: Source of Strength of Socialist Cooperation" (editorial), *Kommunist Ukrainy,* no. 8 (August 1968), pp. 3–13.

30. The differences of opinion among the Soviet bureaucracies regarding the outcome of the Čierna and Bratislava negotiations were probably reflected in Soviet periodicals. While *World Marxist Review* published the text of the Bratislava Declaration, it did not publish the Warsaw Letter. On the other hand, *Politicheskoe samoobrazovanie* (published by the Depart- ment of Propaganda of the Central Committee) ignored the Bratislava Declaration. The editorial board of this periodical, like that of *Kommunist Ukrainy,* seemed to consider the declaration not "relevant" and probably only a temporary document.

31. See "Removal of Shelest," *Listy* 2, no. 4 (July 1972): 33; "The Unexpected Soviet Ini- tiative: Thaw in Prague," *Le Monde,* June 17–18, 1973; *Svědectví* 12, no. 46 (1973); "Is Shelest Responsible for the Intervention?" *Listy* 3, no. 1 (February 1973): 49. It would be misleading, however, to fully accept stories, told by Soviet diplomats in Czechoslovakia and in the West, that Shelest deceived the Politburo at the meeting of August 15 by presenting the situation as disastrous. Shelest may have been the most outspoken advocate of the interven- tion, but obviously he alone could not have convinced the entire Soviet Politburo.

32. For more on the KGB, see F. C. Barghoorn, "The Security Police," in *Interest Groups*

Soviet Politics, ed. H. Gordon Skilling and Franklyn Griffiths (Princeton: Princeton University Press, 1971), pp. 93–129; and John Barron, *KGB: The Secret Work of Soviet Secret Agents* (New York: Reader's Digest Press, 1974).

33. Bittman, *The Deception Game,* p. 214.

34. Mlynář, *Nachtfrost,* p. 217 and an interview with Mlynář, Vienna, October 6, 1978, and Pelikan, *Ein Frühling, der nie zu Ende geht,* pp. 257–58. Also see M. Cikán's report, "Who Stirs Up Mud and for What Purpose? The Letter from Slovnaft a Falsification," *Práce,* uly 22, 1968; and *Večerní Praha,* July 4, 1968.

35. During the Prague Spring several leading Czechoslovak figures of Jewish and non-Jewish origins received a letter allegedly sent by the head of the Jewish Documentation Center in Vienna, Simon Wiesenthal. The letter praised the Prague Spring as an "advantageous thing for the interests of Jews around the world," and the recipients were asked to cooperate with Wiesenthal in a "struggle against anti-Semitism." An investigation of this affair by Czechoslovak Minister of the Interior Pavel led to the conclusion that the letter was fraudulent. Wiesenthal believes it was produced by the Polish intelligence service, headed by M. Moczar, a man who in 1968 organized an anti-Semitic campaign in Poland (interview with Wiesenthal, Vienna, September 2, 1973; Wiesenthal to Valenta, February 13, 1976). Dubček took a copy of the falsified letter to the negotiations at Čierna, where he presented it to the Soviet leaders as proof of the Warsaw Pact secret service organization's provocations against Czechoslovakia. See Jan Sieredzki, "Can They Be at All Forgiven?" *Reporter* 4 (April 10, 1969): 23–24.

36. See the testimony of a former official of the Czechoslovak intelligence service, Major František August, in *Listy* 8, nos. 3–4 (July 1978): 35–36.

37. Frolik, *The Frolik Defection,* p. 148.

38. See *Rudé právo,* March 13, 1970.

39. Robert Littel, ed., *The Czech Black Book* (New York: Praeger, 1969), prepared by the Institute of History of the Czechoslovak Academy of Science, pp. 80–81.

40. See the interview with Smrkovský, *Listy,* p. 17.

41. P. Tigrid, *Le Monde,* March 23–24, 1969.

42. "The Moscow Protocol" in Tigrid, *Why Dubcek Fell,* p. 214.

43. See Frolik, *The Frolik Defection,* p. 150.

44. Tigrid, *Why Dubcek Fell,* p. 59.

45. Erickson, in Kusín, *The Czechoslovak Reform Movement,* p. 57.

46. R. Kolkowicz, "The Military," in Skilling and Griffiths, *Interest Groups in Soviet Politics,* p. 165.

47. See S. M. Shtemenko, *Nedelia,* no. 6 (January 31–February 6, 1965) (*Nedelia* is a weekly supplement to *Izvestiia);* Iakubovskii, "Ground Forces," *Krasnaia zvezda,* July 31, 1967. For an analysis *see* Wolfe, "Doctrinal Developments," *Soviet Power and Europe: 1945–1970,* pp. 451–58; also see John Erickson, *Soviet Military Power* (London: Whitehall, 1971), p. 67. Iakubovskii and Shtemenko were among the few Soviet generals who would, after the invasion, talk about it as a "brilliant demonstration of proletarian internationalism" and as an example of a Warsaw Pact mission in "suppression of counterrevolution." See Iakubovskii, "The Battle-ready Community of Armies of the Socialist Countries," *Kommunist,* no. 5, 1970, pp. 99–100; and Shtemenko, *Za rubezhom,* 19 (May 7–13, 1976): 6.

48. For example, see "An Invincible Friendship of Fighters" (editorial), *Krasnaia zvezda,* July 12, 1968.

49. Mlynář, *Nachtfrost,* pp. 203–4; interview with Mlynář, Vienna, October 6, 1978; interview with Josef Hodic, former head of the Department of Social Sciences of the Klement Gottwald Military-Political Academy in Prague, Vienna, October 7, 1978.

50. During the 1968 crisis, Shtemenko published a history of staff work in World War II *(General 'nyi shtab v gody voiny,* Moscow) which provided a positive appraisal of Stalin's wartime activity.

51. John R. Thomas, *Soviet Foreign Policy and Conflict within Political and Military Leadership* (McLean, Va.: Research Analysis Corporation, 1970), p. 9.

52. Ibid. Soviet sources maintained that Kazakov retired "at his own request for reasons of ill health" (Radio Moscow, August 4, 1968; *New Times,* no. 33 [August 21, 1968]).

53. Interview with General P. Grigorenko, *Die Welt* (Bonn), March 28, 1978.

54. See the Bratislava Declaration in *Pravda,* August 4, 1968.

55. Erickson, in Kusín (ed.), *Czechoslovak Reform Movement*, pp. 34–35.

56. In June 1968, for example, General Iakubovskii stressed the necessity for "further rai, ing of combat readiness," and for "revolutionary vigilance," in part because NATO had, i December 1967, adopted a strategy of "flexible response." See his article "Friendship Born i Battle," *Krasnaia zvezda*, June 23, 1968.

57. Mlynář, *Nachtfrost*, p. 188.

58. P. Chudožilov and Z. Pinc, "We Saw," *Literární listy* 1, no. 24 (August 8, 1968).

59. Erickson, in Kusín, *Czechoslovak Reform Movement*, p. 62.

60. General James H. Polk, "Reflections on the Czechoslovakian Invasion, 1968," *Strategic Review* 5 (1977): 32. There are three categories of Soviet divisions. Category I div sions are fully operational in terms of both men and equipment, and are ready to fight withou delay. Category II divisions have all of their equipment but perhaps only 75 percent of their re quired manpower; these divisions could be ready within a week or less, depending on when th reserves arrive. Category III divisions have all of their equipment but only a nucleus of traine men. Again, reserves would be required to bring these divisions up to full strength. *U.S. Arm Intelligence Center and School, Handbook on the Soviet Ground Forces* (unclassified). For Huachuca, Arizona: USAICS, August 1976, p. 81. In this context, equipment refers to suc combat items as tanks and artillery. Noncombat items such as motor transport vehicles, use by category II and III divisions and the Rear Service, come from civilian resources. Here I an indebted to research conducted by my student, Captain Donald R. Vik, U.S. Army.

61. General S. S. Mariakhin, "The Combat Test of the Rear Service," *Krasnaia zvezda* August 14, 1968.

62. Reported by K. Shoppen, *Deutschlandfunk*, August 23, 1968. Also from an interview with Tatu, Paris, August 7, 1973. The military newspaper *Krasnaia zvezda*, while repeating questions of Western observers, asked pathetically on August 18, "Who won and who lost ir Bratislava? Who made concessions and what were they?" The answer to this question ir *Krasnaia zvezda* was ambiguous. The writer pointed out that in the West the Bratislava Declaration was considered a "banal declaration of no practical importance."

63. "A Document of Enormous Importance" (editorial), *Krasnaia zvezda*, August 8, 1968.

64. Paris AFP, August 9, 1968.

65. Radio Moscow, August 19, 1968.

66. General S. P. Vasiagin, "Loyalty to International Duty," *Krasnaia zvezda*, August 15, 1968.

67. Radio Moscow, August 27, 1968.

68. "The Moscow Protocol" in Tigrid, *Why Dubcek Fell*, p. 212.

69. *Neues Deutschland* asserted, even at that time, that "a quiet counterrevolution" was taking place in Czechoslovakia *(Neues Deutschland*, July 30, 1968). See also *Neues Deutschland*, August 2, 1968.

70. Robert Havemann, *Svět v obrazech*, May 21, 1968, p. 2.

71. Radio Belgrade, August 1, 1968.

72. Philip Windsor, *Germany and the Management of Détente* (London: Chatto and Windus, 1971), p. 159.

73. Ponomarev reportedly said this, in September 1968, to Czechoslovak leader J. Lenárt (Tigrid, *Why Dubcek Fell*, p. 128).

74. Beer, *Die Zukunft funktioniert noch nicht*, p. 340; *Neues Deutschland*, August 21, 25, 1968; and an interview with Hodic, Vienna, October 7, 1978.

75. Reported by Pelikán, *Ein Frühling, der nie zu Ende geht*, p. 263.

76. The content of Ulbricht's report has never been revealed, but the Czechoslovak leaders were able to grasp its importance, judging from the various references made to it by Soviet leaders after the intervention. See Tigrid, *Why Dubček Fell*, p. 95.

77. See "The Year 1968: Parliament on the Invasion; A Secret Transcript of the Session of the Presidium of the National Assembly," *Listy* 8, no. 5 (September 1978): 56. See also Karol Klawitter, *Army of Revenge: Ulbricht's Occupation Forces in Czechoslovakia* (Cologne: Markus, 1968), 5.

78. Melvin Croan, "After Ulbricht: The End of an Era?" *Survey* 17, no. 2 (Spring 1971): 80. See also idem, "Czechoslovakia, Ulbricht, and the German Problem," *Problems of Communism* 18 (January-February 1969): 1–5.

79. Jan B. Weydenthal, "Polish Politics and the Czechoslovak Crisis in 1968," *Canadian avonic Papers* 14, no. 1 (1972): 46.

80. *Trybuna Ludu,* August 16, 1968, quoted by Weydenthal, "Polish Politics," p. 47.

81. See "Edward Gierek," *Mezinárodní politika* 12, no. 7 (May 15-June 15, 1968): 28.

82. *Le Monde,* August 22, 1968.

83. See Weit, *At the Red Summit,* p. 205.

84. *Le Monde,* August 22, 1968; *New York Times,* October 31, 1968, quoted by Weyden-ʌal, "Polish Politics," p. 46. Polish General W. Barański, deputy head of the Polish General ʈaff, gave similar reasons for Polish concern about developments in Czechoslovakia and ex-ʀessed Polish willingness to help *(Krasnaia zvezda,* August 14, 1968).

85. Interview with A. Indra, Radio Prague, August 9, 1968.

86. For the blacklist, see *Tribuna,* October 8, 1969; and a report of J. Rumel in *Večerní ʀaha,* August 19, 1968.

87. See Moravus [pseud.], "Shawcross's Dubček: A Different Dubček," *Survey* 17, no. 4 ʌutumn 1971): 44.

88. Interview with Silnický, Tel Aviv, September 24, 1973.

89. *Pravda* (Bratislava), August 17, 1968. It seems probable, however, that the Slovak ʌarty Congress of August 26 would have resulted in a substantial change in Slovak leadership, ʌcluding the replacement of Bilak by Husák and the removal of Bilak's antireformist sup-orters.

90. See Littel, *The Czech Black Book,* p. 26.

91. Interview with Havlíček, Geneva, June 8, 1974. Also see Kolder's speech, *Svědectví* 10, ɔ. 38 (1970): 292.

92. For Kašpar's report, see *Tribuna,* February 5, July 2, 1969; *Rudé právo,* July 2, 1969. or a detailed analysis, see Skilling, *Czechoslovakia's Interrupted Revolution,* p. 328.

93. Ibid.

94. See Littel, *The Czech Black Book,* pp. 24-26. For Dubček's similar version, see his ɔeech at the Central Committee Plenum in September 1969, as reported in *Svědectví,* no. 38, . 277.

95. See the discussion in the next chapter.

96. See J. Hofman, *Reportér* 3 (August 21-28, 1968): 10.

97. *Rudé právo,* August 17, 19, and 20, 1968.

98. *Rudé právo,* August 14, 1968.

99. Y. Zhukov, "Instigators," *Pravda,* August 16, 1968. In an interview ten years after the ʌvasion, Zhukov stated that "the complexity and contradictions inherent in the situation in ʈzechoslovakia were felt especially after the Bratislava meeting." *Rudé právo,* August 8, 978.

100. This suggestion is supported by evidence from Hungarian sources: e.g., István Kulcsar, Y. Zhukov: Who Is He and Why Does What He Says Command Such Great Attention?" ʈadio Budapest, February 8, 1975.

101. Moravus, "Shawcross's Dubček," p. 210.

102. Ibid.

103. Mlynář, *Československý pokus o reformu, 1968,* p. 237.

Chapter 5

1. For a general discussion of Soviet diplomatic channels of information and communica-on, see Aspaturian, "Soviet Foreign Policy," in Macridis, *Foreign Policy in World Politics,* . 185; and Sir William Hayter (formerly British Ambassador to Moscow), *Russia and the ʋorld* (New York: Taplinger, 1970), pp. 16-25.

2. Tigrid, *Why Dubcek Fell,* p. 98.

3. Horský, *Prag 1968,* p. 139.

4. Chervonenko graduated from Kiev University in 1936 and served in the Ukrainian ʌarty bureaucracy from 1949 to 1959. In his last position he was responsible for ideological ʌatters. From 1959 to 1965, during the period when the Sino-Soviet dispute erupted, he was mbassador to China. He was later (1965-74) ambassador to Czechoslovakia and, since 1974, as been ambassador to France.

5. Tigrid, *Kvadratura kruhu,* p. 12.

6. Chervonenko, in a conversation with M. Voslensky at the Soviet embassy in Pragu Voslensky's diary, *Der Spiegel,* no. 34 (August 21, 1978), p. 126.

7. Ibid.

8. Tigrid, *Why Dubcek Fell,* p. 98.

9. Voslensky's diary, p. 126.

10. Tigrid, *Why Dubcek Fell,* p. 128.

11. See Michel Gordey, *L'Express* (Paris), August 9–15, 1976, p. 55.

12. See an interview with Smrkovský, *Listy,* p. 15; and Pelikan, *Ein Frühling, der nie z Ende geht,* p. 257.

13. An interview with Smrkovský, *Listy,* p. 8.

14. Pelikán, " 'Prague Spring' and the International Communist and Revolutionar Movement," *Sborník, systémové změny,* pp. 229–30.

15. Indra's secretary reportedly saw him sending messages to Chervonenko on the teletyp on August 15; the secretary informed the Czechoslovak ministry of the interior (Chapmar *August 21st: The Rape of Czechoslovakia,* p. 37).

16. See an interview with Kolder in *Rudé právo,* September 10, 1969; and Littel, *Th Czech Black Book,* pp. 24–25.

17. See "The Defense of Socialism: A Supreme International Duty" (editorial), *Pravda* August 22, 1968.

18. See Dubček's letter *(Listy* [Rome], no. 3 [April 1975], p. 10).

19. "Letter of A. Dubček to Comrade A. Smrkovský," *Listy* 4, no. 2 (May 1974): 4–6

20. Ibid.

21. Mlynář, *Nachtfrost,* p. 205.

22. *Le Monde,* June 17–18, 1973.

23. See J. L. Beam (U.S. ambassador to the Soviet Union 1969–72), in *The Soviet Union Yesterday, Today, Tomorrow,* ed. Foy D. Koehler and Mose L. Harvey (Miami, Fla.: Univer sity of Miami, Center for Advanced International Studies, 1975), p. 146.

24. This message was conveyed by the Czechoslovaks to the U.S. government (interviev with Walt W. Rostow, Austin, Tex., July 26, 1974).

25. Ibid. President Johnson admitted: "The Czechs themselves had indicated they did no plan to resist with military force, and that they would not welcome any response from th West" *(The Vantage Point,* p. 486). On Johnson's warning to the Soviet leadership regardin Rumania and Soviet "assurances," see *Public Papers of the Presidents of the United States* pp. 919–20, 930.

26. Interview with Rostow, Austin, Tex., July 26, 1974.

27. Newhouse, *Cold Dawn,* p. 114.

28. After the first Soviet military intervention, in Hungary on October 24, 1956, Presiden Eisenhower had demanded that the Soviet Union abstain from further force; but Presiden Johnson made no public reference to Czechoslovakia during the crisis in 1968 until after th intervention.

29. Only two days before the intervention (August 19) President Johnson again go "tough" on the Vietnam issue, in a speech in Detroit. See his remarks in *Public Papers of th Presidents of the United States,* pp. 898–902. At that time, the Soviet decision to interven seems to have been already made. Under such circumstances, it might have been easier fo Soviet advocates of intervention to get "tough" with Czechoslovakia.

30. Adam B. Ulam, *The Rivals: America and Russia since World War II* (New York: Vik ing, 1971), p. 380.

31. Interview with Secretary Rusk, Athens, Ga., July 31, 1974. See also Ronald Steel, "Up against the Wall in Prague," *New York Review of Books* 11 (September 26, 1968): 13–16.

32. Interview with Rostow, Austin, Tex., July 26, 1974. See also Philip Ben, "How the Czechs Got a U.S. Brush-off," *New Republic* 159, no. 9 (August 31, 1968): 8.

33. *Czechoslovak Digest* (Prague), no. 29 (July 18, 1968), pp. 19–20.

34. Bohlen, *Witness to History,* p. 529.

35. Johnson, *The Vantage Point,* p. 486; interview with Rusk, Athens, Ga., July 31, 1974; interview with Rostow, Austin, Tex., July 26, 1974; interview with Henry Owen, chairman of the State Department Planning Committee, Washington, D.C., March 22, 1974; Bohlen,

Witness to History, pp. 529–31; and General James H. Polk, "Reflections on the Czechoslovakian Invasion, 1968," *Strategic Review* 5 (1977): 33.

36. Interview with Rusk, Athens, Ga., July 31, 1974. Rusk denied, as he had in 1968, "any suggestion that the U.S. government gave any kind of advance approval to the Soviet intervention in Czechoslovakia in 1968."

37. Polk, "Reflections on the Czechoslovakian Invasion," p. 33.

38. Radio Moscow, August 7, 1968.

39. Kenneth A. Myers and Dimitri Simes, *Soviet Decisionmaking, Strategic Policy, and SALT,* ACDA/PAB–293 (Washington, D.C.: The Center for Strategic and International Studies of Georgetown University, 1974), p. 9.

40. A. Grigoriants and V. Rogov, "Leninist Ideas Are Invincible; The Policy of Anticommunism Meets with Failure; Richard Nixon Again," *Trud,* August 13, 1968.

41. In the early 1970s, a senior Soviet analyst of U.S. foreign policy stated in a lecture at the Central Committee Institute of World Economy and International Relations that the results of the American presidential election would have been quite different had it not been for the invasion of Czechoslovakia. See Dimitri K. Simes, "The Soviet Invasion of Czechoslovakia and the Limits of Kremlinology," *Studies in Comparative Communism* 8, nos. 1–2 (Spring/Summer 1975): 178.

42. As late as August 20, Assistant Secretary William Bundy finished drafting several secret diplomatic notes to be sent to all major U.S. allies abroad informing them of the impending Johnson-Kosygin summit (Theodore H. White, *The Making of a President: 1968* [New York: Pocket Books, 1969], p. 346).

43. William Griffith, "U.S. Policy and the Invasion of Czechoslovakia," in *Czechoslovakia: Intervention and Impact,* ed. William I. Zartman (New York: New York University Press, 1970), p. 55.

44. As reported by Šnejdárek, in Kusín (ed.), *The Czechoslovak Reform Movement,* p. 56.

45. Reported by Czechoslovak leader M. Vaculík at the Fourteenth Extraordinary Party Congress. See Pelikán, *The Secret Vysočany Congress,* pp. 26–27.

46. Reported by Šnejdárek, who received this impression from his own discussions with Soviet officials in Moscow at the time of the crisis, in Kusín (ed.), *The Czechoslovak Reform Movement,* p. 51.

47. "The Failure of Absurd Hopes," *Za rubezhom* 34 (August 17, 1968): 8.

48. *Dokumenty k československé zahraniční politice,* pp. 288–89.

49. Interview with Jiří Hájek in *Reportér* 3 (October 16–23, 1968): 45. For Hájek's appraisal of Czechoslovak foreign policy and Soviet policy toward Czechoslovakia in 1968, see his book *Dix ans après: Prague, 1968–1978* (Paris: Éditions du Seuil, 1978).

50. See, for example, J. Hanák, "A Little Entente: A Healthy Idea," *Reportér* 3 (July 24–31, 1968).

51. The Letter of Warning from the CPSU Politburo, Radio Prague, August 20, 1969.

52. See the interview with J. B. Tito, "War or Peace," *Paris Match,* November 16, 1968, pp. 92–95, 104.

53. For Ceausescu's speech expressing support for Czechoslovakia and hinting disapproval of the Soviet and Warsaw Pact policies, see *Scînteia* (Bucharest), August 15, 1968 (*FBIS,* August 16, 1968). An editorial in the Albanian Party newspaper concluded: "The Soviet Union emerged more weakened from Bratislava," where the agreement symbolized "the scandalous retreat of the Soviet revisionists." See "The Defeat of the Soviet Revisionists in Bratislava" (editorial), *Zeri i popullit,* August 10, 1968, as reported in *FBIS—East Europe,* August 12, 1968.

54. Letter of Warning from the CPSU Politburo.

55. G. Husák's speech, Radio Prague, September 28, 1969.

56. Letter of Warning from the CPSU Politburo.

57. Radio Moscow, August 21, 1968.

58. "The Defense of Socialism: A Supreme International Duty" (editorial), *Pravda,* August 22, 1968. Emphasis added. Smrkovský, in an interview, expressed his belief that the main reason for the intervention was the Soviet decision to prevent the Party congress and the dismissal of the antireformist coalition. See *Vie Nuove Giorni,* September 16, 1971.

59. A. Sovetov, "The Present Stage in the Struggle between Socialism and Imperialism," *International Affairs,* no. 11 (November 1968), p. 5. Brezhnev stated in his address to the Polish Party Congress, in November 1968, that the invasion was "an extraordinary measure dictated by necessity" (*Pravda,* November 13, 1968).

60. Reported by a Czechoslovak leader, J. Piller, Radio Prague, September 17, 1969.

61. *Pravda,* August 22, 1968. Emphasis added.

62. Sidney Verba, "Assumption of Rationality and Non-rationality in Models of International Systems," in *The Shaping of Foreign Policy,* ed. H. K. Jacobson and W. Zimmerman (New York: Atherton Press, 1969), p. 198.

63. See Khrushchev's interview with the editor of the *New York Times,* Catledge, in *Pravda,* May 14, 1957. Another Soviet leader, F. R. Kozlov, told Vice President Nixon during a visit to the United States in 1959 that "there is never a day we [in the Kremlin] don't argue" (*Time,* July 13, 1959, p. 13).

64. Aspaturian, "Soviet Foreign Policy," in Macridis, *Foreign Policy in World Politics,* p. 159.

65. Pravda, May 14, 1957.

66. New York Tims, June 15, 1973.

67. Radio Paris, August 12, 1968.

68. This session was reported in *Sueddetedeutsche Zeitung,* August 20, 1968, and by Beer *Die Zukunft funktioniert noch nicht,* p. 343.

69. Shelest was the first Soviet leader to make a speech in the Soviet Union after the invasion referring to counterrevolution in Czechoslovakia; at that time most of the Soviet leaders including Brezhnev, kept silent. On September 9, 1968, he said: The recent events in Czechoslovakia have clearly shown the results when the counterrevolutionary and antisocialist elements attempt to seize key positions in the Party" (Radio Kiev, September 9, 1968). Afterwards, Shelest displayed unusual enthusiasm for the process of "normalization" in Czechoslovakia. See, for example, *Pravda Ukrainy,* June 8, 1971.

70. Mlynář, *Nachtfrost,* p. 301.

71. See Il Alexandrov, *Pravda,* August 18, 1968. The modification of *Pravda's* moderate (August 5) line on Bratislava to the hostile line expressed on August 18 was in some respect similar to the modification of its line during the Hungarian crisis between October 31 and November 3, 1956. After Suslov and Mikoian concluded their agreement with Nagy on October 31, 1956, *Pravda* announced the withdrawal of Soviet troops from Budapest and a return to "normalcy" for Hungarian life (*Pravda,* November 1, 1956). Three days later, however *Pravda* reported "the massacre and murder of communists throughout all Hungary" (*Pravda,* November 3, 1956). In both cases, *Pravda's* modifications probably reflected the changing perceptions in the Soviet Politburo.

72. Some of the arguments presented in the press defended the Bratislava conference and the resulting Soviet-Czechoslovak compromise on the grounds that a conflict would have been exploited by the West and by China. See "Loyalty to Lenin" (editorial), *Izvestiia,* August 13, 1968; V. Matveev, "Poison Pens," *Izvestiia,* August 17, 1968; and the very unusual editorial in *New Times,* no. 34 (August 28, 1968), which seemed to draw an analogy between the Politburo debate on the Brest Litovsk Treaty of 1918 and the Czechoslovak issue.

73. Piller, Radio Prague, September 17, 1969. See also the speech of another Czechoslovak official, B. Chňoupek, *Tvorba,* January 6, 1971.

74. Tigrid, *Why Dubcek Fell,* p. 96.

75. Shub, *The New Russian Tragedy,* p. 102. D. Voslensky was given similar information during a visit to the editorial office of the journal *Kommunist.* Voslensky's diary, p. 127. The Italian Communist newspaper *L'Unità* also listed Suslov, Shelepin, and Kosygin among those Soviet leaders who "expressed a view contrary to the decision to send troops to Czechoslovakia" *(L'Unità,* August 22, 1968; also reported by AFP, August 22, 1968). A similar report came from an East European source in East Berlin quoting a Soviet secretariat official *(New York Times,* March 4, 1969). Suslov's opposition to the intervention was also reported by the Hungarian ambassador to Italy, J. Szall. See Sulzberger, *An Age of Mediocrity,* p. 464.

76. *Le Monde,* August 26, 1969. Suslov and Ponomarev's reluctance to accept the notion that the counterrevolution in Prague required military intervention can be seen in their speeches during the postintervention period. Both tried to avoid the subject as much as possible. I was able to find only one reference to the Czechoslovak crisis of 1968 in Suslov's

speeches and essays. See Michael Suslov, *Izbrannoe* (Moscow: Izdateľstov Politicheskoi Literatury, 1972). I did not find any reference to the Czechoslovak crisis in Ponomarev's speeches.

77. "The Defense of Socialism: A Supreme International Duty" (editorial), *Pravda*, August 22, 1968.

78. Tigrid, *Why Dubcek Fell*, p. 97; Kusák and Künzel, *Der Sozialismus mit menschlichen Gesicht*, p. 209. Isolated cases of reluctance to approve the decision to intervene were reported from various research institutions of the Central Committee, such as the Institute of the International Workers' Movement (IWM), IMEMO, and probably several others in which some party members found the courage to vote against, or to refrain from voting on, the Soviet decision (Reddaway, *Uncensored Russia*, p. 97).

79. Sulzberger, *An Age of Mediocrity*, pp. 476–7. Kádár's reluctance was further indicated by his failure to comment publicly on this subject for a long time, and by postintervention reports of the Hungarian press, which tried to avoid East German and Polish attacks against "revisionism" and personal attacks against Dubček and his supporters. Kádár restated implicitly his stand on the Czechoslovak issue in *Rudé právo*, May 27, 1971.

80. Pelikán, *Ein Frühling, der nie zu Ende geht*, p. 262.

81. Mlynář, *Nachtfrost*, p. 299.

82. Ibid., p. 298.

83. Tigrid, *Why Dubček Fell*, p. 97.

84. Mlynář, *Nachtfrost*, pp. 207–8.

85. Ibid., pp. 214–15.

86. *L'Unità*, August 22, 1968; Luděk Pachman, *Jak To Bylo* (Toronto: 68 Publishers, 1974), pp. 127–28.

87. See Ponomarev's statement in Tigrid, *Why Dubcek Fell*, p. 127.

88. Official sources in the Johnson administration believed this, as did several former advisers and supporters of Dubček. West German Chancellor K. Kiesinger also said that "all the information we have indicates that the Soviet leaders did not make their decision until shortly before the actual event." See *International Review Service* 14, no. 9 (December 27, 1968): 87.

89. Littel, *The Czech Black Book*, p. 77.

90. Shtemenko, *Krasnaia zvezda*, August 21, 1968.

91. Polk, "Reflections on the Czechoslovakian Invasion," p. 32.

92. Interview with a former high East European official.

93. See *Českoslovenko 1968*, p. 143; *Mezinárodní politika* 12, no. 9 (September 1968): 1.

94. It is interesting to note the Chinese claim that "around August 20" Soviet military aircraft of various types unexpectedly and unprecedentedly "flew a succession of twenty-nine sorties intruding into China's air space." See *Peking Review*, no. 38 (September 20, 1968), pp. 41–42.

95. Newhouse, *Cold Dawn*, p. 130. Also from interviews with Rusk and Rostow.

96. See Johnson, *The Vantage Point*, p. 488 (emphasis added); also the similarly worded Soviet note to West German Chancellor Kiesinger, in *International Review Service* 14: 87–88.

97. Polk, "Reflections on the Czechoslovakian Invasion," p. 36.

98. There are several eyewitness accounts of this session: an interview with Smrkovský, in *Listy*, pp. 12–16; by Mlynář, *Nachtfrost*, pp. 251–56; by Presidium member Švestka, in *Tribuna*, August 20, 1969; and by D. Havlíček, in Littel, *The Czech Black Book*, pp. 23–29. I also rely here on interviews with Z. Mlynář, D. Havlíček, and other former officials of the Czechoslovak Communist Party.

99. Pelikàn, *Ein Frühling, der nie zu Ende geht*, pp. 268–69.

100. This is the particular view of the eyewitness Mlynář, *Nachtfrost*, pp. 251–52.

101. Ibid., pp. 186, 254–55.

102. At this session of the Central Committee three members, Jakeš, Pavlovský and K. Mestek, argued that "the Soviet Union had probably been justified in taking the action it had taken" (Pelikàn, *The Secret Vysočany Congress*, p. 25). Indra and Kolder had indeed tried to organize their supporters at the Central Committee level. Kolder's assistant R. Kaška (later Czechoslovak minister of the interior) was helping KGB agents on the first day of intervention to divide the personnel of the Czechoslovak Central Committee into "healthy" and "counterrevolutionary" forces (Littel, *The Czech Black Book*, p. 82).

103. See an interview with Smrkovský, *Listy*, p. 17.

104. *Pravda* (editorial), August 22, 1968. Nagy was charged with "having paid lip service to the danger from the counterrevolutionary instigators, and in fact proved objectively to be an accomplice of the reactionary forces" ("Block the Road of Reaction in Hungary" [editorial], *Pravda,* November 4, 1956).

105. See an interview with Smrkovský, *Listy,* pp. 15–19.

106. In the mid 1970s, Moscow viewed Dubček's policies as being "counterrevolutionary." See "Support for the Party Line," *Pravda,* April 30, 1975.

107. While most Soviet newspapers maintained that the Czechoslovak working class had welcomed "fraternal assistance," *Trud,* the trade union newspaper, reported rather accurately the anger of the Czechoslovaks with the occupation forces. See Novikov, "Colossal Vigilance Is Still Necessary," *Trud,* August 27, 1968.

108. Tigrid, *Why Dubcek Fell,* p. 111.

109. Instead of the long-expected announcement of the start of SALT talks, President Johnson called on the Soviet Union to withdraw its troops from Czechoslovakia on August 21 (*Public Papers of the Presidents of the United States,* p. 905).

110. Chinese Premier Chou En-lai condemned the Soviet intervention (Radio Peking, August 23, 1968).

111. Mlynář, *Nachtfrost,* p. 301.

112. Tigrid, *Why Dubcek Fell,* p. 114.

113. Ibid, p. 219.

114. The negotiations between the two teams finally enabled the Czechoslovaks to bring Kriegel back to Czechoslovakia. Originally, the Soviets wanted to keep him in Moscow (interview with Smrkovský, in *Listy,* p. 22).

115. See an interview with Smrkovský, *Listy,* p. 22. For the text of the Moscow Protocol, see Tigrid, *Why Dubcek Fell,* pp. 210–14.

116. Tigrid, *Why Dubcek Fell,* p. 125.

117. An interview with Smrkovský, *Listy,* p. 20.

118. Ibid.

119. See, for example, "Betrayal of Bratislava," *Neues Deutschland,* August 25, 1968.

120. Tigrid, *Why Dubcek Fell,* p. 128.

121. Mlynář, *Nachtfrost,* p. 307.

Chapter 6

1. Mlynář, *Nachtfrost,* p. 194.

2. Pelikan, *Ein Frühling, der nie zu Ende geht,* p. 261.

3. See the discussion of Arnold L. Horelick, A. Ross Johnson, and John D. Steinbruner, *The Study of Soviet Foreign Policy,* pp. 49–57.

4. Interview with Rusk, Athens, Ga., July 31, 1974.

5. See Medvedev, *On Socialist Democracy,* p. 28.

6. Santiago Carrillo, *"Eurocommunism" y Estado* ["Eurocommunism" and the State] (Barcelona: Editorial Crítica, 1977), pp. 166–67.

7. *L'Unità,* July 14, 1977.

8. *Corriera della Sera,* June 15, 1977.

9. See my "Eurocommunism and Eastern Europe," *Problems of Communism,* no. 2 (March–April 1978), pp. 41–54.

10. Willy Brandt, *People and Politics: The Years 1960–1975* (Boston: Little, Brown, 1976), pp. 214–15, 299.

11. Medvedev's essay as quoted in *Newsweek,* December 25, 1978, pp. 28–29.

12. See *Le Monde,* June 17–18, 1973, and Smrkovský's letter to Brezhnev, Listy 5, no. 2 (March 1975): 26–28.

13. As reported in the *Los Angeles Times,* December 13, 1978.

A Bibliographic Note

In writing this manuscript I consulted all available books that have been published in Russian, Czech, Slovak, English, German, and French on the USSR and the Czechoslovak crisis of 1968. Of the studies that focus primarily on internal events in Czechoslovakia at that time, the most outstanding are H. Gordon Skilling's *Czechoslovakia's Interrupted Revolution* (Princeton: Princeton University Press, 1976); Galia Golan's *Reform Rule in Czechoslovakia: The Dubček Era, 1968–1969* (Cambridge: Cambridge University Press, 1973); and Robin A. Remington, ed., *Winter in Prague: Documents on Czechoslovak Communism in Crisis* (Cambridge, Mass.: MIT Press, 1969). In addition to my own doctoral dissertation, three earlier studies which analyze briefly the Soviet management of the Czechoslovak crisis and which were very helpful are Fritz Ermarth's *Internationalism, Security, and Legitimacy: The Challenge to Soviet Interests in East Europe 1964–1968* (Santa Monica, Calif.: The Rand Corporation, March 1969), RM–5909–PR; Philip Windsor and Adam Roberts' *Czechoslovakia 1968* (New York: Columbia University Press, 1969); and William F. Robinson's "Czechoslovakia and Its Allies," *Studies in Comparative Communism* 1, nos. 1 and 2 (July–October 1968), pp. 141–70.

The main sources for my research were the newspapers, journals, documents, and books that appeared in the USSR, Czechoslovakia, and Eastern Europe primarily in 1968–69, but also in the decade following the invasion, I was able to supplement these sources by recourse to memoirs and letters (both published and unpublished), and verbal accounts of former members and advisers of Dubček's leadership, various members of the Johnson administration, Soviet citizens living abroad and in the USSR, and Soviet and East European emigrants living in several Western countries.

Radio broadcasts such as those published in *Foreign Broadcast Information Service (FBIS)* were drawn upon only when other sources were not available or when dealing with news reports in languages not commonly used in research (Albanian, Hungarian, Rumanian).

Only those books that I found helpful in arriving at a conceptualization of Soviet foreign policy decisionmaking or that I used extensively are listed in the bibliography that follows. The same rule applies to periodicals and newspapers used in research. Also listed are the most important documents, reports, analyses, articles, and speeches of the Soviet and Czechoslovak Communist parties which are relevant to the subject. A more comprehensive list of the sources used may be found in the notes.

Bibliography

Scholarly and Interpretative Studies, Reportage

Allison, Graham T. *Essence of Decision: Explaining the Cuban Missile Crisis.* Boston: Little, Brown, 1971.

Aspaturian, Vernon V. "Soviet Foreign Policy," in *Foreign Policy in World Politics,* 2d ed., ed. Roy C. Macridis. Englewood Cliffs, N.J.: Prentice-Hall, 1962.

_____. *The Union Republics in Soviet Diplomacy.* Geneva: Librarie E. Droz; Paris: Librarie Minaro, 1969.

Barghoorn, Frederick C. *Politics in the USSR,* 2d ed. Boston: Little, Brown, 1972.

_____. "Trends in the Top Political Leadership in the USSR," in *Political Leadership in Eastern Europe and the Soviet Union,* ed. R. Barry Farrell. Chicago: Aldine, 1970.

Beer, Fritz. *Die Zukunft funktioniert noch nicht: Ein Porträt der Tschechoslowakei, 1948–1968.* Frankfurt: S. Fischer, 1969.

Bertleff, Erick, *Mit blössen Händen.* Vienna: Fritz Molden, 1968.

Bethell, Nicholas. *Gomułka: His Poland, His Communism,* New York: Holt, Rinehart & Winston, 1969.

Brahm, Heinz. *Der Kreml und die ČSSR, 1968–1969.* Stuttgart: Kohlhammer, 1970.

Browne, Michael, ed. *Ferment in the Ukraine.* London: Macmillan, 1971.

Brzezinski, Zbigniew, and Huntington, Samuel P. *Political Power: USA/USSR.* New York: Viking, 1964.

Československo 1968: Přehled událostí. Prague: Vědecko-Informační Kabinet Ustavu Dějin Socialismu, 1969.

Chapman, Colin. *August 21st: The Rape of Czechoslovakia.* Philadelphia: Lippincott, 1968.

Chornovil, Vyacheslav, comp. *The Chornovil Papers.* New York: McGraw-Hill, 1968.

Cohen, Stephen F. *Bukharin and the Bolshevik Revolution: A Political Biography 1888–1938.* New York: Knopf, 1973.

Conquest, Robert, ed. *The Soviet Political System.* New York: Praeger, 1968.

Czerwinski, E. J., and Piekalkiewicz, Jaroslaw A., eds. *The Soviet Invasion of Czechoslovakia: Its Effects on Eastern Europe,* New York: Praeger, 1972.

Dinerstein, Herbert S. *The Making of a Missile Crisis, October 1962.* Baltimore: Johns Hopkins University Press, 1976.

Dornberg, John. *Brezhnev: The Mask of Power.* London: Andre Deutsch, 1974.

Dziuba, Ivan. *Internationalism or Russification?* London: Weiderfeld and Nicolson, 1968.

Erickson, John. *Soviet Military Power.* London: Royal United Services Institute, 1971.

Ermarth, Fritz. *Internationalism, Security, and Legitimacy: The Challenge to Soviet Interests in East Europe, 1964–1968.* Santa Monica, Calif.: The Rand Corporation, March 1969. RM–5909–PR.

Golan, Galia. *The Czechoslovak Reform Movement: Communism in Crisis, 1962–1968.* Cambridge: Cambridge University Press, 1971.

_____. *Reform Rule in Czechoslovakia: The Dubček Era, 1968–1969.* Cambridge: Cambridge University Press, 1973.

Haefs, Hanswilhelm, ed. *Die Ereignisse in der Tschechoslowakei, vom 27.6.1967 bis 18.10. 1968: Ein dokumentarischer Bericht.* Bonn: Siegler & Co. KG. Verlag für Zeitarchive, 1969.
Halperin, Morton H. *Bureaucratic Politics and Foreign Policy.* Washington, D.C.: Brookings Institution, 1974.
Hodnett, Grey, and Potichnyj, Peter J. *The Ukraine and the Czechoslovak Crisis.* Canberra: Australian National University, 1970.
Horský, Vladimír. *Prag 1968: Systemveränderung und Symstemverteidigung.* Stuttgart: Ernst Klett, 1975.
Jakobson, Max. *The Diplomacy of the Winter War: An Account of the Russo-Finnish War, 1939–1940.* Cambridge, Mass.: Harvard University Press, 1961.
Kaplan, Frank, *Winter into Spring: The Czechoslovak Press and the Reform Movement, 1963–1968.* Boulder: East European Quarterly, 1977, distributed by Columbia University Press.
Klaiber, Wolfgang. *The Crisis in Czechoslovakia in 1968.* Arlington, Va.: Institute for Defense Analyses, 1969. Research Paper P–570.
Klawitter, Karol. *Army of Revenge: Ulbricht's Occupation Forces in Czechoslovakia.* Cologne: Markus, 1968.
Korbel, Josef. *Twentieth-Century Czechoslovakia.* New York: Columbia University Press, 1977.
Král, Václav. *Československo a Sovětský svaz, 1917–1971.* Prague: Práce, 1971.
Kusák, Alexej, and Künzel, Franz Peter. *Der Sozialismus mit menschlichen Gesicht.* Munich: Südwest, 1969.
Kusín, Vladimír V., ed. *The Czechoslovak Reform Movement, 1968.* London: International Research Documents, 1973.
Leonhard, Wolfgang. *The Kremlin since Stalin.* New York: Praeger, 1962.
Levy, Alan. *Rowboat to Prague.* New York: Grossman, 1972.
Löbl, Eugen, and Grünwald, Leopold. *Die intellektuelle Revolution.* Düsseldorf: Econ, 1969.
Maxa, Josef. *A Year Is Eight Months.* Garden City, N.Y.: Doubleday, 1970.
Medvedev, Roy A. *On Socialist Democracy.* New York: A. A. Knopf, 1975.
Medvedev, Roy A. and Medvedev, Zhores A. *Khrushchev: The Years in Power.* New York: Columbia University Press, 1976.
Mlynář, Zdeněk. *Československý pokus o reformu, 1968: Analýza jeho teorie a praxe.* Cologne: Index-Listy, 1975.
Molnar, Miklos. *Budapest, 1956.* London: George Allen Unwin, 1971.
Morozov, Michael. *Leonid Breschnev.* Stuttgart: V. Kohlhammer, 1973.
Newhouse, John. *Cold Dawn: The Story of SALT.* New York: Holt, Rinehart & Winston, 1973.
Ostrý, Antonín. *Československý problém.* Cologne: Index, 1972.
Piekalkiewicz, Jaroslaw A. *Public Opinion Polling in Czechoslovakia, 1968–69: Results and Analysis of Surveys Conducted during the Dubček Era.* New York: Praeger, 1972.
Reddaway, Peter. *Uncensored Russia: Protest and Dissent in the Soviet Union.* New York: American Heritage Press, 1972.
Remington, Robin A., ed. *Winter in Prague: Documents on Czechoslovak Communism in Crisis.* Cambridge, Mass.: MIT. Press, 1969.
Riker, William H. *The Theory of Political Coalitions.* New Haven: Yale University Press, 1962.
Sakharov, Andrei D. *Progress, Coexistence, and Intellectual Freedom,* ed. Harrison E. Salisbury. New York: Norton, 1968.
Salomon, Michel. *Prague Notebook: The Strangled Revolution.* Boston: Little, Brown, 1971.
Sborník, Systémové změny. Cologne: Index, 1972.
Schmidt-Häuer, Christian, and Müller, Adolf. *Viva Dubček.* Cologne: Kiepenheuer & Witsch, 1968.
Schwartz, Harry. *Prague's 200 Days.* New York: Praeger, 1969.
Shawcross, William. *Dubček.* London: Weidenfeld & Nicolson, 1970.
Shub, Anatole. *The New Russian Tragedy.* New York: Norton, 1969.
Skilling, H. Gordon. *Czechoslovakia's Interrupted Revolution.* Princeton: Princeton University Press, 1976.

Slusser, Robert M. *The Berlin Crisis of 1961*. Baltimore: Johns Hopkins University Press, 1973.
Smolar, Boris. *Soviet Jewry Today and Tomorrow*. New York: Macmillan, 1971.
Stárek, Jiři. *Briefe aus der Tschechoslowakei*. Vienna: Styria, 1975.
Steiner, Eugen. *The Slovak Dilemma*. Cambridge: Cambridge University Press, 1973.
Sterling, Claire. *The Masaryk Case*. New York: Harper & Row, 1969.
Sulzberger, C. L. *An Age of Mediocrity: Memoirs and Diaries, 1963–1972*. New York: Macmillan, 1973.
Szulc, Tad. *Czechoslovakia since World War II*. New York: Viking, 1971.
Tatu, Michel. *L'hérésie impossible*. Paris: B. Grasset, 1968.
Thomas, John R. *Soviet Foreign Policy and Conflict within Political and Military Leadership*. McLean, Va.: Research Analysis Corporation, 1970.
Tigrid, Pavel. *Kvadratura Kruhu*. Paris: Svědectví, 1970.
_____. *Why Dubcek Fell*. London: MacDonald, 1971.
Triska, Jan F., and Finley, David D. *Soviet Foreign Policy*. New York: Macmillan, 1968.
Tucker, Robert C. *Stalin as Revolutionary*. New York: Norton, 1973.
Ulam, Adam B. *The Rivals: America and Russia since World War II*. New York: Viking, 1971.
Veselý, Ludvík. *Dubček*. Munich: Kindler, 1970.
Vital, David. *The Survival of Small States*. London: Oxford University Press, 1971.
White, Theodore H. *The Making of a President: 1968*. New York: Atheneum, 1969.
Windsor, Philip, and Roberts, Adam. *Czechoslovakia 1968*. New York: Columbia University Press, 1969.
Wolfe, Thomas W. *Soviet Power and Europe: 1945–1970*. Baltimore: Johns Hopkins University Press, 1970.
Zartman, I. William, ed. *Czechoslovakia: Intervention and Impact*. New York: New York University Press, 1970.
Zimmerman, William. *Soviet Perspectives on International Relations*. Princeton, N.J.: Princeton University Press, 1969.
Zinner, Paul E., ed. *National Communism and Popular Revolt in Eastern Europe: A Selection of Documents of Events in Poland and Hungary, February–November 1956*. New York: Columbia University Press, 1956.

Newspapers and Periodicals

Soviet Newspapers and Periodicals
Agitator, Ekonomicheskaia gazeta, International Affairs (Moscow), Izvestiia, Khronika tekushchikh sobytii [Chronicle of current events], *Kommunist Belorussii, Kommunist Estonii, Kommunist Sovetskoi Latvii, Kommunist* (Lithuania), *Kommunist Moldavii, Kommunist* (Moscow), *Kommunist Ukrainy, Komsomol'skaia pravda, Krasnaia zvezda, Literaturnaia gazeta, Mirovaia ekonomika i mezhdunarodnye otnosheniia, New Times, Novyi mir, Politicheskii dnevnik* [Political diary], *Politicheskoe samoobrazovanie, Pravda Ukrainy, Radians'ka Ukraina, Sovetskaia Belorussiia, Sovetskaia Estoniia, Sovetskaia Rossiia, Trud, Voprosy ekonomiki, Voprosy filosofii, Voprosy istorii KPSS, World Marxist Review, Za rubezhom.*

Czechoslovak Newspapers and Magazines
Czechoslovak Digest, Lidová demokracie, Literárni listy, Listy (Rome, Italy), *Mezinárodní vztahy, Mezinárodní politika, Mladá fronta, Nová mysl, Obrana lidu, Politika, Práca* (Bratislava), *Práce* (Prague), *Pravda* (Bratislava), *Reportér, Rudé právo, Směna, Student, Svědectví* (Paris), *Svět v obrazech, Svobodné slovo, Tribuna, Tvorba, Večerní Praha, Volkszeitung, Zemědělské noviny, Život strany.*

Other Selected Newspapers and Periodicals
L'Humanité, Le Monde, L'Unità, Neue Zürcher Zeitung, Neues Deutschland, New Left Review, New York Times, Peking Review, Trybuna Ludu, Vie Nuove Giorni, Washington Post.

Press and Radio Broadcasts in Translation

U.S. *Foreign Broadcast Information Service (FBIS), Daily Report: The USSR and Eastern Europe.*

U.S. *Joint Publication Research Service, Eastern Europe.*

Selected Soviet Party Documents, Speeches, Reports, and Studies

Brezhnev, Leonid Ilich. *Following Lenin's Course: Speeches and Articles.* Moscow: Progress, 1972.

Kommunisticheskaia partiia Sovetskogo Soiuza v rezoliutsiiakh i rescheniiach s"ezdov Konferencii i plenumov Ts. K. 1966–1968, no. 7. Moscow: Izdatel'stvo Politicheskoi Literatury, 1972.

K sobytiiam v Chekhoslovakii, fakty, dokumenty, svidetel'stva pressy i ochevidtsev. Moscow, 1968. The so-called White Book.

Materialy XXIV s"ezda KPSS. Moscow: Izdatel'stvo Politicheskoi Literatury, 1971.

Mrackhovskaia, I. M. *From Revisionism to Betrayal.* Moscow: Progress, 1972. Criticism of Ota Šik's economic views.

Pravda pobezhdaet. Moscow: Izdatel'stvo Politicheskoi Literatury, 1971.

Silin, M. A. *A Critique of Masarykism.* Moscow: Progress, 1975.

Sovetsko Chekhoslovatskie otnosheniia, 1961–1971. Moscow: Izdatel'stvo Politicheskoi Literatury, 1975.

Suslov, Michael A. *Brilliant Teacher and Leader of the Working Class.* Report by Michael A. Suslov, Member of the Politburo and Secretary of the Central Committee of the CPSU, at a meeting in Moscow on May 5, 1968, to commemorate the 150th Anniversary of the birth of Karl Marx. Moscow: Novosti Press Agency Publishing House, 1968.

——————. *Izbrannoe.* Moscow: Izdatel'stvo Politicheskoi Literatury, 1971.

Trapeznikov, Sergei P. *At the Turning Points of History.* Moscow: Progress, 1972.

Zagladin, Vadim V. *Lektsii po nauchnomu kommunizmu.* Moscow: Politicheskoi Literatury, 1971.

Czechoslovak Party Documents, Speeches, Reports and Studies

Akční, program kommunistické strany Československa přijatý na plenárním zasedání ÚV KSČ dne 5, dubna 1968. Prague, 1968.

Bilak, Vasil. *Pravda zůstala pravdou: Projevy a články, říjen 1967–prosinec 1970.* Prague: Svoboda, 1971.

Dokumenty k československé zahraniční politce. Prague: Ministerstvo Zahraničnich Věcí, 1967–69.

Dubček, Alexander, *K otázkám obrodzovacieho procesu v KSČ, vybrané prejavy prvého tajomníka ÚV KSČ súdruha Alexandra Dubčeka.* Bratislava, 1968.

Husák, Gustav. *State a prejavy April 1969–1970.* Epocha, 1970.

Littell, Robert, ed. *The Czech Black Book.* New York: Praeger, 1969. Translation of the publication *Sedm pražských dnů, 21.–27. Srpen 1968, Dokumentace* (Prague, Sept. 1968), originally prepared by the Institute of History of the Czechoslovak Academy of Sciences.

Pelikàn, Jiří, ed. *The Secret Vysočany Congress: Proceedings and Documents of the Extraordinary Fourteenth Congress of the Communist Party of Czechoslovakia.* London: Allen Lane, 1971.

——————. *The Czechoslovak Political Trials, 1950–1954: The Suppressed Report of the Dubček Government Commission of Inquiry, 1968.* London: MacDonald, 1971.

Poučeni z krizového vývoje v straně a společnosti po XIII sjezdu KSČ. Prague, 1971.

Rok šedesáty osmý: V usneseních a dokumentech ÚV KSČ. Prague: Svoboda, 1969.

Personal Memoirs, Interviews, Diaries, and Letters

Bittman, Ladislav. *The Deception Game: Czechoslovak Intelligence in Soviet Political Warfare.* Syracuse: Syracuse University Research Corporation, 1972.

Bohlen, Charles E. *Witness to History, 1929–1969.* New York: Norton, 1973.

Dubček, Alexander, Dubček's letter to the Federal Assembly of Czechoslovakia and the Slovak National Council of October 28, 1974. *Listy* (Rome), no. 3 (April 1975), pp. 3–16.

Frolík, Josef. *The Frolik Defection*. London: Leo Cooper, 1975.
Hájek, Jiří. *Dix ans aprés: Prague, 1968–1978*. Paris: Éditions du Seuil, 1978.
Johnson, Lyndon B. *The Vantage Point*. New York: Holt, Rinehart & Winston, 1971.
Interviews with Czechoslovak leaders Vasil Bilak, Drahomír Kolder, Jan Piller, Oldřich Čer-
    ník, and Oldřick Švestka on Prague Radio and in *Rudé Právo* in 1969; and in *Fakta nelze*
    zalmčet: Svědectví lidí a dokumentů (Prague: Knihovna Rudého Práva, 1971).
Mlynář, Zdeněk. *Nachtfrost: Erfahrungen auf dem Weg vom realen zum menschlichen*
    Sozialismus. Cologne: Europäische Verlagsanstalt, 1978.
Pelikan, Jiri. *Ein Frühling, der nie zu Ende geht: Erinnerungen eines Prager Kommunisten*.
    Frankfurt: S. Fischer, 1976.
Smrkovský, Josef. An interview, *Listy* (Rome) 5, no. 2 (March 1975), pp. 4–25.
Voslensky, Michail. "This Will Only Help the Americans" (excerpts from Voslensky's diary),
    Der Spiegel, no. 34 (August 21, 1978), pp. 126–27.
Weit, Erwin. *At the Red Summit: Interpreter behind the Iron Curtain*. New York: Macmillan,
    1973.

Unpublished Sources: Interviews and Letters

Dušan Havlíček, former head of the press department of the Central Committee of the
    Czechoslovak Communist Party. Interview, Geneva, June 8, 1974.
Josef Hodic, former head of the Department of Social Sciences of the Klement Gottwald
    Military-Political Academy in Prague and an adviser of Czechoslovak Premier Černik.
    Interview, Vienna, October 7, 1978.
Přemysl Janýr, member of the Preparatory Committee of the Czechoslovak Social Demo-
    cratic Party in 1968. Interview, Vienna, May 25, 1974.
Karel Král, former ČTK reporter in New York. Interview, New York, October 27, 1971.
Franz Marek, former Politburo member of the Austrian Communist Party, expelled after
    the Czechoslovak intervention. Interview, Vienna, May 27, 1974.
Zdeněk Mlynář, former secretary of the Central Committee of the Czechoslovak Communist
    Party. Interviews, Vienna, October 6 and 9, 1978.
Henry Owen, chairman of the Policy Planning Staff of the State Department in Johnson's
    administration. Interview, Washington, D.C., March 22, 1974.
Jiří Pelikán, former chairman of the Czechoslovak Assembly's Foreign Affairs Committee
    and director of Czechoslovak Television. Interview, Rome, May 28, 1974.
Walt W. Rostow, national security adviser of President Johnson. Interview, Austin, Tex.,
    July 26, 1974.
Dean Rusk, secretary of state under President Johnson. Interview, Athens, Ga., July 31, 1974.
Radoslav Selucký, adviser to the Central Committee of the Communist Party of Czechoslo-
    vakia and the Economic Council of the Czechoslovak Government. Letter, Ottawa,
    October 23, 1974.
Ota Šik, former deputy prime minister of Czechoslovakia. Interview, St. Gallen, June 5, 1974.
Larisa Silnický, former interpreter for the Czechoslovak leadership. Interview, Tel Aviv,
    September 24, 1973.
Antonín Šnejdárek, former director of the Institute of International Politics and Economics
    (UMPE), and foreign policy adviser to Dubček's regime. Interview, Paris, June 6, 1974.
Simon Wiesenthal, head of the Jewish Documentation Center in Vienna. Interview, Vienna,
    September 2, 1973; letter, Vienna, February 13, 1976.

Index

Abrasimov, Peter, 43
Academy of Sciences (USSR), 62
Action Program, 37; circulation of (USSR), 31, 99; Czechoslovak Party acceptance of, 12, 20; features of, 12, 168 n. 28; and GFR Social Democrats, 24, 89; 2000 Words on, 41. *See also* Reform process (Czechoslovakia)
Advocates of military intervention, 48, 52, 92, 142; antireformists as allies of, 39, 141; in armed forces, 108–14, 152, 156; and bureaucrat-ideologists, 97–101; at Čierna, 72; consensus-building by, 155; criticism of, 95; and dissatisfaction with Čierna-Bratislava accord, 156; East European supporters of, 23–25, 53, 114–18; first appeal of, 22; in KGB, 104–8; members of, 21–23, 141, 156; and mobilization of support at July session CC/ CPSU, 59–63; persuasion of wavering members by, 42, 101, 145, 155; pressure on Kosygin by, 80; and timing of decision, 139; and Ukrainian Party bureaucracy, 102–4; and use of press to prejudice Czechoslovak-Soviet reconciliation, 35
Air Forces (USSR), 6
Al-Ahram, 10
Albania, 89; and armed resistance, 158; and Warsaw Pact Organization, 163
Alexandrov, I. (pseud.), *Pravda* articles of: on August 18, 142; on July 11, 50–52, 54; on March 28, 36
Alliance obligations (Czechoslovakia): Action Program on, 12; Bratislava Declaration on, 89; and neutrality, 116. *See also* COMECON; Warsaw Treaty Organization
Allison, Graham, 2, 4, 7
Angola, 10, 158
Antireformist coalition, 36–39; appeal for assistance by, 134, 137–38; and April CC session, 36, 38; attempts to form anti-Dubček government by, 79, 147, 149–50; at August 6, 13 Presidium sessions, 119; and August 21 CC session, 149–59; Bratislava accord as defeat for, 118; and

Chervonenko, 122, 126; and Čierna Conference, 78, 83, 84; defeat of, at August 20 Presidium session, 149; defeat of, at district and regional conferences, 41–42; defeat of, at July 19 CC session, 65–66, 68, 70; efforts to prevent 14th Congress by, 37–39, 119, 156; formation of, 36; and Kašpar's report, 120; labeled "conservatives," 37, 137; at May 7–9 Presidium sessions, 38; members of, 37–38; and Prchlík's dismissal, 75; relations of, with Soviet and East European allies, 38, 116, 122, 126 (*see also* Chervonenko, S. V.; Shelest, P. E.; Ulbricht, Walter); as Soviet alternate information channel, 37–39, 122, 124, 127–28, 137–39, 157; Soviet press support of, 51, 121; Soviet sympathizers in, 38, 51, 78, 136; and 2000 Words, 41–42; use of press by, 121. *See also* "Healthy forces," fifth column, pro-Soviet
Anti-Semitism: and Polish Intelligence Service, 106, 181 n. 35; and Ukraine, 79–80, 170 n. 55
"Antisocialist forces," 5, 38, 57, 82, 86, 98, 103, 112, 121, 137. *See also* Reformists, coalition of
Appeal for assistance, 127, 134, 137–38. *See also* "Fraternal assistance"
Arab-Israeli war, 130
Armed forces (Czechoslovakia): dismissal of GRU representatives from, 109; Soviet avoidance of confrontation with, 146; and stationing of Soviet Ground Forces, 110–11; and weak morale as threat to Warsaw Pact and Soviet forces, 16, 22–23. *See also* Armed resistance
Armed forces (USSR), 110, 182 n. 60; and implementation of decision, 145; interventionists in, 108–14, 141; psychological pressure by, 13, 49, 51, 69, 94, 105, 122; represented at Moscow talks (August), 113, 152; and willingness to assist, 22, 23, 111, 113, 171 n. 85; and withdrawal from Czechoslovakia, 56, 83–84, 179 n. 72. *See*

Fourteenth Extraordinary Party Congress
(continued)
137; preparations for, 118, 138, 148; Soviet
agreement to, 33, 83–84, 88, 92; and
validation of reform, 30, 84, 136, 157
France, 130; Communist Party of, 27, 67, 78,
161, 163. *See also* Garaudy, Roger;
Rochet, Waldeck
"Fraternal assistance": Bratislava Declaration on, 87–88; and "Brezhnev doctrine,"
87; Czechoslovak "appeal" for, 127, 137,
152; and Epishev, 22, 109, 125; Podgorny
on, 64, 67; and proletarian internationalism, 66; Vasiagin on, 113; Warsaw Letter
on, 57; Zhadov on, 23. *See also* Appeal for
assistance; "Brezhnev doctrine"
Freedom of press (Czechoslovakia), 12, 53
Frolík, Josef, 105
Furtseva, E. A., 19

Galanskov, Yu., 98
Galuzzi, C., 67
Garaudy, Roger, 78
General Agreement of Tariffs and Trade
(GATT), 131
German Democratic Republic (GDR), 49, 85,
117, 159; anti-Dubček campaign in press
of, 25, 29, 36, 152, 175 n. 58; and GFR,
53, 56, 115; intelligence service of, 106; and
interventionist coalition, 23, 114–16, 141;
and military maneuvers, 13, 33, 73–74,
113, 116; reformist influence in, 2, 105,
114; and Soviet information channels, 128,
157; and Soviet-West German rapprochement, disapproval of, 25, 34, 49–50, 53,
89, 114; Warsaw delegation of, 53, 56, 174
n. 38, 175 n. 33. *See also* Ulbricht, Walter
German Federal Republic (GFR), 8, 20, 134,
147; Czechoslovak relations with, and
invasion, 24, 56, 89, 102, 114, 116–17,
135; and dialogue with USSR as linked to
Czechoslovakia, 16, 43–45, 49–50, 52, 56;
and Gromyko's speech, 45; invasion and
risk of confrontation with, 129, 147, 158;
and revanchist threat to Eastern Europe,
50, 56, 89, 134–35, 156; and signals of
noninvolvement, 73; and Soviet national
security, 2–3, 5; Soviet rapprochement
with, 25, 34, 49–50, 53, 89–90, 114,
161–62; Ulbricht's overtures to, 115. *See
also* Brandt, Willy
Gerö, E., 121
Gierek, E., 117
Ginzburg, A., 98
Glassboro Summit, 45–46
Gomułka, Władysław, 54, 77, 113; and
Bratislava Declaration, 87–88; domestic
position of, 26, 116–17, 118; and Dubček,
24–25; as interventionist, 2, 23, 33, 81;
and Moscow Protocol, 152; post-Bratislava pressures of, and invasion, 156;
reports of, 124, 139, 141; and Warsaw
Conference, 53, 57. *See also* Poland

Great Britain, 130, 147
Grechko, A. A., 64, 73–74, 113, 151. *See
also* Ministry of Defense
Greek-Catholic Church, 15
Gribachev, N. M., 16, 34, 61–62, 100
Griffith, William, 133
Grigorenko, P. G., 16, 99, 110
Grishin, V. V., 22, 31–32, 61
Gromyko, Andrei, 10, 43–46, 50, 56, 89, 94,
129, 151
Ground Forces, Soviet, 6, 108, 110, 139, 157;
and implementation of decision, 145; and
June exercises, 33; and logistic exercise
Nemen, 73; and pressures for stationing
troops, 26, 110–11. *See also* Military
maneuvers

Hager, K., 29
Hájek, Jiří, 135
Halperin, M., 4
Hamouz, 67
Havemann, Robert, 114
"Healthy forces," 22, 37, 50, 57, 105, 137–
38, 148. *See also* Antireformist coalition
Hebrang, A., 79
Heikal, Mohamed, 10
Hodnett, Grey, 61, 102
Hoffman, H., 74
Honecker, 174 n. 33
Hoxha, E., 78. *See also* Albania
Human rights movement (USSR), 98, 107
Humphrey, Hubert H., 132
Hungarian crisis (1956), 67; and coalition
politics, 18–19; and collective decision-
making, 10, 71; compared to Czechoslovak
crisis, 13, 25, 30, 49–50, 66, 69, 91–92, 95,
103–4, 110, 112, 121, 126, 130, 149, 169
n. 48; and U.S. noninvolvement, 130, 158.
See also Nagy, Imre
Hungary, 85; armed forces of, and maneu-
vers in, 113; domestic reform in, 27, 96,
163; press of, 36, 40, 174 n. 43, 179 n. 6,
187 n. 79; and relations with Czechoslovakia, 49, 53; and role in Czechoslovak
crisis, 27. *See also* Kádár, János
Husák, G., 119, 137

Iakubovskii, I. I., 23, 32, 49, 64, 108, 113,
181 n. 47; and deployment of Warsaw Pact
troops in Czechoslovakia, 30, 111; and importance of combat readiness, 109–10, 182
n. 56
Ideological Commission, 16
Il'nitskii, Yu. V., 60–61, 79, 97, 102
Imperialism, 44, 46, 53–54, 56, 60, 62, 86,
89–90, 97–98, 112, 121
Implementation of decision, 3, 58, 145–53
Indra, A., 36–38, 118, 120, 143, 187 n. 102;
and appeal to Party organizations, 41–42;
and communications with Chervonenko,
38, 184 n. 15; during Presidium session of
August 20 and post-invasion, 148–49; and
elections, 41, 119; and People's Militia, 38.
See also Antireformist coalition